THE
GREEN COOK'S
ENCYCLOPEDIA

THE
GREEN COOK'S
ENCYCLOPEDIA

Janet Hunt

GREEN
PRINT

First published in 1991 by
Green Print
an imprint of The Merlin Press
10 Malden Road, London NW5 3HR

ISBN 1 85425 057 4

1 2 3 4 5 6 7 8 9 10 :: 99 98 97 96 95 94 93 92 91

Phototypeset by Computerset Ltd., Harmondsworth

Printed in England by Biddles Ltd., Guildford, Surrey on recycled paper

ALPHABETICAL LIST OF RECIPES

All recipes are for 4 average servings, except where otherwise stated.
Measurements are given in metric and imperial, and are not interchangeable, so use one or the other, not a mixture.

LETTER FROM THE AUTHOR

To whom it may concern

Concern for the planet is undoubtedly on the increase. The Green movement – once little more than a twitch – has become a strong and unstoppa-
ble surge forwards.

Why now? Because, maybe, there is something to the saying that we
never really value what we have until we are in imminent danger of losing
it. And certainly this is true of beautiful Planet Earth.

In just the last century man has increased his numbers to plague
proportions, and as a result is polluting and destroying everything around
him. More animals and plants become extinct each day. Rainforests are
hacked and burned, turned into vast and arid wastelands. The seas are
black with oil. Our water and air, essentials of life, can kill.

There are those who continue to use up resources as if they were infinite,
constantly renewing themselves, there for the taking. Many of us just avert
our eyes. Others have blind faith that it will be alright in the end. *They* will
find a way, haven't they always? People must have panicked during the
times of plague and pestilence, yet here we all are today, proof that it wasn't
the end of the world, right?

Right. But this is different. This is destruction on a worldwide scale, it's
happening fast and all around us, and soon there will be nothing anyone
can do to stop it.

And when our planet dies, so will we.

We talk about ecology as though it was something separate from us, and
yet we are part of it. We, the planet and everything on it are linked, inter-
dependent. It is how we choose to live our lives right now that will
ultimately decide whether future generations have the chance to enjoy
many of the things we take for granted – trees, open spaces, birds – or
whether their world will be sterile, artificial, something out of science
fiction. Whether, in fact, there will be a world.

Of all the things we can do to put our concern into action, one of the most
immediate – and relatively easy – is to eat with care. Because our eating
habits are set early in life, this tends to be something to which we give little
thought, choosing and cooking the same foods automatically, day after day,
year after year. Maybe it is time to change this.

Processed foods, for example, constitute about 70% of the food consumed in Britain. They contain massive amounts of additives and little nourishment, and are invariably over-packaged. Could you cut back on them? Cut them out altogether?

Meat is another bone of contention. Many confirmed Greens see no harm in eating meat, especially if it has been reared organically. They point out that in any case, an entirely vegetarian world would not work. Others feel that there is no valid excuse for continuing to eat a product that not only treats defenceless living creatures as commodities, but that is a major cause of pollution.

The question of cash crops is another one to which there is no easy answer. On the surface it seems wrong that native people should be moved away from their land so that it can be used to grow luxury crops for the tables of the affluent West. Especially when the land to which they are sent – as in Ethiopia – fails them, and they starve. Put like that, who can dispute it? But not every case is as black and white. Should you avoid all exotic food imports, or buy them in the hope that you will be helping the people of other countries? How can you decide which is which?

Looking at cash crops from another angle completely, it is surely illogical to import crops that we can grow perfectly well in our own country. And yet that is exactly what we do. Much of the Southeast of England was, not that long ago, supplying London with excellent crops of a whole range of produce. Now many of the small-scale farmers have gone out of business, pushed out by imports of the very same crops. There is a story of one of them, a celery grower, now living a life of luxury in Spain where he advises the locals on growing celery. The celery is sent to Britain. Isn't this economics gone mad?

This book is written in the hope that it will help you make some sense of it all. It aims to prove that you can eat in a way that does least harm to the environment without sacrificing pleasure, without having to go hungry. It lists, in alphabetical order, all the eco-friendly foods you may find at your local shops, tells you how to choose, store and cook them.

Hopefully, it will also answer at least some of your questions about other aspects of food. But better still, I hope it encourages you to ask a lot more. Of your local retailer, food manufacturers, politicians. As a consumer you have far more power than you may realise. You have the power to help save the planet. Do it now.

J.H.

ADDITIVES

Concern about the additives and preservatives used in food is a phenomenon of recent times, yet the original reasons for using them were sound enough. It was in the 1870s that science and technology made concerted efforts to find a way of preserving foods so that they could be transported from places where there was plenty to places where they was none. They were highly successful. Little did they realise what they had started.

Now food production is a sophisticated science. Whereas there were about 50 permitted additives in use at the turn of the century, there are now nearer 3,500, the number having doubled in just the last decade. Nor is it easy to judge which foods contain them. Processed foods do, certainly, but so may innocent seeming items such as vegetables (sprayed to prevent sprouting), lemons and oranges (often dyed and waxed), strawberries (sprayed with hormone mixtures to promote growth). Egg yolks can be dyed via colouring in chicken feed. Foods sold for use in catering establishments are allowed to contain 10% more sulphur dioxide than food sold for home use. The list goes on.

In brief there are five main groups of additives. Antioxidants prevent spoilage in processed oils and fats, so can be found in products such as crisps, ice cream, commercially-made cakes and biscuits. Emulsifiers and stabilisers stop oil and water-based liquids separating – they are used in margarines and low fat spreads. Flavourings are used to replace flavours lost or destroyed during processing. Some of them are from natural sources such as essential oils, herbs and spices, but many of them are synthetic. It is estimated that flavourings account for about 3,000 of the additives now used in our foods! Flavour enhancers bring out the natural flavours of food, or replace those lost during processing – one of the most often used is monosodium glutomate. Colourings, mostly from coal tar dyes, improve the appearance of foods that look less than attractive.

Add to these additives such as improvers, artificial sweeteners, fortifiers, and you begin to see that food production today really is a science.

Even worse, many of the foods that are actually grown will have been treated with chemical fertilisers and sprays before they were even picked.

Are such additives safe? The food industry insists they are, at least in the quantities used. Careful monitoring by two major organisations – the World Health Organization and the Food and Agriculture Organization of the United Nations – means that any suspect chemical may be struck off the list at any time. Yet are these controls enough? How, in truth, can any control be kept over so many additives being used by thousands of companies, and in such diverse combinations?

An alternative way to approach the problem is to ask if such foods are necessary in your diet. They might have been at a time when there was no other choice. Now, however, there is. As more people express concern about the items in their shops, and make it clear they would prefer food that is both safer and richer in nutrients – and that they are prepared to pay for it, whatever it costs – so more wholefoods are becoming available. As the range grows so even more people are tempted to try eating this way. And the more powerful the trend becomes, the more effective those that follow it will be in stopping the adulteration of a nation's food. Governments and manufacturers will be forced to listen. You will have done something to help.

ADUKI BEANS

A small red-brown bean which is the seed of a bushy plant native to Japan. It has a sweet taste, and is easier to digest than most beans. It is thought that drinking the juice may help in kidney complaints. Aduki beans frequently feature in macrobiotic cooking, and are considered to be the king of beans by those who follow this way of eating.

Buying/Storing: Buy regularly in small quantities from a retailer who has a fast turnover. Store in a sealed container in a cool place.

How to use: Allow approximately 1 hour to cook, fast-boiling them for 10 minutes before reducing the heat and simmering them until tender. Add to soups, stews, salads and rice dishes. Do as they do in China and Japan, and mash cooked beans to a purée, then make into cakes. Fry as burgers. Use in sweet dishes – aduki are particularly good with apples.

ADUKI AND LEEK ROLL

115g/4oz/¹/₂ cup aduki beans, cooked and drained
1 tablespoon vegetable oil
1 onion, finely chopped
1 large leek, washed and finely chopped
55g/2oz/3³/₄ cups mushrooms, washed and chopped

good pinch crushed rosemary
seasoning to taste
pastry:
115g/4oz/2 cups wholemeal flour
55g/2oz/¹/₄ cup margarine
2-3 tablespoons cold water
milk to glaze

Mash the beans slightly. Heat the oil, gently fry the onion and leeks for 5 minutes, then add the mushrooms and cook a few minutes more. Mix the vegetables with the beans, add rosemary and seasoning – the mixture should be thick and moist.

To make the pastry, rub the margarine into the flour to make a mix resembling fine breadcrumbs. Add just enough water to bind to a dough, knead lightly, then wrap in kitchen foil and leave in the fridge for at least 30 minutes.

On a lightly-floured board roll out the pastry to make an oblong. Spread the bean mixture over it, leaving a small space around the edges. Roll the pastry up so that it looks like a long thin swiss roll, then dampen the edges with water and press them together to seal. Lay the roll on a lightly-greased baking sheet – if you like you can brush the top with a drop of milk.

Bake the roll at 200°C/400°F (Gas Mark 6) for 30 minutes or until the pastry is cooked. Serve cut in thick slices.

Optional extras – a thick tomato sauce, and a garnish of watercress.

AGAR AGAR
See also **Carrageen**

Made from the dried purified stems of kelp, it has exceptionally strong jelling properties that make it ideal for use in such recipes as moulded jellies. Available as either powder or flakes. It is unbleached and therefore light-grey in colour, though this does not affect the appearance of the finished dish. A nutritious and vegetarian alternative to gelatine. Agar agar has long been used in Japan, where there is a tradition of cooking with seaweed. As gelatine becomes more expensive, agar agar is now being used increasingly by sweet manufacturers.

Nutrition: It is rich in iodine and other minerals.

Buying/Storing: Buy in packets from wholefood and healthfood shops. Store in a cool dry place. The flakes are sun-bleached and processed in a natural way, the powder is made with chemicals, so although the former is a little more expensive it is worth it.

How to use: Can be used to make sweet and savoury jellies. Add 2 teaspoons of agar agar to 570ml/1 pint of liquid (or follow the instructions given on the pack). Bring the liquid almost to the boil, then simmer for 3 minutes. The liquid can be water, stock, vegetable or fruit juice – agar agar is especially good with acid fruits.

MOULDED SALAD

570ml/1 pint/2¹/₂ cups water
3-4 tablespoons lemon juice
1 tablespoon raw cane sugar, or to taste
2 teaspoons agar agar
55g/2oz/¹/₂ cup walnuts
1 small cucumber
2 sticks celery
2 dessert apples

Bring the water to the boil and add the lemon juice, then stir in the agar agar until it dissolves. Simmer briefly. Leave to cool slightly. Coarsely chop the nuts, slice the cucumber and celery, chop the apples. Add them to the lemon mixture.
Rinse a mould with cold water, shake off any excess, pour in the mixture. Leave to cool, then stir to distribute the salad ingredients evenly. Put in a cold place to set. When ready to serve, dip the mould quickly into hot water, then invert over a plate. Surround with lettuce, watercress, or other greenery.

See also Blackcurrant mousse.

ALCOHOL
See **Beer, Wine**

ALES
See **Beer**

ALFALFA

The seeds of one of the oldest cultivated plants, which has deep roots enabling it to get extra minerals that other plants cannot reach.
Nutrition: Alfalfa seeds contain up to 19% protein, compared with 16% in beef, though you would be unlikely to eat your way through a quarter-pound lump of alfalfa! One of the best ways to eat the seeds is to sprout them, which boosts their protein content to 40%. In the Third World, alfalfa is used as a food supplement.
Buying/Storing: Buy regularly in small quantities from a retailer who has a fast turnover. Store in a sealed container in a cool place.
How to use: The seeds can be sprinkled onto savoury or sweet dishes, or can be sprouted and used as a crispy, moist sandwich filling. Also good in salads, but if you stir them into other ingredients, do so gently – they are very fragile.

AUTUMN SALAD

1 red pepper, sliced
1 small parsnip, peeled and grated coarsely
1 large carrot, peeled and grated coarsely
2 sticks celery, chopped
1 bunch watercress, washed
55g/2oz alfalfa sprouts
55g/2oz/¹/₂ cup peanuts, preferably roasted

dressing:
170g/6oz/³/₄ cup silken tofu, drained
3 tablespoons vegetable oil
3 tablespoons wine vinegar or lemon juice
seasoning to taste

In a small bowl combine the red pepper, parsnip, carrot, celery and watercress. Stir in the nuts.

Make the dressing either by mashing the tofu well and then mixing with the other ingredients, or by putting them all into a blender. The dressing should be creamy but not too thick, so adjust accordingly.

Pour some of the dressing over the salad, toss lightly, top with the alfalfa sprouts.

ALLERGIES

Food is one of the main causes of the many allergies that now affect literally millions of us, causing anything from minor irritations to chronic and debilitating illness. Hyperactivity in children, for example, can often be traced directly to a wide range of foods, the majority of them processed, many of them coloured and flavoured specially to attract children. At a correction home in the USA, youngsters who were switched to a wholefood diet and given no processed foods (including white flour and sugar) showed a marked improvement in behaviour.

Clinical ecologists, specialists in such allergies, report an increase in cases of adults with catarrh, headaches, skin problems, digestive upsets, mouth ulcers, constipation, diarrhoea, colitis, high blood pressure, fainting fits, convulsions, impotence, anxiety – a list that goes on and on. It is estimated that some 5¹/₂ million people in Britain suffer in this way, probably many more. And though there may well be other causes, it is also believed that the majority of these allergies are caused by chemicals in our water, air and food.

Tracking down the exact cause of an allergy is not easy. Neither is getting many doctors to even accept that this is what a patient is suffering from – though the medical profession *is* gradually beginning to admit there might be something to the allergy theory.

If you think you may be allergic to some food, do seek help from a clinical ecologist or other alternative practitioner.

ALLSPICE

Not, as many people think, a mixture of spices, but the berry of a tree native to the West Indies, which explains why allspice is also known as Jamaica pepper. The small brown berries are usually ground into a powder and have a flavour that is like a mixture of cinnamon, cloves and nutmeg. This is one of the milder spices.

How to use: Good in curries. Also ideal for use in cakes, stewed fruit and fruit pies. Try in fruit-based punches.

GREEN TOMATO CHUTNEY

1 kilo/2 lb green tomatoes
455g/1 lb apples
455g/1 lb onions
455g/1 lb/2¹/₂ cups sultanas
1 teaspoon ground ginger
1 teaspoon allspice
570ml/1 pint/2¹/₂ cups cider vinegar
340g/³/₄ lb/2 cups raw cane sugar

Peel and chop the tomatoes, apples and onions. Put into a large saucepan with the sultanas, spices, and 190ml/1/3rd pint cider vinegar. Simmer the mixture gently for about an hour, or until everything is well cooked, adding more vinegar if necessary. Stir in the rest of the vinegar and the sugar and cook steadily until the chutney thickens.

Transfer to warmed jars, making sure you fill them right to the top, cover with waxed paper, then screw on the tops firmly (metal tops will rust if they come into contact with the chutney). Store in a cool, dry, dark place. This is a mild and rather sweet chutney. Use more spices and less sugar, if you prefer.

See also Pakora, Zucchini bread.

ALMONDS

The attractive almond tree with its pink flowers grows in Britain, but the nuts it produces are usually of the bitter variety and therefore not edible, though the oil can be extracted to use as a flavouring agent. Sweet almonds are grown in Spain, India, North Africa and America.

Varieties: You can buy almonds whole, blanched and flaked. They are also available ground to a powder.

Nutrition: Almonds have one of the highest protein contents of all nuts and are also an excellent source of calcium. Yogis are said to breakfast on a few almonds soaked overnight in milk.

How to use: Use them in cakes, biscuits and dessert dishes. Add roasted chopped almonds to ice cream. Sprinkle whole almonds over salads and vegetable dishes, or stir them into chop suey.

ALMOND BISCUITS

85g/3oz/³/₄ cup ground almonds
30g/1oz/1 good tablespoon sesame seeds
115g/4oz/³/₄ cup rice flour
few drops natural vanilla essence
2 egg whites
pinch of salt
115g/4oz/³/₄ cup raw cane sugar
blanched almonds – optional

In a bowl mix together the ground almonds, sesame seeds, rice flour and vanilla essence. Whisk the egg whites lightly with the salt, stir in the sugar, and add to the dry ingredients, stirring well.

Drop spoonfuls of the mixture onto a greased tray (or better still, rice paper). Press lightly. Top each biscuit with a nut if liked. Bake at 180°C/350°F (Gas Mark 4) for 20 minutes or until golden. Leave to cool before removing carefully from tray. If using rice paper, tear round each biscuit.

See also Cinnamon honey cake, Curried nuts nibbles, Caramellised satsumas, Skordalia, Dried fruit compôte, Lemon honey squares, Almond vegetable crumble, Wheat berry salad.

ALUMINIUM SAUCEPANS
See **Utensils, Cooking**

ANGELICA

A white-flowered plant that originated in the Baltic, so grows best in cold climates. It can reach up to 2.4 metres/8 feet in height.

Varieties: Angelica roots are used to flavour gin, vermouth and liqueurs such as benedictine. However, it is the candied stalks that are best known, for their pleasantly aromatic taste and attractive green colouring.

Buying/Storing: When buying the candied variety, make sure it looks fresh and bright and is not damaged. Wrap it well to keep out the air and store somewhere cool.

How to use: Often used for decoration on cakes. Try adding angelica when cooking fruit such as apples, pears or rhubarb. Gives an interesting flavour to marmalades and jams.

ANISEED

A decorative annual plant that can be grown in Britain, though the seeds need a warm, dry summer to ripen. Much of the aniseed on sale in Britain is imported from Spain, where it is grown commercially.

Buying/Storing: Buy the seeds frequently and in small quantities. Store in a sealed container. When using crushed seeds, do the crushing yourself (with a mill, rolling pin or heavy weight) just before they are needed, so as to retain maximum flavour.

How to use: The sweet taste, reminiscent of liquorice, makes a delicious tea that is widely believed to be good for helping the digestion. Sprinkle the seeds on bread, cakes and biscuits. Crushed seeds go well with vegetables.

CABBAGE WITH ANISEED

1/2 white cabbage, coarsely sliced
2 carrots, peeled and sliced
30g/1oz/2 1/2 tablespoons margarine or butter
approx. 6 tablespoons vegetable stock
seasoning to taste
1-2 tablespoons aniseed, or to taste

Put the cabbage and carrots in a small lightly-greased ovenproof dish. Dissolve the fat in the stock, add seasoning and aniseed, and pour over the vegetables. Cover, either with a lid or with silver foil, and bake at 180°C/350°F (Gas Mark 4) for about 20 minutes.

This is a nice vegetable accompaniment to such dishes as nut roast. So you could use the oven economically and cook the two at the same time (maybe with jacket potatoes?).

Alternatively, to make it into a complete snack on its own, add some nuts, tofu or hardboiled eggs. Or top with grated cheese and grill for a few minutes before serving.

APPLES
See also **Crabapples**

One of the most popular fruits in Britain, it is thought the apple may have been around since the Stone Age. The climate is well suited to this fruit, and there are now many different kinds available throughout the year.

Varieties: Apart from numerous varieties of succulent dessert apples there are a number of different kinds of cooking apples. Dried apple slices are also on sale in most wholefood stores.

Buying/Storing: Apples should be bright and firm, with no blemishes or bruises. Both dessert and cooking apples can be stored in the bottom of the fridge, though they will also keep for a limited time in a fruit bowl. Dessert apples are best eaten at room temperature.

How to use: Chop raw apples and add to salads. Mix with cheese and use to fill an omelette. Sprinkle grated apple over your morning muesli. Cook apple with red cabbage, or put it in a curry sauce. Make apple sauce for a quick topping, to mix into yogurt, or to spread on bread or gingerbread. Crabapples can be used for jams and jellies. Dried apples are good in a compôte with other dried fruit, especially prunes. Or chop them and add to breakfast cereals, or bake in a cake.

MOLASSES TOFFEE APPLES

4 medium-sized eating apples
225g/¹/₂ lb/1 1/3rd cups raw cane sugar
4 tablespoons molasses
55g/2oz/¹/₄ cup margarine
good teaspoon vinegar

Wipe the apples and – if they are extra shiny – use a fine grater to roughen the skin a little. Remove the stalks.
In a large heavy-based saucepan stir together the sugar, molasses, margarine and vinegar. Bring the mixture gently to the boil, stirring all the time to make sure the sugar dissolves completely. Continue boiling for about 20 minutes until it reaches hard crack stage. To test this, drop a teaspoonful into a cup of very cold water – it should separate into hard brittle threads.
Remove the pan from the heat at once.
Spear each apple with a small stick and then dip them one at a time into the toffee, turning them so that the apples are completely and evenly coated.
Leave them to cool and firm up. You can lay them on a greased tray to do this, or stand them in a mug or jar.

See also Moulded salad, Muesli, Green tomato chutney, Apple oatmeal biscuits, Red cabbage with sour cream, Dried fruit compôte.

APRICOTS

Apricot cultivation began in China around 4,000 years ago, where the apricots grew wild around Peking. From there it spread to the Middle East, the fruit being taken by Arabs to the Mediterranean countries where it is now widely grown. The climate of southern Spain is particularly suitable for the growing of apricots. The name itself comes originally from a Latin word and means 'that which ripens quickly'.

Varieties: As well as fresh apricots, look out for dried ones which are available as whole fruit, halves and pieces. For best flavour try hunza apricots which are wild and need only to be soaked before eating.

Nutrition: They are a good source of vitamin A and some minerals. As well as containing more protein than any other dried fruit, apricots are rich in iron.

Buying/Storing: Choose apricots that are firm but not hard, with a good colour and no blemishes. Also avoid any with a green tinge as they are unlikely to ripen. If soft, eat at once, as they don't keep well. If unripe, leave at room temperature for a few days.

How to use: Apart from the obvious fruit salad, apricots are nice raw with celery and walnuts. Less perfect ones can be cooked to make a purée (try adding vanilla), or put into a chutney. Halves can be used in a French style flan, maybe topped with almonds and whipped cream. Fresh apricots make a tasty crumble. Dried apricots can be chopped and added to a coleslaw or Waldorf salad, or used with rice as a stuffing. Hunza apricots can be lightly cooked (or even just soaked), the stones removed, and then re-filled with almonds or hazelnuts for a bufffet party.

APRICOT RICE

340g/12oz/1¹/₄ cups long grain brown rice
570ml/1 pint/2¹/₂ cups water
¹/₂ teaspoon turmeric
2 spring onions, finely chopped
1 small red pepper, finely chopped
1 stick celery, finely chopped
55g/2oz/1/3rd cup dried apricots, well soaked and chopped
55g/2oz/¹/₂ cup almond flakes, lightly roasted
1 tablespoon oil, preferably olive
good squeeze of lemon juice

Put the rice into a saucepan with the water and turmeric, bring to the boil, then cover and simmer until all the water has been absorbed. The rice should be just tender. (Check that it does not boil dry, but if necessary add only the minimum amount of water or the rice will be soggy.)
Immediately stir in all the other ingredients. This can be served as a sort of hot salad, or left to get completely cold before serving. Delicious with yogurt.

See also Stuffed dates, Dried fruit compôte.

ARAME
See **Seaweed**

ARROWROOT

This is a white, starchy powder that is made from the underground stalks of a plant that is grown on a large scale in the West Indies. In this form it makes an ideal food for babies and anyone who is ill, as it is not only nutritious, but is especially easy to digest. In general, though, it is used as a thickening agent for sauces, soups, glazes. It has no taste.

Buying/Storing: Buy from a retailer who has a fast turnover. Keep it in an airtight container in a cool spot.

How to use: Always blend it with a drop of cold liquid before adding the paste to the dish you are cooking. How much you use will vary – as a guide start with 2 tablespoons to 570ml/1 pint of liquid.

BUTTERSCOTCH CREAM

30g/1oz/¹/₄ cup arrowroot
570ml/1 pint/2¹/₂ cups milk
115g/4oz/2/3rd cup raw cane sugar
knob of butter
1 teaspoon vanilla essence

Mix the arrowroot with a little of the cold milk to make a smooth paste. Heat the rest of the milk and pour it onto the paste, stir well, then return to the saucepan. Bring the milk mixture to the boil, still stirring continually and cook gently for 5 minutes. Remove from heat and stir in the sugar, butter and vanilla essence. When these ingredients have completely dissolved it can be served hot, either alone or as a creamy sauce with fruit or sponge pudding.

Alternatively, pour into individual glasses and leave until cold, then serve with single cream. Or top with grated raw sugar, chocolate or chopped nuts. Also good poured over ice cream.

See also Glazed carrots almondine, Lemon curd (eggless).

ARTICHOKES, GLOBE

An unusual vegetable with a globe-shaped head. It is usually imported from Mediterranean countries or Egypt, though it can be grown in Britain. **Buying/Storing:** Buy when the leaves look firm and are closely folded together. (Fully opened leaves are a sign that the artichoke is past its best.) At least a few inches of stalk should still be attached. Often only the subtly-flavoured heart is served, but the leaves are also tasty, and can be dipped into sauces, dressings or melted butter. Only the fleshy base of the leaves is eaten. Store in a cool place and eat as soon as possible after purchasing. **How to use:** Can be baked whole and served with a sauce, or stuff the centre with a favourite filling. Alternatively, simply boil until tender and serve hot or cold with a selection of dips.

STUFFED GLOBE ARTICHOKES

4 medium-sized globe artichokes
lemon juice
15g/¹/₂oz/1 flat tablespoon margarine
1 small onion, chopped
1 stick celery, chopped
2 mushrooms, chopped
2 tomatoes, coarsely chopped
vegetarian 'bacon bits' – optional
2 tablespoons cooked grain (i.e. bulgur, rice)
1 egg, lightly beaten
seasoning to taste
chopped parsley

To prepare the artichokes, remove the tough outer leaves, cut off the stems, trim the spiked points of the leaves with scissors. Rub the surfaces with lemon juice to prevent discolouring. Rinse in cold water. Then cook in a large pan of boiling water for 30 minutes or until a leaf comes away when gently pulled. Drain well. Use a spoon to carefully remove the inner leaves and the chokes (these are tucked in the centre of the artichokes and look like small thistles). Leave the outer leaves. Stand the artichokes close together in a small greased ovenproof dish.

Melt the margarine and sauté the onion, celery and mushrooms for 5 minutes. Add the tomatoes, 'bacon bits' if using them, grains, lightly beaten egg, seasoning and parsley. Mix well. Divide this mixture between the artichokes. Cover the dish and bake at 190°C/375°F (Gas Mark 5) for 15 minutes. Serve hot. Makes an unusual starter.

▓▓▓ ARTICHOKES, JERUSALEM ▓▓▓

A knobbly looking vegetable which is actually the tuber of a species of sunflower. It originated in North America, grows well in Britain, though is not widely-known. Look out for it during the winter months. Jerusalem artichokes have firm white flesh and a smoky flavour.

Buying/Storing: Do not buy if they look wrinkly or damaged in any way. If they are very misshapen they will be difficult if not impossible to peel. Store in a dark, dry place where they should keep for up to a week.

Nutrition: Artichokes have a high potassium content.

How to use: To make peeling easier, cook them briefly first. A drop of lemon juice in the water will help keep the flesh white. Jerusalem artichokes can be boiled and served with butter or a sauce. Slice them very thin and deep-fry to make crisps. Purée them and use to thicken winter soups. Added to stir-fried vegetables they have a taste and texture something like water chestnuts. They make an unusual soufflé.

ARTICHOKE SALAD

455g/1 lb Jerusalem artichokes
squeeze of lemon juice
1 small red pepper, sliced
1 stick celery, chopped
1 small leek, cleaned and finely sliced
mayonnaise
4 hardboiled eggs, quartered
green leaves to serve
parsley to garnish

Scrub the artichokes under cold water, remove any damaged parts, leave to stand for a few minutes in cold water with lemon juice added.

Transfer to a saucepan and steam or boil the artichokes for 15 to 20 minutes, or until just tender. Use a sharp knife to peel them. (You can do this first, but it is easier to

peel cooked artichokes, and they retain more flavour.) Cut into large chunks and leave to cool.
In a bowl mix together the artichokes, pepper, celery, leek, and enough mayonnaise to moisten. Arrange some green shredded leaves in a salad bowl, top with the artichoke mixture, decorate with egg quarters and sprigs of fresh parsley.

ASPARAGUS

The very young shoots of a plant which is a member of the lily family. Though it is now grown around the world, most of the asparagus available in Britain is imported from Mediterranean countries. As it is available only for a short period at the beginning of the summer, and is expensive, it is usually considered to be a luxury item rather than a day-to-day vegetable.

Varieties: There are two main varieties, one with white spears, the other with purple or green spears. The larger the spears, the higher will be the price. Sprew is a thinner kind of asparagus that is most often used in dishes such as soup.

Buying/Storing: Don't buy asparagus if it looks woody, wrinkled or dry. Choose a bunch with even-sized spears. Fresh asparagus should be cooked as soon as possible after purchasing.

How to use: The best way to eat asparagus is to cook it lightly, then serve it with butter or hollandaise sauce. Can also be used in quiches and flans, or in soufflés – it goes especially well with eggs. Try serving it in a cheese sauce. Cold cooked spears are delicious in salads.

ASPARAGUS WITH HOLLANDAISE SAUCE

455g/1 lb young asparagus

sauce:
30g/1oz/2¹/₂ tablespoons margarine
55g/2oz/¹/₂ cup wholemeal flour, sifted to remove the bran
425ml/³/₄ pint/2 cups hot water
seasoning to taste
1 tablespoon hot milk
1 egg yolk
1 tablespoon lemon juice
1-2 teaspoons fresh tarragon, chopped fine

Wash the asparagus, cut off any woody stalk ends. Trim so they are equal lengths. Tie into neat bundles of about 6 stalks, heads at the top, and steam in an asparagus pan for about 10 minutes until tender.
Meanwhile, make the sauce. Melt the margarine, add the flour, and cook briefly. Pour in the water, stir, season well, and cook until the sauce begins to thicken. Combine the milk and egg yolk. Add the lemon juice to the sauce, stir in the milk and egg mixture, and heat gently, stirring all the time so that the egg does not curdle. Add tarragon to taste.

Either serve the sauce in a jug, or in small individual dishes. The asparagus should be dipped in the sauce – you eat the tip and soft part of the stem. Don't forget the napkins!

Note: An asparagus pan is especially tall so that the asparagus stalks can stand upright in water whilst the tender tops are steamed. If you do not have one, try inverting one saucepan on top of another, or simply use silver foil to cover the tops.

AUBERGINE

This shiny, dark-purple, oval-shaped vegetable is a member of the same family as the deadly nightshade. Though it has been known since the 13th century, it was for many years cultivated as an ornamental plant rather than as something to be eaten. Grown in much of the world – and with large quantities now also being grown under glass in Britain – it is available all year round. In America it is called eggplant.

Varieties: Though aubergines are usually dark-purple in colour, some of the imported varieties are white, others a mixture of white and purple. Despite this, the taste is much the same.

Nutrition: Aubergines are low in calories, though most of the traditional methods of cooking them involve using oils, so the calorie count can increase considerably. Not especially nutritious, they do contain some vitamins plus traces of potassium, iron and calcium. Macrobiotics will not eat them.

Buying/Storing: Buy only firm, unshrivelled aubergines. The skin should look polished. Store in the fridge, preferably for no more than 2 or 3 days.

How to use: The water content in aubergines is high, and it can be bitter. To remove this bitterness, slice the aubergine, sprinkle with salt, leave 30 minutes, then rinse with water and pat dry before proceeding to cook them. Cube and then fry aubergine with onions and tomatoes, as in ratatouille. Cut aubergines in half, stuff with a nut and breadcrumb mixture, and bake. Use to make moussaka, or blend with garlic and make into a dip.

AUBERGINE FRITTERS

1 medium aubergine, peeled and coarsely chopped
salt
1 small onion, peeled and chopped
115g/4oz/¹/₂ cup tofu, drained and well mashed
2 tablespoons wholemeal flour
chopped parsley
good pinch garlic salt
vegetable oil to cook

Put the aubergine into a bowl and sprinkle with salt. Leave for 15 minutes then drain well. Stir in the onion, tofu, flour, parsley and garlic salt. Keep stirring the mixture until well blended.

Heat the oil and, when it is very hot, drop large spoonfuls of the mixture into it. Deep-fry them until the fritters are crisp and brown. Drain well before serving. Can accompany a main savoury dish, or serve them as a starter with a sauce such as tomato.

Note: These fritters are ideal for vegans. Vegans who like a firmer textured fritter can use egg substitute to hold the ingredients together. Others might like to replace the tofu with one or two eggs.

See also Moussaka.

AVOCADO PEARS

Now grown widely in the tropics and sub-tropics, the avocado was also a favourite of the Aztecs, who introduced it to Mexico back in the 13th century. Though it is a fruit it is used most often as a vegetable. Avocados on sale in Britain are usually imported from Israel or South Africa.

Nutrition: Avocados are a natural 'super food', rich in protein, vegetable oils, B complex vitamins, vitamin E, and minerals. They are also low in carbohydrate and cholesterol-free.

Buying/Storing: To check if ripe, press gently. The flesh should yield slightly. If very soft the avocado is over-ripe. If still hard, wrap in paper and leave in a warm place for 2 or 3 days.

How to use: The simplest way to serve is to halve and serve with a vinaigrette or herb dressing. Alternatively cut avocados in half, brush with lemon, then fill with cottage cheese or sour cream and sprinkle with nuts. Can also be chopped up and added to salads, savoury or fresh fruit. Try blending or mashing over-ripe avocados to make a dip or salad dressing. Avocado soup is good chilled on summer days. Or bake avocados and eat hot.

GUACAMOLE DIP

2 ripe avocados
2 tablespoons lemon juice
1/4 small onion
seasoning to taste
pinch of paprika
pinch of chilli powder
parsley to garnish

Mash the avocado flesh with the lemon juice. Finely chop the onion and stir into the avocado mixture with the seasoning and spices to taste. Chill briefly.

Serve in a dish garnished with fresh parsley sprigs. Surround it with corn chips, potato crisps, crackers, raw vegetables such as carrot, cauliflower, pepper and

celery, all to be dipped in the guacamole before being eaten.
You can make guacamole in a blender if you prefer.

BABY FOOD

The first food a baby consumes is of course milk, preferably mother's milk. For several months this may be all baby needs. Between 4 and 6 months he or she may start taking such foods as yogurt, vegetable broth and fruit juice. By 6 months you will be able to start introducing solid foods.

It is at this stage that many mothers choose to feed their babies – at least part of the time – on the ready-prepared baby foods that are popular and widely available. If you wish to do this, do so with care. Read the labels. It has been claimed that the levels of pesticide in commercially-prepared baby foods are well within maximum residue levels set by the government, and undoubtedly manufacturers take their responsibility seriously. Just the same, the vulnerability of a baby should not be underestimated.

The way to be sure is to make up your own foods from ingredients you know you can trust. If circumstances prevent this much or part of the time, consider organic foods.

There is now a selection of organic baby foods on the market, including such things as fruit purées and juices, ground cereals, rusks and vegetables with noodles, most of them also salt and sugar free. You may have to search for them, though an increasing number of wholefood and healthfood shops are stocking them. If you cannot see them do ask – most enlightened stockists will be only too grateful to have their omission pointed out to them.

BAKING POWDER
See **Raising agents**

BANANAS

An ancient food originating in the tropics, yet not known in Britain until the 1860s. Now they are the second most popular fruit here – apples are the first. The name is derived from the Arabic word for 'finger'.

Varieties: Yellow bananas are best used in sweet dishes. For savoury dishes look out for the larger green bananas that are called plantains; these, in fact, should not be eaten raw. Perfect for children's lunchboxes are tiny fat apple bananas – though expensive as they are the young ones and are therefore especially sweet. Bananas are also available cut into strips and sun-dried, which makes them a high energy and natural alternative to sweets. Try freezing them to make them chewier. Banana chips have been fried or baked so that they are crisp, some are also sweetened.

Nutrition: As bananas are a good source of natural carbohydrates and dietary fibre, they make a filling and satisfying snack for comparatively few calories (a small one contains about 80). They are also a good source of potassium.

Buying/Storing: Nowadays bananas are usually picked when green and allowed to ripen en route to their destination. The pulp is ready and at its sweetest when brown spots appear on the skin; even a completely brown banana may be edible, provided that the skin has not been damaged (the riper the fruit, the easier it will be to digest). Always leave bananas to ripen in the room, do not put them in a fridge. For cooking in savoury dishes choose the plantains that are firm to touch and still green.

How to use: Chop and add to salads; bananas are especially good with rice salads. Mash and add to yogurt, or use in a milkshake (bananas are just as good with soya milk, and are nice with tofu). Hot bananas in honey sauce make a quick dessert. Serve them with curry, or fry them and serve them American-style with sweetcorn. Plantains are much used in West Indian cookery. Banana chips are good mixed with dried fruit and nuts, or added to a breakfast cereal. Chop dried bananas and add them to a curried rice salad.

FROZEN BANANA YOGURT

3 ripe bananas
6 tablespoons honey
55g/2oz/1/3rd cup raw cane sugar
1/2 teaspoon finely grated lemon rind
425ml/3/4 pint/2 cups natural yogurt
roasted hazelnuts, coarsely chopped

Mash the bananas and mix with honey, sugar and lemon rind. Lightly blend in the yogurt, and turn into a tray. Freeze until it begins to firm. Beat the mixture, then return to the tray, cover, and freeze until set firm. Serve in scoops, garnished with roasted hazelnuts.

See also California salad, Parsnip and banana chutney, Tropical fruit salad, Banana milkshake.

BARBECUES

Until recently barbecues were not popular in Britain, mainly because of the climate. Now, however – with our summers seeming to be a little more reliable – more people are discovering the pleasure of not only eating outdoors, but cooking over a real fire. With this interest has come a wide range of equipment, most of which is over-priced and unnecessary. All you need to have a barbecue are a few bricks to build up the sides and a grill rack suspended over the heat. Though you can use wood as a fuel, charcoal or briquettes are best as they reach a good heat quickly and then maintain it. A sheet of aluminium foil spread under the barbecue rack will speed up the heating of the coals, and to raise the heat even higher, simply stir them.

What foods you cook over your barbecue is, of course, your choice. In countries where the climate allows barbecues to be a regular part of everyday life, the most often cooked food is meat. If, however, you are vegetarian there are still plenty of things you can cook. Try threading vegetables and tofu onto kebab sticks and cooking briefly, turning frequently. Young corn-on-the-cobs are another idea. Nut or bean burgers are excellent cooked this way, as are any of the vegetarian sausages you can now buy (or make yourself, of course). Potatoes can be scrubbed, wrapped in foil, and cooked in their jackets. Try also more exotic foods such as Indian breads, koftas and bhajis, Middle Eastern pita bread and falaffels, or Italian rice balls. Remember that smaller items, especially vegetables, will cook more quickly. And do brush the grill rack well with vegetable oil before you start, and lightly oil the foods too to prevent them sticking.

Add fresh bread and a selection of salads and you have a delicious barbecue that will be enjoyed by everyone – including the cook.

See Vegetable kebabs with herbs, Borlotti bean burgers.

BARLEY

This small whole grain was used by the Egyptians 5,000 years ago for the brewing of beer. It is still used for this purpose, especially in Scotland, where it is also used to make whisky and vinegar and to feed livestock. In America it is used in the production of bourbon.

Varieties: Pot barley is the whole grain. Pearl barley has had the outer two layers removed which makes it quicker to cook, but less nutritious. When barley is malted during the first stage of the beer making process, a by-product is malt extract which can still be found in some shops and is a valuable food.

Nutrition: It is a highly nutritious grain, easy to digest, and ideal for slimmers since it has the lowest calorie count of all grains. Be sure to buy pot barley, which still contains the valuable bran and germ.

How to use: Because it is easy to digest, barley is excellent when cooking for invalids, or for adding to baby foods. Use barley in soups, stews, scotch broth, bean hotpot, or to make barley water. Use quick-cooking barley flakes to make milk puddings or to add to muesli. Barley flour is fine and sweet when made from pearl barley, darker and coarser when made from the whole grain. Add it to bread dough. Look out for barley syrup and barley malt, both of which are hard to find in shops these days, but which are excellent food supplements.

MIXED GRAIN GRANOLA

115g/4oz/1 cup barley flakes
115g/4oz/1 cup wheat flakes
115g/4oz/1 cup rye flakes
115g/4oz/1 cup rolled oats
70ml/¹/₈th pint/¹/₄ cup honey
4 tablespoons vegetable oil
peel of half an orange, coarsely chopped
55g/2oz/¹/₂ cup coconut flakes
115g/4oz/1 cup chopped nuts, one kind or mixed
115g/4oz/1 cup chopped dates

Mix together the flaked grains. Heat the honey and oil in a large saucepan, stir, add the grains. Transfer the mixture to a shallow heat-proof dish or tin and bake at 170°C/325°F (Gas Mark 3) for about 30 minutes, stirring occasionally. Add the orange peel, coconut flakes and nuts, and cook 15 minutes more, or until the mixture is light gold in colour.

Remove from the heat, stir in the dates, and set aside to cool. Transfer to a large screw-top jar. Can be eaten as a breakfast cereal with milk or fruit juice, or used to top fruit purées, ice cream or yogurt.

BASIL

Sweet basil is a garden herb that can grow well in our climate, though it needs to be carefully tended. It is said to have originated in India, but nowadays it is particularly popular in Mediterranean countries, especially Italy, where its delicate and slightly sweet taste is an essential part of many traditional dishes.

Buying/Storing: Dried it will keep for some time in dark well sealed jars, though it is best to buy small quantities and use them within a reasonable time. Fresh basil should be used as soon as possible after it has been picked or purchased.

How to use: Basil is the perfect herb to use with tomatoes, also courgettes. Try it with scrambled eggs, rice and other grain dishes. Good when shredded coarsely and sprinkled over salads. Mix into cheesespread or dips for a change. Add to sauces.

TOMATO BASILICA WITH MOZZARELLA

455g/1 lb large tomatoes
225g/¹/₂ lb/2 cups mozzarella cheese
olive oil
seasoning to taste
fresh basil

The tomatoes should be ripe but still firm. Wipe them to clean, then cut crossways into evenly-sized slices. Slice the mozzarella. Arrange attractively on a serving dish, overlapping the tomatoes and cheese.
Mix together the olive oil, seasoning and a good amount of finely-chopped basil. Trickle this over the other ingredients. Chill before serving topped with sprigs of basil.

See also Minestrone alla Milanese, Pesto sauce, Tomato sauce.

BAY

A well-known evergreen garden shrub that can grow up to 3.60 metres/12 feet in height. Its leaves have been used in cookery in Britain for hundreds of years.

Buying/Storing: Freshly picked leaves can be used at once, or dried and then stored in dark airtight jars. Like all herbs, bay leaves will lose their strength if left too long.

How to use: The very distinctive flavour is good on its own, though it also combines well with that of other herbs. Bay is an essential ingredient of bouquet garni. Add a whole leaf to stews, casseroles, soups, and remove before serving. Or use to flavour milk before making a sauce. Crush and add to vegetable dishes – goes especially well with cabbage.

VEGETABLE KEBABS WITH HERBS

1 large green pepper
12 button mushrooms
2 large courgettes
8 cherry or small tomatoes
6 small unpeeled potatoes, steamed until just cooked
1 large onion
8 stuffed olives
bay leaves

marinade:
3 tablespoons vegetable oil
1 tablespoon white wine vinegar
pinch garlic salt
1 teaspoon dried basil
1 teaspoon dried rosemary, crushed
1 teaspoon dried oregano
seasoning to taste

Cut the stem from the pepper, remove the seeds, and cut the flesh into large cubes. Wipe the mushrooms to clean. Cut the courgettes into thick slices. Wash and dry the tomatoes. Halve the potatoes (skins should be left on). Cut the onion into thick segments and then separate the layers. Put all the vegetables into a bowl and pour on the marinade. Leave overnight in the fridge.
Thread all the ingredients onto skewers, arranging them attractively, and including the olives and bay leaves. Lay them on a baking sheet. Cook under the grill for 10-15 minutes or until all the ingredients are just tender, turning the skewers frequently, and basting with any left-over marinade. Serve with rice.

BEAN CURD
See **Tofu**

BEANS, FRESH
See also **Broad beans**

There are a number of varieties available fresh from spring through to autumn, most of them homegrown. Runner beans and broad beans are probably the best known, along with French beans which are a dwarf green bean variety.
Nutrition: All contain vitamins A and C, calcium and potassium. Beans are also a reasonably good source of folic acid.
Buying/Storing: The shells should look smooth, free of blemishes, and a good colour. Store in the fridge for a few days if not needed at once.
How to use: Young broad beans are good raw or very lightly cooked, and added to green salads, potato salad, or mixed with other beans and eaten hot. Older broad beans go well in creamy sauces, or add them to vegetable hotpots or casseroles for a quick source of protein. Runner beans combine well with tomatoes. Add them to a salad niçoise. Serve in a cheese sauce, or use as a filling for quiche.

MARINATED BEANS
455g/1 lb green beans
2 tablespoons cider vinegar
6 tablespoons vegetable oil

seasoning to taste
good pinch dried marjoram
1/2-1 teaspoon honey
30g/1oz/1/4 cup chopped cashew nuts, roasted

Wash the beans and, if necessary, cut off any stringy sides. Steam the beans for about 15 minutes, or until just cooked but still crisp. Drain well.
In a small screw-top jar combine the vinegar, oil, seasoning, marjoram and honey, making sure they are thoroughly blended. Or put them into a bowl and whisk well.
Pour the marinade mixture over the beans, toss lightly. Leave in a cool place for an hour or two, even overnight, for the beans to take up the flavour of the marinade.
Serve sprinkled with nuts.

See also Three bean salad, Sorghum and green bean stew, Bean salad niçoise.

BEANS, DRIED
See **Pulses**

BEAN SPROUTS
See **Sprouted seeds, grains and beans**

BEER

Originally beer was a simple drink made from fermented malted barley with hops added. Like wine, however, it has changed over the years. Certainly it still contains barley and hops. But with the consumption of beer rising, and vast amounts being consumed each day – and profits, as usual, being a key factor – the process has undergone various changes. Nowadays chemicals are used to speed up the germination of the barley. Anti-foam agents are pumped into the vats to reduce the size of the yeast head, foam stabilisers are also being used to produce the thick white head of foam that looks so good on the top of a glassfull. Other additives known to be included by some brewers are hydrogen peroxide, sulphites, corn grits (to replace some of the more expensive barley), potato starch, sugar syrup. Even the barley and hops that are used have almost certainly been grown using chemicals.

Although all additives are used in small quantities, and the brewers claim that they are safe, no one can deny that whatever variety you drink – bottled, canned or draught – beer is a dubious product. And as no labelling is required at the moment, you have no way of judging if the pint in your hand contains something you would sooner avoid. Vegetarians might prefer not to know that virtually all traditional draught beer is fined with isinglass, which is a fish product.

As with so many aspects of the food and drink industry, however, things are looking up. Public demand has encouraged a number of small brewers to start production of additive free and naturally produced beers. A few are already available. No doubt as more natural brews appear in pubs and off-licenses you will hear about them.

BEETROOT

Victorians not only ate them but used them also to rinse hair and as a clothes dye. These plum-coloured round-shaped vegetables grow best in cool regions and so feature often in Polish, Russian and Scandinavian cookery. In this country they are traditionally sold ready-cooked, the peel left to be removed just before you serve it. Beetroots are at their best in the late summer, though they are available for most of the year.

Buying/Storing: Both cooked and raw beetroots should have a good colour and look firm and damage-free. The smaller ones are sweeter. If cooked, the skin should rub off easily. Store beetroot in a cool, dark place. Cooked beetroot will keep in the fridge for a few days.

How to use: Young, raw beetroot can be grated and used in a salad – delicious combined with celery, apple and nuts. Cooked beetroot should be sliced or diced and served with dressings, or hot in a white sauce. Complimentary flavours include ginger, caraway and sour cream. Borscht is an exotic beetroot soup. Beetroot tops are nice too. Cook them like spinach.

SWEET AND SOUR BORSCHT

2 tablespoons vegetable oil
1 small onion, chopped
2 carrots, peeled and grated
1/4 small red cabbage, grated
3 small raw beetroot, peeled and grated
70ml/1/8th pint/1/4 cup lemon juice
2 tablespoons raw cane sugar
good pinch dried dill
850ml/1 1/2 pints/3 3/4 cups vegetable stock
seasoning to taste
sour cream, natural yogurt, cottage cheese or tahini to serve

Heat the oil and lightly fry the onion, carrots and red cabbage for 5 minutes or until soft.

Stir in the beetroot, lemon juice, sugar, dill and vegetable stock. Bring to a gentle boil, then lower the heat and simmer for about 30 minutes, or until everything is cooked. Add seasoning to taste. Serve very hot.

Traditionally borscht is served with a spoonful of sour cream swirled into each helping. Yogurt makes a good alternative, or stir in a spoonful or two of cottage cheese. Tahini gives a delicious nutty taste to it.

See also Caraway beetroot pancakes.

BERGAMOT

A herb that grows well in Britain, bergamot has medium-sized leaves and attractive red flowers. The leaves are most often used added to drinks such as a summer fruit cup. For an unusual touch, sprinkle a few of the flower petals over a salad.

LEMON SQUASH

3 lemons
approx. 2 tablespoons honey or raw cane sugar
850ml/1¹/₂ pints/3³/₄ cups boiling water
fresh bergamot flowers

Halve the lemons and squeeze as much juice as possible from them. Put this aside.
In a separate jug combine the honey or sugar and boiling water, stirring to dissolve the sweetener.
Chop up the lemons and add to the sweetened water. Leave to cool.
Strain the liquid from this mixture and add it to the lemon juice, stirring well. Chill.
Serve in 4 glasses, floating a few bergamot flowers on the top of each.
Note: For an especially refreshing lemon squash, add chopped mint to the boiling water along with the sugar or honey – not too much, though, or the flavour will be overpowering.

BERRIES
See also **Cranberries, Mulberries**

Berries come in numerous different colours and sizes, and many are grown in Britain where the temperate climate suits them particularly well. Favourite for flavour are raspberries, the majority of which are cultivated in Scotland. Loganberries are a hybrid between a raspberry and a Pacific blackberry; with a sharper taste they are ideal for cooking. Strawberries are also very popular, and though the local crops are available for only a limited time, imported crops mean that you can now have fresh strawberries midwinter as well as mid-summer. Gooseberries have a distinctive taste yet are relatively unknown outside Europe. And picking wild blackberries is an autumn tradition even in cities (these hardy plants grow just about anywhere!).
Buying/Storing: All berries are fragile fruits, best eaten within 24 hours of being bought or picked. If you cannot use them at once, store them in the

fridge, and do not wash them until just before they are to be used. They freeze well.

How to use: Traditionally they were used in jams, and when there is a glut this is a good way to preserve them for later. However, berries are also delicious in crumbles, pies and tarts, in sauces (try serving gooseberry sauce with a nut roast) and fruit fools. Young raw berries are, of course, the perfect ingredient for fruit salad.

GOOSEBERRY BRULÉE

455g/1 lb gooseberries
sugar to taste
grated peel of 1 orange
approx. 55g/2oz/1/3rd cup raw cane sugar
140ml/¹/₄ pint/²/₃rd cup sour cream

Clean the fruit, remove the stalks. Put into a saucepan with the orange peel, add sugar to taste. The exact amount will depend on how ripe the gooseberries are, and what variety you use. Add a drop of water and cook gently until only just tender. Check to see that the saucepan does not boil dry, but do not use more water than is necessary.

Divide the fruit between small heatproof ramekins, or pile it into one large dish. Top with the cream and then the sugar, spreading it evenly.

Put the ramekins or the dish under a hot grill and cook until brown on top. Serve hot.

See also Tropical fruit salad, Red fruit salad.

BICARBONATE OF SODA
See **Raising agents**

BLACK BEANS

These are a member of the kidney bean family, much used in the cookery of the Caribbean, South America and Africa; a bigger, 'meatier' bean that makes more of a meal. They are available here only as dried beans.

How to use: Allow approximately 1¹/₂-2 hours to cook. Use in stews and winter savouries. Make into a loaf, or combine with onions and rice. Black beans go especially well with spiced and curry sauces. Can be re-fried Mexican style.

BLACK BEAN AND PUMPKIN STEW

115g/4oz/2/3rd cup black beans, soaked overnight
2 tablespoons vegetable oil
1 red pepper, sliced
1 large onion, sliced

¹/₄ white cabbage, sliced
1 teaspoon mixed herbs
seasoning to taste
pinch of chilli powder to taste
¹/₄ small pumpkin, peeled and sliced

Cover the beans with fresh water, bring to the boil and continue to boil for 10 minutes, then lower the heat and simmer for 1 hour.

Meanwhile, heat the oil and fry the pepper and onion for 10 minutes. Add the cabbage and cook 10 minutes more. Combine the beans with the vegetables in one saucepan, add herbs, seasoning, chilli powder, and extra water if necessary. Add the pumpkin. Continue simmering for about 15 minutes, or until everything is cooked, and serve the stew piping hot. A crisp green salad and some corn bread make this a complete and balanced meal.

BLACKBERRIES
See **Berries**

BLACKCURRANTS
See **Currants**

BLACK EYED PEAS

This medium-sized white dried bean has a distinctive black mark that gives it its name. It originated in Africa, where it is still a staple, the dried seeds being ground to make a coffee substitute and the shoots eaten as a green vegetable. Black eyed peas are also grown in the USA (one variety has pods which reach up to nearly 1 metre/3 feet in length), and feature in a number of the traditional dishes of the southern states.

How to use: Allow approximately 45 minutes-1 hour to cook. Cook with onion, garlic and spices. Add cold to a salad. Mix with vegetables and other pulses for a hearty winter casserole.

HOPPIN' JOHN

170g/6oz/1 cup black eyed peas
2 tablespoons vegetable oil
1 onion
2 tablespoons fresh parsley
170g/6oz/³/₄ cup brown rice
850ml/1¹/₂ pints/3³/₄ cups vegetable stock
3 firm tomatoes
seasoning to taste
parsley to garnish

Put the black eyed peas in fresh water, bring to the boil and cook for 10 minutes. Lower heat, cover pan, and cook for 15 minutes.
Heat the oil and sauté the sliced onion. Add the parsley and cook a minute longer, then stir in the drained black eyed peas together with the rice and stock. Bring to the boil, then simmer for 30 minutes until peas and rice are cooked. Drain off any excess liquid, stir in the quartered tomatoes and seasoning to taste. Serve topped with sprigs of parsley.

BORAGE

A herb that has large, rather hairy leaves with a cucumber-like flavour, and pretty blue flowers that are most widely used in drinks, though they can also be candied and used to decorate cakes. When adding the leaves to food chop them fine to disguise their hairiness.

BORAGE COTTAGE CHEESE

225g/¹/₂ lb/1 cup cottage cheese
approx. 2 tablespoons chopped borage
seasoning to taste
flowers to garnish

Simply combine the cheese, borage and seasoning and leave in the fridge for the flavours to blend.
Serve topped with a few borage flowers.

BORECOLE
See **Kale**

BORLOTTI BEANS

An unusual bean with a pinky flecked skin, another member of the kidney bean family. It has rather a bland taste, and goes floury when cooked. Borlotti beans are popular in Italy where they are added to a variety of dishes.
How to use: Allow approximately 45 minutes-1 hour to cook. Borlotti beans go well with pasta, or in casseroles. As they can easily be mashed to a purée, try borlotti beans in loaves and croquettes. Make into a soup and sprinkle with grated Parmesan cheese.

BORLOTTI BEAN BURGERS

170g/6oz/1 cup borlotti beans, soaked overnight
285ml/¹/₂ pint/1 1/3rd cup vegetable stock
2 spring onions, finely chopped

1 large carrot, peeled and coarsely grated
1 teaspoon yeast extract, or to taste
seasoning to taste
1 egg, beaten
2 tablespoons chopped parsley
approx. 55g/2oz/^{1}/$_2$ cup rolled oats
vegetable oil for frying

Drain the beans, add them to the vegetable stock, bring to the boil and cook for 10 minutes, then lower the heat and cook for a further 30-40 minutes, or until the beans are tender. Check that they do not need more water during cooking, though only add the minimum. If a lot is left when the beans are cooked, continue cooking with the lid off and on a high heat until at least some of it has been absorbed. Drain off any excess. Cool the beans.

Mash the beans to a thick paste and mix with the chopped onion and carrot, the yeast extract and seasoning, the egg and then the parsley. Keep stirring until all the ingredients are thoroughly blended. Add some of the oats to thicken the purée. Divide into 8 equal-size portions, roll into balls and then press them to flatten slightly. Coat lightly with more oats.

Shallow-fry for about 5 minutes on each side, or until crisp and brown. Drain before serving.

BRAN

The tough outer coating of a grain. Wheat bran used to be the one most widely used, but since oats have become such a popular grain (mainly on account of their reputed ability to counteract cholesterol), oat bran is becoming equally popular. Even more recent is the discovery that rice bran may have similar qualities, so this too is now on sale in an increasing number of stores. The bran is removed when the grain is processed. Very bland in taste, crunchy in texture, it can be added to most dishes.

Nutrition: The main value of bran in the diet is as a source of fibre. When Dr. T.R. Allinson discovered, in London in the 1880s, how bran helped his patients, he campaigned to stop it being removed from flour, but he was considered to be a crank and was ignored. Eventually he was struck off the medical register. In the early 1900s the Kellogg Company in the USA sponsored research into the effects of their product All-Bran and came to many of the same conclusions as Dr. Allinson. But it has only been in the last decade that fibre has come to be considered an important and necessary part of our daily diet, and not – as was formerly thought – an irritant which was devoid of nutrients and therefore best avoided.

Bran on its own is not a good source of nutrients. In fact, unprocessed bran prevents minerals such as iron, calcium and zinc being absorbed in the small intestine. When eaten in bread or baked goods, however, bran is a good source of B vitamins, phosphorus and iron. Keeping the bran in grains, or adding bran to flours which have had the bran removed, is believed to help such conditions as constipation, diverticular disease, varicose veins, obesity, piles, hiatus hernia, and possibly some more serious conditions. It is filling, yet contains only about 117 calories per ounce, so it is also a help for those wanting to lose weight. (However, adding large quantities of bran to your food is not a good way to gain health – in fact, it can be positively harmful to those unused to high fibre food.)

Buying/Storing: Available coarse or fine milled. Probably best to start by using the fine milled variety and only in small amounts. Bran is now available from wholefood and healthfood shops, plus chemists and many supermarkets. Buy in small quantities at a time and store in an airtight container. Make sure it is unprocessed natural bran.

How to use: It is recommended by many doctors that one or two tablespoonsful a day should be added to each person's food, though do note that additional bran is *not* necessary if you are already eating wholegrain breads and other wholegrain products. Bran should not be eaten raw, but added to bread, pastry or hot breakfast cereals, or stirred into stews and casseroles. When using bran in baking you may need to add extra water as bran absorbs more than flour alone. For a change, try using it as a coating for fritters, and add it to sauces.

FRUIT AND NUT BRAN MUFFINS

55g/2oz/¹/₄ cup margarine
55g/2oz/1/3rd cup raw cane sugar
1 large egg, beaten
285ml/¹/₂ pint/1 1/3rd cups milk
30g/1oz/¹/₄ cup bran
170g/6oz/1¹/₂ cups wholemeal flour
2 good teaspoons baking powder
30g/1oz/2 tablespoons candied peel
30g/1oz/2 tablespoons sultanas
30g/1oz/2 tablespoons walnuts, chopped

Melt the margarine and stir together with the sugar. Add the egg and milk. Sift together the bran, flour and baking powder and stir into the first mixture. Add the fruit and nuts, then beat the batter to lighten. If it seems too thick add a drop more milk.

Grease 12 muffin tins and pour in the batter, filling each one two-thirds full. Bake at 200°C/400°F (Gas Mark 6) for about 20 minutes. The muffins should then be well risen and golden. Check that they are ready by pushing a sharp knife into one of them; it should come out clean.

Cool slightly, then transfer to a wire rack. Eat them warm or cold. Good just as they are, but even better spread lightly with butter.

See also Bran and rosemary biscuits.

BRAZIL NUTS

This large white nut comes in a tough angular shell, and these in turn are clustered together in larger shells rather like coconuts in appearance, the clusters each weighing up to 4 lbs. Originating in the Amazon forests of Brazil, some are still grown there on trees that can reach 45 metres/150 feet in height. These are said to have the best flavour and texture. With the destruction of the rainforests, however, they are in short supply these days, most imported brazil nuts now coming from other parts of South America and Africa.

Nutrition: Though a good source of protein, and rich in zinc and vitamin B1, brazil nuts are one of the few varieties that contain saturated fats. They are still worth eating regularly for their smooth creamy taste, but go sparingly.

Buying/Storing: Best to buy nuts in their shells and crack them as you need them. Otherwise, buy a small quantity at a time from a stockist who has a fast turnover, and store in a dark and airtight container. If grinding the nuts, do so just before you use them.

How to use: Make a brazil nut roast. Grind them to make sweets, or to add to pastries or biscuits. Chop them coarsely and sprinkle them over fruit salads, muesli or a fruit flan.

STUFFED MUSHROOMS

12 large mushrooms
55g/2oz/¹/₄ cup butter or margarine
55g/2oz/1 cup dried wholemeal breadcrumbs
2 spring onions, chopped
1 tablespoon capers
3 tablespoons brazil nuts, coarsely chopped
seasoning to taste
extra fat for topping – optional
watercress to garnish

Clean the mushrooms, remove the stalks carefully. Arrange the mushroom cups side by side in a greased ovenproof dish.

Melt the butter and stir in the finely chopped stalks, breadcrumbs, onion, capers, nuts and seasoning. Remove from the heat at once and divide the mixture between the mushrooms. Top each with a small knob of extra fat if the mixture seems very dry.

Bake at 180°C/350°F (Gas Mark 4) for about 20 minutes, or until the mushrooms are cooked and the top is crisp.

Serve as a starter garnished with fresh watercress and accompanied by warm fresh rolls.

See also Spicy plum crumble.

BREAD

Since the dawn of civilisation bread of one kind or another has been a staple food in just about every corner of the world. Originally bread was flat and heavy, probably baked on hot stones. With the development of the oven, and then the discovery of yeast and its ability to make bread rise (both attributed to the Egyptians), it became not just nutritious and filling – it even tasted good.

In Britain, bread was made in much the same way, and using stone-ground grains, until about a hundred years ago. Then roller mills were introduced, mills that removed the valuable germ and bran from the grain, giving it the ability to stay 'fresh' for ages. White flour became fashionable. Bleaches were added to ensure whiter than whiteness. As the oils had been lost, additives were used to improve its texture and taste. Today's commercial white bread had been born – and was taken to our hearts and tables with joy.

It is only in very recent years that there has been a movement away from what is virtually a 'dead' food back to the bread that really deserves to be called a staple food. Though the majority of British people still prefer their bread to be white and flabby, there is a growing interest in breads made with wholemeal flour, preferably organic, better still stoneground. As this spreads not just to wholefood and healthfood shops, but to the high street supermarket too, the range of such breads expands. There are breads made with combinations of different flours, others with whole grains added to provide interest, others sprinkled with seeds.

Baking your own bread, though, is an experience not to be missed. Try it and it might even become a habit. There are so many pluses: the therapy of kneading the dough, the monetary savings, the delicious smell that fills the house, the opportunity to be creative. And, of course, you get to eat it hot out of the oven!

Each country has its own traditional breads, many now also available here. Try pita bread, popular in the Middle East – a flat bread that, when cut in half, opens out to form pockets into which you can stuff such fillings as hummus or salad. Indian breads include pappadums (thin and crispy), chapatis (like puffed-up pancakes), and the heavier naan bread. Mexican tortillas look like pancakes but are used much as we use bread.

WHOLEMEAL BAPS

680g/1¹/₂ lbs/6 cups wholemeal flour
pinch of salt
15g/¹/₂oz/1 tablespoon fresh yeast or 7g/¹/₄oz/¹/₂ tablespoon dried yeast
good 425ml/³/₄ pint/2 cups warm water
sesame seeds, poppy seeds or crushed grain – optional

Sieve together the flour and salt into a large, warmed mixing bowl. In a cup cream together the yeast, sugar and a few spoonfuls of the water. When the yeast has dissolved completely set it aside in a warm spot and leave for 5 minutes, or until it froths up.

Use a wooden spoon to stir the yeast into the flour, then add the rest of the water and mix well. The dough should be heavy and not too dry. Transfer it to a floured board and knead for 5 to 10 minutes. In this way you fold air into the dough, so the more kneading you do the lighter your baps will be. When the dough is supple and smooth divide it into 8 even-sized pieces and shape them into slightly flattened rounds. Sprinkle with seeds if using them. Place them on a lightly-greased baking sheet, cover with a tea towel, and leave in a warm draught-free spot until they have doubled in size.

Bake at 200°C/400°F (Gas Mark 6) for about 15 minutes or until cooked.

See also Wheatgerm bread, Brown bread ice cream, French toast with maple syrup.

BREADFRUIT

Native to Sri Lanka, Malaysia and China, breadfruit is now a very popular food in the West Indies, though it is not well-known in Britain. Occasionally it can be found in ethnic or speciality stores. It is about the size of a small melon, has a thick waxy skin that is rough to the touch, and a sweetish taste that really is reminiscent of bread.

Nutrition: Breadfruit provides a reasonable supply of most vitamins and of mineral salts, and with a fairly high starch content, is a natural source of energy.

Buying/Storing: Check that the fruit has not been damaged, and that it has no soft spots. If it has a green tinge it is under-ripe; when ripe it will be more of a brown colour. (Some say it has more flavour if eaten before it is fully ripe.) Once ripe, eat it as soon as possible – breadfruit does not keep well.

How to use: It can be fried, boiled, sliced and baked, and then served as a vegetable. In Thailand it is an important ingredient in *poi*, a fermented paste usually made from yams. It goes well in curries such as dal. Try it too in sweet dishes – it goes especially well with the taste of coconut.

BAKED BREADFRUIT

1 medium breadfruit
butter
good pinch of mixed spice

Put the unpeeled breadfruit in the centre of the oven on a baking tray. Bake it for about 45 minutes at 180°C/350°F (Gas Mark 4).

Cut it in half, remove the centre core, and then scoop out the flesh and mash together with the butter and spices. Serve as a vegetable accompaniment.

BREWER'S YEAST
See **Yeast, brewer's**

BROAD BEANS

Large flat beans which, when dried, are a brownish colour. They were a staple food for the Egyptians, Greeks and Romans, and are still widely grown in many areas including South America, where they are roasted and ground into flour. Locally-grown broad beans are usually served as a fresh vegetable.

How to use: Dried broad beans should be soaked overnight and then will need to cook for approximately 1½ hours. Both dried and fresh broad beans can have tough skins which may need to be rubbed off after cooking. A good choice for winter casseroles and stews. Broad beans can also be served in a white sauce as a vegetable, or cooked with tomatoes, onions and garlic. In early summer try using young, fresh broad beans raw in a salad with a creamy mild-flavoured dressing.

COCONUT BEANS

1 kilo/2 lb young broad beans
1 tablespoon vegetable oil
¹/₂ small onion, finely chopped
1 teaspoon powdered cumin
approx. 200ml/1/3rd pint/³/₄ cup water
55g/2oz/2/3rd cup desiccated coconut
seasoning to taste
4 tomatoes, quartered

Shell the broad beans and cook in boiling water for 15 minutes, or until just tender. Drain them well.

In another pan, heat the oil and fry the onion to soften. Stir in the cumin and cook a minute more. Add the water and bring it to the boil; add the coconut and drained beans. Continue cooking for a few minutes more, spooning the coconut over the beans to ensure they are evenly coated. Season to taste.

Transfer to a serving dish and decorate with the tomato quarters.

BROCCOLI

Though broccoli is one of the less well-known British vegetables, it is becoming more popular, and some varieties grow well in this country. There are three main types of broccoli. Sprouting broccoli has small tender shoots. Cape broccoli has a single larger head shaped rather like a cauliflower, usually purple. Calabrese has a very good flavour and is imported mostly from Italy – hence it tends to be expensive.

Nutrition: Broccoli is a good source of vitamins A, B2 and C. It also supplies a good amount of iron.

Buying/Storing: Choose broccoli heads which are a good colour and look fresh. Can be kept in the fridge for a day or so, but broccoli deteriorates quickly and is best used as soon as possible.

How to use: All broccolis go well in salads, especially with mayonnaise dressing. Make fritters by dipping the heads into a batter and deep-frying – good in a tempura vegetable mix. Add to stir-fries. Serve with cheese sauce and a sprinkling of walnuts.

BAKED BROCCOLI GRATIN

680g/1 1/2 lbs broccoli, trimmed
55g/2oz/1/4 cup margarine
115g/4oz/2 cups mushrooms, cleaned and sliced
2 tablespoons wholemeal flour
285ml/1/2 pint/1 1/3rd cups milk
115g/4oz/1 cup Cheddar cheese, grated
seasoning to taste
15g/1/2oz/1/8th cup Parmesan cheese, grated
3 tablespoons wholemeal breadcrumbs
good pinch ground nutmeg

Cook the broccoli by standing it upright in a saucepan and covering just the stalks with water, so that the delicate heads are steamed. After 10 minutes, drain well and arrange in a greased ovenproof dish.

Melt half the margarine and fry the mushrooms until just tender, then add them to the broccoli. Melt the remaining margarine, sprinkle in the flour, cook briefly and then pour in the milk. Simmer until the sauce thickens. Stir in the grated Cheddar cheese, season to taste. Spread the sauce over the vegetables.

Sprinkle with the Parmesan cheese, breadcrumbs and nutmeg. Bake at 180°C/350°F (Gas Mark 4) for about 20 minutes. For an extra brown topping, pop the dish under the grill for a minute or two before serving.

See also Chinese fried vegetables with eggs.

BRUSSELS SPROUTS

These tiny cabbages are thought to have originated in Belgium near Brussels in the 13th century, which explains their name. They are a good vegetable for winter, with a nut-like flavour that is actually improved by a touch of frost – cold weather keeps the heads tight.

Nutrition: A valuable winter source of vitamin C.

Buying/Storing: Choose small, evenly-sized sprouts with no sign of wilting around the edges. Keep in the fridge for a few days if not needed at once.

How to use: Good in soups, vegetable hotpots and flans. Brussels go well with mushrooms. Nuts to add are brazils, almonds and peanuts as well as the traditional chestnuts. A little ground nutmeg seems to bring out the flavour. Young Brussels sprouts, finely grated, are tasty if served raw in a salad. For a change try them in a curry.

BRUSSELS SPROUTS PATÉ

455g/1 lb Brussels sprouts
1 onion, chopped
285ml/¹/₂ pint/1 1/3rd cup vegetable stock
squeeze of lemon juice
approx. 3 tablespoons peanut butter
approx. 30g/1oz/¹/₂ cup wholemeal breadcrumbs
seasoning to taste
a few raw peanuts to garnish

Trim, wash and slice the Brussels sprouts. In a saucepan combine the sprouts with the onion and vegetable stock, bring to the boil and cook covered for about 10 minutes. When they are tender, drain them and set aside to cool slightly.
Mash the vegetables together with lemon juice, peanut butter and enough crumbs to thicken the mixture to a paté-like consistency. Season generously.
Spoon the mixture into a small bowl, smooth the top, sprinkle with chopped peanuts. Chill before serving.

See also Winter hotpot with miso.

BUCKWHEAT

Buckwheat is technically not a grain, but is related botanically to dock and rhubarb. It comes from a plant that has heart-shaped leaves and attractive pink flowers. It is, however, used as a grain, and has much the same nutrients. Buckwheat was brought to Europe from Asia by the Crusaders – hence its other name, Saracen corn. It is now grown in many countries, but especially in Russia, where it is used in a variety of ways. Buckwheat honey is also very popular there.

Nutrition: High in protein. Also contains rutic acid which is said to have a good effect on the circulatory system. As it does not contain gluten it is a useful grain for anyone who needs to avoid this.

Varieties: Choose between the whole grain or buckwheat groats, which are the crushed hulled grain. Kasha is buckwheat that has been dry-roasted and has a stronger taste. Some shops also sell buckwheat flour. Buckwheat spaghetti makes a change from the more traditional kind which is made with wheat, but it has a heavier texture and takes longer to cook.

How to use: Use buckwheat to make pilaffs, as an accompaniment to vegetables, or add egg and make a savoury loaf. Kasha has more flavour –

make this yourself by putting grain into a dry pan and cooking over a medium heat, shaking it often, until the grains begin to colour. Buckwheat flour can be used to make Russian-style blinis, also muffins and biscuits (mix with wheat flour for the best results).

KASHA AND CABBAGE

225g/¹/₂ lb/1 cup kasha
2 tablespoons vegetable oil
1 large onion, sliced
1 small clove garlic, crushed
¹/₄ red cabbage, shredded
seasoning to taste
soy sauce
tahini, puréed tofu or cottage cheese to serve

Put the kasha into a saucepan and add enough water to just cover the grains. Bring to the boil, cover the pan, lower the heat and simmer until all the water is absorbed. If it still seems too hard, add a drop more water, but do not over-cook or it will be mushy.

Meanwhile, heat the oil and fry the onion and garlic to soften. Stir in the red cabbage and continue cooking and stirring for a few minutes. Add seasoning and soy sauce, plus a drop of cold water, bring to the boil, then cover and cook over a high heat for 5 minutes more.

Combine the kasha and cabbage and serve topped with a swirl of tahini or puréed tofu, or a few spoonfuls of cottage cheese.

▌BULGUR▐

Bulgur (sometimes called burghul) is actually cracked wheat. It was much used in eastern Europe at one time, and it is said that Ghengis Khan celebrated his victories by loading the tables with bulgur dishes, including a fermented version to drink! It is especially quick cooking, which makes it an ideal choice for anyone who has little time to spend in the kitchen.

Nutrition: Bulgur is a good source of protein.

How to use: This delicate-flavoured grain can be used as a base for pilaffs and risottos, and is an ideal replacement for rice with stir-fried vegetables. Try it also in bazargan, an Eastern salad where the grain is not cooked but soaked. Bulgur flour is interesting but rather heavy.

BAZARGAN

225g/¹/₂ lb/1 cup bulgur
soy sauce
¹/₂ small onion
fresh parsley
fresh mint

2 tablespoons olive oil
2 tablespoons lemon juice
pinch mustard powder
seasoning to taste
55g/2oz/¹/₂ cup walnuts
4 tomatoes
lettuce to serve

Put the bulgur in a bowl and cover with boiling water. Add soy sauce, cover, and leave until cool, by which time the bulgur should be cooked.
Meanwhile, finely chop the onion, parsley and mint and add to the cooled bulgur. Mix the oil, lemon juice, mustard powder and seasoning, and pour over the bulgur. Stir well, add the chopped nuts and quartered tomatoes. Cover the mixture and chill overnight for the flavours to mingle. Serve on a lettuce base.

BURGHUL
See **Bulgur**

BUTTER

A fat made by agitating creams so that the fat globules coalesce into progressively larger grains of butterfat. It takes the cream from ten pints of milk to make ¹/₂ lb butter. Salt and colourings are frequently added. As dairying is a traditional farming practice in temperate climates, most of the butter consumed in Britain today comes from Northern Europe, though some still comes from New Zealand.

Nutrition: Butter is approximately 80% fat and 20% water. It also contains vitamins A, D and E. As the fat is highly saturated – the kind suspected of building up in the arteries – butter should be used sparingly. However, a thin scraping of natural butter (preferably the un-salted, un-dyed variety) will do little harm, especially for people who do not eat meat. Many of the recent spate of factory-produced 'spreads' (including a new low fat butter!) are tasteless, strange in texture and, of course, highly processed.

Buying/Storing: Best bought frequently and in small quantities. Store in a cool place, preferably a fridge.

How to use: Keep butter for use only when you are going to appreciate its flavour. Delicious spread on fresh bread or muffins, or on young vegetables, especially sweetcorn. Some baked goods, shortbread for example, taste far better when made with butter.

BUTTER SHORTBREAD
115g/4oz/1 cup wholemeal flour
55g/2oz/¹/₄ cup rice flour
55g/2oz/1/3rd cup raw cane sugar

115g/4oz/¹/₂ cup butter
4 tablespoons currants – optional

Combine the flours, then add the sugar. Use a knife to cut the butter into the other ingredients – it should be small lumps. Then knead the mixture well to make a stiff dough. Gradually work in the currants, if using them.

Grease a large round sponge tin and press the mixture into it, making sure it is smooth and even. Alternatively, divide the mixture into two, roll out circles about 6mm (¹/₄ inch) thick, and transfer them to greased trays. Prick the dough with a fork. Bake at 170°C/325°F (Gas Mark 3) for about 40 minutes, or until just firm. Mark into segments. Leave to cool slightly before transferring to a cooling rack.

Can be stored in an airtight tin.

BUTTER BEANS

One of Britain's most popular dried beans, the butter bean originated in Peru. (The Americans call them Lima beans.) It is now grown in many tropical areas including Florida, and in Africa, where it is an important source of protein. A large flat white bean, it is a member of the kidney bean family, though is much more subtle in taste, and goes floury when cooked. **How to use:** Allow approximately 45 minutes-1 hour to cook. Add to soups, stews and vegetable casseroles. Can be used in salads, or served in a white or cheese sauce, adding lots of herbs. Mash, add egg, and make into burgers, or stir mashed beans into a tomato sauce to make it thick and creamy, and serve with pasta. Make a butter bean paté.

BUTTER BEAN PIE

115g/4oz/2/3rd cup butter beans, soaked and cooked
2 tablespoons vegetable oil
1 small onion, sliced
1 small green pepper, sliced
2 tablespoons wholemeal flour
approx. 200ml/1/3rd pint/³/₄ cup milk
115g/4oz/1 cup Edam cheese, grated
seasoning to taste
4 tomatoes, quartered

rough puff pastry:
115g/4oz/¹/₂ cup margarine or butter
170g/6oz/1¹/₂ cups wholemeal flour, sifted
approx. 6 tablespoons iced water

Drain the butter beans. Heat the oil and gently fry the onion and pepper slices until they begin to soften. Sprinkle in the flour and cook briefly, then stir in the milk. Bring gently to the boil. Add the cheese. The sauce should be quite thick but if it is too heavy, dilute it with a drop more milk. Season to taste, add the beans, and gently stir in the tomato quarters. Transfer the mixture to an ovenproof dish.

To make the pastry, put the fat into a bowl with the flour and use a knife to cut it into small pieces. Add some iced water and continue mixing with the knife – you should end up with a lumpy fairly soft dough.

Turn this onto a floured board and sprinkle with extra flour. Use hands to shape it quickly into a rectangle, then roll this out so that it is larger and the dough thinner. Fold the top third down, the bottom third up, and press down the edges to seal. Give the dough half a turn so that the folds are at the sides and repeat this folding and rolling process once more, then wrap it in a polythene bag and chill for 30 minutes. Repeat this whole process once more, chill again.

When ready to use, roll out the dough and cut into a circle. Place this over the bean filling, pressing down the edges with damp fingers. Lightly prick the top.

Bake at 220°C/425°F (Gas Mark 7) for 30 minutes or until brown, then serve at once.

Note: Rough puff pastry is best made with a lighter flour, so either sift out the bran from wholemeal flour (use the bran in another recipe), or make it with unbleached white flour. As the process is lengthy and fiddly, you could make up double the quantity and keep the extra in your fridge or freezer until needed.

See also Endive and butter bean soup.

BUTTERMILK

A by-product of the butter-making process, buttermilk is the residue left after churning. It has a slightly acid flavour. Not widely used in Britain, it is popular in many other countries including Germany and Scandinavia, America, India and the Middle East.

Nutrition: Buttermilk is low in fat and calories, high in protein. It is especially easy to digest.

Buying/Storing: Like most dairy products, buttermilk is best bought in small quantities, and should be kept in a cool place. Available from some healthfood and wholefood shops, also delicatessen and supermarkets. It can easily be made at home.

How to use: Use buttermilk in baking cakes and pies. Blend it with fruit juice or fresh fruit and ice for a summertime drink. Add it to sauces to serve with vegetables, or curry sauce.

BUTTERMILK MUFFINS

340g/³/₄ lb/3 cups wholemeal flour
4 good teaspoons baking powder
pinch of salt
55g/2oz/1/3rd cup raw cane sugar
2 eggs
285ml/¹/₂ pint/1 1/3rd cups buttermilk
85g/3oz/¹/₂ cup raisins
approx. 4 tablespoons vegetable oil

Sift together the flour, baking powder and salt, then add the sugar. Whisk the eggs lightly, make a well in the centre of the dry ingredients, and add the eggs. Lightly

whisk the buttermilk and add it to the mixture, stirring well. Mix in the raisins. Add enough oil to make the batter fairly liquid, taking care not to over-mix.
Grease a tray of muffin tins and fill each one three-quarters full with the batter. Bake at 200°C/400°F (Gas Mark 6) for about 20 minutes, or until well risen. Test by inserting a fine knife into one of the muffins, which should come out clean. Cool on a wire rack.

CABBAGE

Cabbages have been eaten for thousands of years. As far back as 200 BC the builders of the Great Wall of China were maintaining their stamina with pickled cabbage! The word itself comes from the Latin and means 'head'.

Varieties: Though most cabbages on sale in Britain are grown in this country, an increasing number are being imported, making the varieties that are now available too numerous to list. Sufficient to say that cabbages can be white, all shades of green, red or purple; they can be shaped round or conical, can be tightly-packed or loose-leaved.

Nutrition: All cabbages are excellent sources of vitamin C and minerals, provided they are not over-cooked.

Buying/Storing: Buy in season, choosing those that are firm and a good colour. Avoid any that are blemished or damaged. Store either in a vegetable rack or the salad drawer of a fridge. How long your cabbage will stay fresh depends on the variety – the hard, tightly-packed kind will keep longest.

How to use: All can be thinly sliced and used in salads, white and red cabbage together making an interesting combination – in a coleslaw for example. Red cabbage combines well with apple and sweetcorn. It needs to be cooked slowly as it is quite hard. You can also pickle it. Add white cabbage to soups and stews, or serve with carrots. Mix cooked cabbage and potatoes with a little cheese, make into cakes, and fry. Stuff cabbage leaves with a cooked grain, beans and onions.

RED AND WHITE SLAW

1/2 small red cabbage
1/2 small white cabbage
1 apple
1/4 small onion
55g/2oz/1/3rd cup cooked sweetcorn
55g/2oz/3 good tablespoons peanuts
55g/2oz/1/3rd cup raisins

dressing:
4 tablespoons vegetable oil
2 tablespoons cider vinegar
1 teaspoon honey
seasoning to taste

In a bowl mix together the finely shredded cabbages, grated apple and onion. Stir in the drained sweetcorn, peanuts and raisins. Combine the salad dressing ingredients in a screw-top jar and shake well, then pour over the cabbage. Toss gently, then chill for 1 hour before serving.

See also Cabbage with aniseed, Kasha and cabbage, Sweet and sour borscht, Stir-fried vegetables with seaweed.

CALABRESE
See **Broccoli**

CANNELLINI BEANS
See **Haricot beans**

CAPERS

These tiny wizened seeds are actually from the nasturtium, and are preserved in brine. They have a soft texture and sharp, distinctive taste that you either love or hate. Add just a few to savoury dishes such as pizza, pies, sauces, or to salads (add too many and you will find they overpower other flavours).

SPAGHETTI WITH CAPER SAUCE

285g/10oz spaghetti, preferably wholemeal
5 tablespoons olive oil
2 tablespoons lemon juice
2 tablespoons capers
1 tablespoon parsley, chopped
seasoning to taste

Cook the pasta in a pan of boiling water – the time will depend on the pasta you are using, so follow instructions on the pack.
Meanwhile put all the ingredients for the sauce into a screw-top jar and shake well.
When the pasta is ready, drain it well, return it to the pan, pour on the sauce and leave for literally a minute or two to warm through. Serve at once.

Note: This pasta recipe is very low in protein. Served in the way the Italians serve it – as a starter – this is not important. If, however, you are having it as your main meal, either add some nuts and/or grated cheese, or accompany it with, for example, a salad with a protein-rich dressing such as blue cheese or tofu.

See also Bean salad niçoise, Stuffed mushrooms.

CAPSICUM
See **Sweet peppers**

CARAMBOLA
See **Star fruit**

CARAWAY

The small brown seeds of a plant which is usually cultivated, though is sometimes found growing wild. The oil from the seeds is used to make kummel, the famous liqueur.

Buying/Storing: The seeds are best bought in small quantities from retailers who have a fast turnover. Store them in a sealed jar in a cool place. If using crushed seeds, crush them just before using so as to retain maximum flavour.

How to use: The slightly sharp taste of these seeds goes well with many ingredients, though they should be used sparingly. Add them to rye bread, seed cake, or sprinkle over homemade bread rolls. They also go well with sauces, cheese spreads, and a variety of vegetables, cabbage in particular. The fresh-picked leaves of the caraway plant can be chopped and added to salad.

CARAWAY BEETROOT PANCAKES
batter:
115g/4oz/1 cup wholemeal flour
pinch of salt
1 egg
285ml/¹/₂ pint/1 1/3rd cups half milk, half water

filling:
455g/1 lb cooked beetroot
1 small carton natural yogurt or sour cream
seasoning to taste
1-2 teaspoons caraway seeds
extra yogurt or sour cream to top
fresh dill or parsley to garnish

Sift together the flour and salt. Add the beaten egg, then gradually whisk in the liquid. Beat to get air into the mixture. Put in the fridge for 30 minutes.
When ready to make the pancakes, whisk the batter lightly again. Heat a little oil in a heavy-based pan and pour in a few spoonfuls of the batter, tipping the pan so that it spreads. Cook gently, and when the underside is set, flip by hand or with a spatula and cook the other side for a minute or two. Keep the pancake warm whilst making the other pancakes in the same way.
Meanwhile, dice the beetroot and put into a small pan, stir in the yogurt or sour cream, and heat very gently. Add seasoning and caraway seeds to taste. Fill each pancake with some of the beetroot mixture, fold carefully, and top with a spoonful or two of yogurt or sour cream and a good sprinkling of herbs. Serve hot.

CARDAMOM

A plant native to the East Indies and China, though the seeds are best known in this country for the distinctive aromatic flavour they give to many popular Indian dishes, sweets in particular. They are excellent for the digestion.

Buying/Storing: The tiny black seeds are bought in their fibrous pod from which they are usually extracted just before use. Store them in a cool dark place. If grinding the seeds, do so just before using them as they lose their flavour very quickly.

How to use: Add to vegetable and bean curries, use in Indian desserts and sweets. Cardamom is also popular in Scandinavian dishes, and it gives a unique flavour to coffee as it is drunk in the Middle East. Especially good with baked apples. Add one or two pods to a cup of tea – with or without milk.

CARDAMOM AND ROSEWATER ICING
15g/¹/₂oz/1 tablespoon margarine or butter
¹/₂-1 tablespoon rosewater
¹/₄ teaspoon vanilla essence
1-2 tablespoons creamy milk or concentrated soya milk
¹/₂ teaspoon ground cardamom seeds
approx. 170g/6oz/1 cup raw cane sugar, powdered in a grinder

Melt the fat and remove from heat. Stir in the rosewater, vanilla essence, milk and ground cardamom. Now use a fork to stir in the powdered sugar, mixing well. You

need to add enough to make the mixture thick and smooth. Adjust the flavour if necessary.
Use the icing to top or sandwich two halves of a plain wholemeal sponge cake.
Delicious with a few chopped cashews or almonds added.

See also Kiwi raita.

CAROB

A dark-brown powder used as a substitute for chocolate. It is made from the beans of a tall evergreen tree (sometimes called locust bean tree), which are dried and then ground. St. John the Baptist is said to have lived in the wilderness on honey and locusts (not, as is often indicated, the insects!), which is surely proof enough of its nutritional value. Because of this, it is also used in animal feed, and at one time the seeds were used as currency in the Middle East.

Nutrition: Contains protein, carbohydrate, calcium and phosphorus, also pectin (a type of dietary fibre) which it is thought may help to calm upset stomachs. Unlike chocolate, it contains no caffeine, and is unlikely to cause allergic reactions.

Buying/Storing: You can buy it ready-ground from most healthfood and wholefood shops. Transfer the powder to an airtight container and keep it in a cool place. Look out also for carob bars which are a healthier version of chocolate bars.

How to use: Can be used as a substitute for chocolate in any recipe. Especially good in milkshakes, also cakes and confectionery. Carob bars, when melted, make an ideal coating for biscuits. Mix carob powder with honey, margarine, chopped nuts and a pinch of spice to make a delicious spread.

CAROB CAKE
115g/4oz/¹/₂ cup margarine or butter
115g/4oz/2/3rd cup raw cane sugar
2 eggs
115g/4oz/1 cup wholemeal self-raising flour
55g/2oz/¹/₂ cup carob powder
2 teaspoons mixed spice
55g/2oz/¹/₂ cup candied peel

Blend together the softened fat and sugar. Add the eggs. Sift together the flour, carob powder and spice and stir into the other ingredients. Add the peel, distributing it evenly.
Spoon the mixture into a shallow greased and floured tin, smoothing the top. Bake at 180°C/350°F (Gas Mark 4) for 20-25 minutes or until firm when pressed lightly.
Leave to cool slightly, then cut into squares and transfer to a wire rack.

CARRAGEEN
See also **Agar agar**

This is a powder made from seaweed. Like agar agar it has excellent gelling properties, though when used to set food it gives a lighter, more mousse-like texture. Carrageen is also useful as a thickening agent – try stirring a spoonful into a sauce or soup. Native to Ireland, it is also called Irish moss. Carrageen in seaweed form is also available, and is ideal for use in drinks; try it as a remedy for the misery of coughs and colds.

See Leek and herb mousse.

CARROTS

Way back, before the Middle Ages, carrots were yellow or purple. It was during the reign of Queen Elizabeth I that the Flemish introduced the orange variety to this country, since when they've become one of our most popular root vegetables.

Nutrition: The reputation carrots have for helping you see in the dark is based on the fact that they are an excellent source of vitamin A, a deficiency of which can lead to nightblindness.

Buying/Storing: Look out for well coloured and shaped carrots (though they don't have to look so perfect they could be artificial!). Those with most nutrients and taste will be blemish-free and firm to touch, and the younger the better. Store them in the fridge.

How to use: Carrots are very versatile. Baby carrots are best lightly steamed and served with just a knob of butter, or a simple sauce. Or use them raw in a salad or coleslaw. Older ones can be added to stews, bakes, soups. They are good made into a purée to mix into a soufflé, or serve with a savoury such as a bean loaf. Surprisingly, carrots are also good in sweet dishes. The best known is the American carrot cake, but they also feature often as an ingredient in Indian sweets.

GLAZED CARROTS ALMONDINE
680g/1 ¹/₂ lbs carrots, peeled and cut into strips
30g/1oz/2¹/₂ tablespoons butter
30g/1oz/2 tablespoons raw cane sugar
2 tablespoons cold water
1 teaspoon arrowroot
1 teaspoon dried marjoram, or to taste
55g/2oz/¹/₂ cup flaked almonds

Cook carrots in boiling water for 5-10 minutes, or until just tender, then drain well. Melt the butter, add the sugar and cook gently for a minute or two. Mix the water and arrowroot to a paste and stir into the fat and sugar. Add the marjoram and the

carrots, and mix well. Cook over a low heat for 10 minutes until the carrots are completely cooked and glazed.
Serve topped with almond flakes.

See also Autumn salad, Sweet and sour borscht, Spicy cauliflower, Cabbage with aniseed, Pea and carrot loaf, Parsnip curry.

CASH CROPS

The increasing imports of exotic fruits and vegetables, especially from Third World countries, bothers many people who are concerned that the poor of such countries may be being exploited. If, however, the words cash crops are used – as is usual – to include *all* export crops, then the three main ones are tea, coffee and cocoa, all of which have been part of our lives for many years.

It is when vast areas, even whole countries, are dependent on just one of these three that major problems can occur. Should there be a crop failure, or a sudden drop in the international commodity price, the results can be devastating. This is why many of these countries are now aiming to strengthen their position by diversifying – and why our willingness to take their produce is vital.

Even so, there are undoubtedly many other aspects of cash cropping that should be considered. Employees have a right to expect a fair wage, regular rest periods, and safe working conditions. Individual farmers should be assured of a sale for their products. The use of land to grow cash crops should be looked at in conjunction with the availability of food for local consumption.

These and many more issues are not only well beyond our control; it is unlikely we will even be able to find the true facts about most of them. The situation is, in any case, changing continually. It is good, then, to know that there are a number of organisations monitoring this with a view to improving conditions for those who work to supply the crops, and ensuring that they too benefit from the sale of them.

Meanwhile, should you buy cash crops? This is up to you. Boycotting them all, though, would not necessarily do the workers any good. And rather than picking on certain crops, it would be better to find out all you can about the companies that market them, many of which may already be well-known to you for other products. How fairly (or otherwise) they treat their employees is a key issue; if they do not consider them equal to their counterparts in western countries, it is the company that should be boycotted. In fact, many of the bigger multinationals, used to being in the public eye maybe, do tend to be fairer; it is the smaller companies who may to be less responsible.

There is one crop, though, that will hopefully be appearing in our shops soon, and that deserves your support. This is rainforest fruits. Brazil nuts are an obvious example; it is because of destruction of the forests that these are now in short supply. Pomelos are another. There is a move to export more of these exotic items in the hope that it will bring money to the natives of the area, whilst at the same time encouraging them to save the trees.

One final point. Though cash crops *may* have been grown naturally, they are also sometimes treated with chemicals. To make matters worse, some of the additives that have been banned in Europe and America (because of doubts about their safety) have been sold to Third World countries by manufacturers unwilling to just dispose of them. This means they may have been used on crops imported back to this country. Clean them very carefully before eating them. And if you do find any labelled as organic – though they may cost more – snatch them up. They'll be worth every extra penny.

CASHEWS

This soft, pale, kidney-shaped nut is not strictly a nut, but a legume that grows at the end of a pear-shaped fruit. It originated in Brazil, but is now grown in other countries, including India, which is one of the largest exporters. They are expensive, but well worth buying for their sweet delicate flavour.

Buying/Storing: Buy them in small quantities from retailers who have a fast turnover. Store in a screw-top jar in a dark place. If buying the ready-cooked variety, eat or use them as soon as you have opened the packet.

How to use: Cashews can be roasted and lightly salted to make a delicious snack. They also go well in mixes with dried fruit, seeds and flaked coconut. Add cashews to curry, or make cashew fritters. Grind them and add water or soya milk to make a cream-like liquid to pour over fruit salad.

CASHEW NUT BUTTER

225g/¹/₂ lb/2 cups raw cashew nuts
2-3 tablespoons vegetable oil
pinch of salt – optional
soy sauce – optional
honey – optional

In a grinder, reduce the cashew nuts to a fine powder. Mix in just enough oil to make a creamy butter, making sure it is well mixed. Cashew butter has a light, delicate flavour. If you prefer a more savoury taste, add salt or soy sauce. Or make it sweeter by adding a little honey.

Other nut butters can be made in the same way, using just one kind of nut or different kinds in combination. Try using roasted nuts too. A peanut butter made of half raw and half roasted nuts is delicious.

See also Curried nuts nibbles, Cashew noodles with parsley, Parsnip curry.

CASSAVA

An ugly looking tropical vegetable much used in Africa and Asia, as well as South America, which is where it originated. The plant produces a number of tuberous roots that have a coarse skin, usually brown, and hard white flesh and it is these that are eaten. There are two different kinds of cassava. The bitter variety is poisonous until cooked when it is processed into tapioca flour, flakes and pearls (which are gluten-free and therefore useful for coeliacs). The flour is also popular in the Caribbean. Sweet cassava is eaten as a vegetable rather like potatoes.

How to use: Sweet cassava is the kind you are most likely to find in the shops. Try it baked, or cut into chips and fried.

CASSAVA CRISPS

2 cassavas
vegetable oil for frying

Peel and slice the cassavas – the slices should be as thin as possible. Steep them in cold water for 30 minutes or so, then remove and carefully pat dry.
Heat some oil and drop in the cassava slices a few at a time. Deep-fry for a few minutes by which time they should be crisp and golden. Drain well and eat.

CAULIFLOWER

Cauliflowers are actually members of the cabbage family. They are now available almost all year round, though they are cheaper and better in summer.

Buying/Storing: Look for a firm, close-textured head with no brown flecks. As the caulifower has a delicate flavour, take care not to over-cook. For the same reason, do not keep a cauliflower too long before using it, though if it is fresh when you buy it, and you store it in the fridge, it should keep for a few days without deteriorating.

How to use: Florets can be used raw in salads – try mixing them with Chinese leaves, tomato, banana and nuts. Crème Dubarry is a classic cauliflower soup. Add cheese sauce, top with breadcrumbs and pop under the grill, or use the mixture to fill vol-au-vents or a flan. Dip florets into batter and deep-fry. Cook with garlic and onion in tomato sauce for a completely different taste.

CAULIFLOWER PATÉ

1 tablespoon vegetable oil
$^1/_2$-1 onion
1 medium cauliflower
4 tablespoons tahini
55g/2oz/1$^1/_4$ cups wheatgerm
soy sauce to taste
seasoning to taste
fresh chives to garnish

Heat the oil and sauté the chopped onion until soft. In a separate pan, steam the cauliflower until cooked. Mash the cauliflower or push through a sieve, stir together with the onion, and add tahini to make a smooth paste. Use wheatgerm to thicken, then flavour to taste with soy sauce and seasoning. Spoon into a serving dish and chill. Top with plenty of chopped chives, and surround with raw vegetables, melba toast and corn chips.

See also Spicy cauliflower, Cauliflower cheese meringue, Vegetable stew for couscous.

CAYENNE PEPPER

A hot and pungent-tasting powder made from a blend of various capsicums, including both seeds and pods. It originated in Cayenne in South America.

Buying/Storing: Buy in small quantities, store in an airtight container away from light.

How to use: First tip – use cayenne pepper sparingly until you are used to it and know just how much will give you the degree of 'hotness' you like! It can be used to make devilled eggs, to add bite to some cheese dishes. Ideal for the hotter curries. A little cayenne adds interest to stews and casseroles. Use in yogurt, cheese or tofu dips.

GADO-GADO (INDONESIAN PEANUT SAUCE)

2 tablespoons vegetable oil
1 large onion, chopped
2 cloves garlic, crushed
115g/4oz/$^1/_2$ cup peanut butter
$^1/_2$ teaspoon cayenne pepper
$^1/_2$ teaspoon ground ginger
juice of 1 lemon
1 tablespoon raw cane sugar or concentrated orange juice
1 tablespoon cider vinegar
just over 570ml/1 pint/2$^1/_2$ cups water
seasoning to taste
soy sauce

Heat the oil and gently cook the onion and garlic to soften. Then stir in the peanut butter, spices, lemon juice, sweetener, cider vinegar and water. Continue cooking over a very low heat for 20 minutes, stirring frequently. Add seasoning and soy sauce. If necessary adjust the taste of the sauce by adding more spices or sweetening. Serve very hot.

Gado-gado is spooned over a selection of cooked and raw vegetables, usually with a grain dish as an accompaniment.

See also Vegetable stew for couscous, Cashew noodles with parsley.

CELERIAC

This knobbly root vegetable appears only in winter, and is not well-known in Britain, though it is becoming more so. It is, however, a popular vegetable in France, Italy and Germany. Despite being a member of the parsley family, its creamy-white flesh has a flavour more reminiscent of celery.

Nutrition: It is a very good source of minerals and vitamins including potassium and vitamin C.

Buying/Storing: Choose firm roots that are undamaged and that feel heavy in your hand (light ones may well be stale). Small to medium-sized ones with smoother skins will be easier to prepare and cook; the larger ones can sometimes be woody. Store in a polythene bag in the fridge.

How to use: Most of the goodness is just below the skin, so peel as thinly as possible – a squeeze of lemon juice will help keep the flesh white. Grate and add to salads. Make into fritters. Purée and use as a vegetable, or as a filling for other vegetables or vol-au-vents. Add to bean casseroles. Steam lightly and serve with hollandaise sauce. Par-boil and then fry to make celeriac chips.

CELERIAC SALAD WITH MUSTARD

1 medium head celeriac
lemon juice
4 tomatoes, quartered
4 tablespoons cooked kidney beans (or others)
mayonnaise
made-up mustard
crisp dark-green lettuce leaves
parsley for garnish

Peel the celeriac and grate or shred it coarsely. Mix immediately with lemon juice to stop it going brown.

Put the celeriac into a bowl with the tomatoes and beans. Spoon a few tablespoons of mayonnaise into a dish and stir in just enough mustard to give it a slight flavour. Stir this into the first mixture.

Spoon the salad over a bed of lettuce, and serve decorated with sprigs of parsley.

CELERY

The Romans wore it as a protection against hangovers. Nowadays there are two varieties widely available. The self-blanching kind is on sale during the summer and autumn, the maincrop during the winter. Though dirtier and therefore less attractive looking, the winter celery has a better flavour.

Buying/Storing: Choose crisp, unblemished stalks – if there are leaves, they will indicate how fresh the celery is. Can be kept in the fridge for some days. If it is in plastic wrapping, leave this on until you use the celery.

How to use: Most widely used in salads, or with dips. Celery can also be cooked in soups, and added to stews and casseroles. Mix it into a tomato sauce to add to spaghetti. Use it in stir-fries. Braised celery topped with almonds is delicious. Take care not to over-cook celery or it will lose its crispness and become stringy instead.

CALIFORNIA SALAD

1 small melon
1 large peach
1 banana
squeeze of lemon juice
2 sticks of celery
1/2 cucumber
2 large tomatoes
16 grapes
55g/2oz/1/2 cup pecan nuts
endive lettuce to serve
watercress to garnish

dressing:
115g/4oz/1/2 cup cottage cheese
2 tablespoons desiccated coconut
1 tablespoon honey
milk to mix

Peel and chop the melon, slice the peach and banana. Toss the fruit in lemon juice. Slice the celery and cucumber, quarter the tomatoes. Mix with the fruit plus the grapes and nuts.
Sieve the cottage cheese, stir in the coconut and honey, and add enough milk to make a pouring consistency. Pile the fruit and vegetables onto a base of endive lettuce and spoon on the dressing. Garnish with watercress.

See also Lettuce dolmas, Moulded salad, Sunflower and celery paté.

CEREALS
See **Grains**

CHARD
See **Swiss chard**

CHAYOTE
See **Cho cho**

CHEESE

A versatile high-protein food made from the milk of cows, goats or sheep. Regulations demand that hard cheeses must contain not less than 40% fat on a dry weight basis, which must be milk fat. Cheese other than soft cheeses are cured by being left to mature with salt under a variety of conditions, each producing an individual flavour. There are about 400 different types of cheese.

Cheese was probably first produced by the nomadic tribes of eastern Europe and western Asia, who might have put milk into pouches, slung them over their camels, and let the movement do the rest. Cheese is now one of the most popular foods of all, and is produced all over the world.

Nutrition: The type of nutrients depends on the exact composition of the milk or cream from which the cheese was made, though most cheeses are protein-rich, and contain calcium plus the eight essential amino acids. Hard-pressed cheeses, such as Cheddar, contain nearly twice as much protein, weight for weight, as prime beef, but as most of us eat far more protein than we need anyway, this is no justification for eating vast quantities of cheese! Cottage cheese, the dieters' favourite, can be up to 80% water – for light and fresh-tasting alternatives try fromage frais, quark or curd cheese, all considerably better for you than cream cheese. Dutch cheeses are usually lower in fat than British cheeses, though there is now a variety of reduced-fat versions of our more traditional cheeses coming onto the market.

Cheeses to avoid are those that are rich in saturated fat, plus the highly processed cheeses which usually contain flavourings and emulsifiers. Look out too for highly-coloured cheeses (some colourings are natural but many are chemical). Harder to spot are those cheeses – of which there are a fair number – with exceptionally high salt contents.

Vegetarians may well prefer not to buy cheeses made with animal rennet (the inner stomach lining of a calf). Fortunately, the range of those made with a vegetable rennet starter (made from a microbial enzyme) expands daily – look out for those labelled as suitable for vegetarians. Italian cheeses such as mozzarella and ricotta are usually also vegetarian. So are many soft cheeses.

Cheeses made from goat's and sheep's milk are becoming increasingly popular as a discriminating public tries to avoid the additives that are now so widely used in cheeses made from cow's milk.

Buying/Storing: Buy only a week's supply at a time, wrap it in foil or greaseproof paper, and store it in the lowest part of the fridge. Take it out of the fridge for an hour before serving, so it can regain its flavour. Hard cheeses can be frozen, though may be crumbly when defrosted. Stale cheese can be grated and kept in an airtight jar in the fridge, ready to use in cooked dishes.

How to use: Cheese is a familiar and widely-used food, popular because of its versatility as much as anything. Being a high-protein product, it can be sprinkled over grain and vegetable dishes to make a completely balanced meal. Try it with sweet things too – cottage cheese instead of cream with fruit salad, a chunk of hard cheese with an apple pie or crumble.

RICOTTA CHEESE AND SPINACH PASTIES

pastry:
225g/¹/₂ lb/2 cups wholemeal flour
115g/4oz/¹/₂ cup margarine
pinch of salt
cold water to mix

filling:
225g/¹/₂ lb/1 cup ricotta cheese
225g/¹/₂ lb fresh spinach
1 large egg
good pinch of nutmeg
seasoning to taste
30g/1oz/3 tablespoons walnuts
1 tablespoon sesame seeds

Put the flour into a bowl, rub in the fat to make a crumb-like mixture. Add salt, then enough water to make a firm dough. Wrap in polythene and chill.

Meanwhile, mash the ricotta cheese. Steam the shredded spinach, then drain and chop as finely as possible. Stir it into the cheese with most of the lightly-beaten egg, nutmeg, seasoning and chopped nuts.

Roll out the pastry and cut into large circles. Put a little of the filling on one side of each, fold into a pasty, and press to seal the edges.

Brush the tops lightly with the remaining egg and sprinkle with seeds. Arrange on a baking sheet and bake at 190°C/375°F (Gas Mark 5) for 20-30 minutes, or until the pastry is cooked.

See also Cheese and horseradish fondue, Lovage and feta omelette, Cheese rice balls, Pesto sauce, Yogurt rarebit, Cashew noodles with parsley, Borage cottage cheese, Tomato basilica with mozzarella, Baked broccoli gratin, Stuffed dates, Filo parcels, Walnut cheese roulade, Cauliflower cheese meringue.

CHERRIES

The name is taken from Cerasus, a city in Asia Minor where cherries were discovered by Europeans, though they had been eaten in China and Japan for many centuries. The Romans brought them to Britain, but they are still not widely grown in this country.

Varieties: The large sweet black variety is usually imported from Italy. Cherries can be dark or light red, pale peach or yellow in colour; they can be sugary or sour. Also available as glacé cherries which have been preserved in sugar and, though obviously less nutritious than the fresh fruit, are useful in baking.

Buying/Storing: Choose cherries that are dry and undamaged, preferably with their stems still attached. The glossier their skins the fresher they will be. Best used at once, but they can be stored for a few days in the fridge. Put them in an aerated polythene bag. Glacé cherries are best purchased from a healthfood or wholefood shop.

How to use: Add to fruit salad, use to fill crêpes or to top a flan. Make a cherry compôte and pile into tart shells. Make jam. For a splendid dessert, cook cherries in sauce, pour on a drop of cognac and set fire to it!

COCONUT CHERRY SLICES

225g/¹/₂ lb/1¹/₂ cups glacé cherries, washed, dried and halved
85g/3oz/³/₄ cup self-raising wholemeal flour
85g/3oz/³/₄ cup plain wholemeal flour
170g/6oz/2/3rd cup margarine
115g/4oz/2/3rd cup raw cane sugar
2 large eggs, beaten
85g/3oz/1 cup desiccated coconut
milk – optional

Grease a small oblong cake tin and line with greaseproof paper. Combine the flours, coat the cherries in flour and then set aside.

In a bowl cream together the margarine and sugar. Add the eggs gradually, mixing well. Carefully fold in the flour, cherries and coconut. The mixture should be of a stiff dropping consistency, so if it is too dry, moisten with some milk. Make sure the cherries are evenly distributed.

Pour the mixture into the tin. Bake at 180°C/350°F (Gas Mark 4) for about 1¹/₄ hours – to tell if the cake is cooked place a sharp knife in the centre, which should come out clean.

Leave to cool in the tin for a few minutes, then transfer to a wire rack. Cut into slices to serve. If liked you can top them with fromage frais mixed with a little raw cane sugar (best powdered first in a grinder) and a few spoonfuls of desiccated coconut.

See also Stuffed dates, Red fruit salad.

CHERVIL

A cultivated herb that grows well in pots, and has attractive crinkly leaves.
Buying/Storing: Said to be the most delicate-flavoured of all herbs. It's
not surprising then, that though this herb can be bought ready dried, and
will retain its aniseed-like taste quite well if stored in a dark airtight jar, it is
at its best when fresh.
How to use: Nice in salads. Also goes well with egg dishes – try adding it
to omelettes and soufflés, maybe with other herbs too. Can also be used as a
garnish.

EGG SOUP AND CHERVIL

30g/1oz/¹/₂ cup wholemeal noodles
2 large eggs, beaten
30g/1oz/¹/₄ cup wholemeal semolina
55g/2oz/¹/₂ cup Parmesan cheese, grated
1.15 litres/2 pints/5 cups vegetable stock
seasoning to taste
4 teaspoons chopped chervil

Cook the noodles in boiling water for 5 minutes, then drain and set aside. In a small
bowl combine the eggs, semolina, cheese, and a few spoonsful of the stock to make
a smooth paste. Season.
Bring the rest of the stock to the boil, add the noodles, then gradually beat in the egg
mixture. Lower the heat and simmer the soup for 3-5 minutes, still stirring
continually. The eggs will cook and set as small flakes.
Stir in the chervil and serve the soup at once.

CHESTNUTS

Though native to the Mediterranean countries, chestnuts have spread to
many other areas, even to Britain (though our climate is not usually warm
enough for the fruits to ripen). Most of the distinctive shiny brown nuts
found on sale in shops have been imported from Spain; they are available
during the winter months. Their sweet taste and floury texture means that
they are very versatile.
Varieties: Apart from fresh chestnuts look out for the dried variety which
need only be hydrated in water or stock. Chestnut flour used to be a
mainstay of many peasants – some shops may have it, though not many.
Marrons glacé are chestnuts which have been cooked and preserved in
sugar to make a wickedly delicious treat.
Nutrition: Fresh chestnuts are lower in calories than many nuts as they
contain a good deal of water. This also means they contain less protein and
fat.

How to use: The best known way is to roast them and eat them straight from the shell. To use in cooked dishes they should first be skinned. To do this, make a small cut across the top, then boil or roast them for 10 minutes until the skins split. Cool slightly before peeling off the shell and then cooking as required. Perfect in soups, or mixed with breadcrumbs and herbs to make a stuffing mix. Excellent combined with Brussels sprouts – make them into a bake or loaf. Also good in sweet dishes. Blanched chestnuts can be frozen.

CHESTNUT PATÉ

340g/12oz chestnuts
30g/1oz/2¹/₂ tablespoons margarine
¹/₂ clove garlic, crushed
1 carrot, peeled and grated
1 small leek, cleaned and finely chopped
55g/2oz/1 cup mushrooms, chopped
1 tablespoon wholemeal flour
approx. 4 tablespoons water
seasoning to taste
¹/₂ teaspoon dried sage
¹/₂ teaspoon dried thyme
1 tomato to garnish
parsley to garnish

Split the chestnuts, cook them in boiling water for about 15 minutes, drain and cool. Use a sharp knife to peel away the outer shell and skin. Mash them to a purée (or, if still too hard, cook them a little longer in fresh water first).
Meanwhile, melt the margarine and cook the garlic for a few minutes. Add the carrot, leek and mushrooms and cook gently just long enough to soften. Stir in the flour, cook briefly, add the water, seasoning and herbs. Simmer to make a thick sauce – if too thick, add a drop more water. Stir in the chestnuts, mixing them thoroughly.
Spoon the mixture into a dish, smooth the top, and chill briefly.
Slice the tomato and arrange around the edges of the dish, putting some parsley in the centre. Serve with melba toast or crispbread.

CHICK PEAS

A beige-coloured pea the size and shape of a hazelnut. It grows in a small twisted pod, and because it is easy to cultivate it is used in many parts of the world, including America, Africa, Australia, India and around the Mediterranean. The Americans call them garbanzos.

Varieties: Chick peas are usually bought dried and need to be soaked, preferably overnight, before use. Gram flour is actually ground chick peas and is used, particularly in India, to make dishes that are equally rich in protein, but easier to digest than those made with the whole peas.

Buying/Storing: Buy in small quantities from a retailer who has a quick turnover. Check that the peas are well rounded and don't look stale or colourless. Store them in an airtight jar in a cool, dry place.

How to use: Boil for 10 minutes, then lower the heat and simmer until the chick peas are tender – allow 45 minutes to an hour. A very versatile pulse, and one that features in the cuisine of many different cultures. Try falafels, deep-fried balls of ground peas, or make the peas into hummus by mashing and mixing with tahini, garlic and lemon juice. Serve with African couscous. Serve chick peas (maybe combined with other pulses) in a white creamy sauce. Good in stews too, or with onions and garlic in a tomato sauce. Dry roasted with spices they made a tasty nibble.

PAKORA (DEEP-FRIED VEGETABLES)

225g/¹/₂ lb/2 cups gram (chick pea) flour
1 teaspoon ground coriander
¹/₂ teaspoon ground cumin
¹/₂ teaspoon ground allspice
seasoning to taste
cold water to mix
approx. 680g/1¹/₂ lbs mixed fresh vegetables
ghee or vegetable oil for frying
soy sauce to serve

Mix together the flour, spices and seasoning. Add enough water to give the consistency of a thin white sauce, beat well, then chill for 1 hour.

Meanwhile, prepare the vegetables. Cut parsnips, carrots and courgettes into strips. Slice onions thickly. Break cauliflower and broccoli into bite-size clusters of florets. Mushrooms should be halved unless they are the button variety.

When ready to cook, heat a pan of oil until it spits when batter is dropped into it. Dip the vegetables into the batter one at a time, making sure that they are completely covered, then drop them into the deep oil and cook until crisp and brown. Give tougher vegetables such as carrots a minute or two longer. Drain at once, and keep them warm while using up the remaining ingredients in the same way. Arrange on a serving dish, sprinkle with soy sauce, and serve with rice and Indian-style side dishes such as yogurt and cucumber, and chutneys.

If you prefer, you can finely chop the vegetables, mix into a spoonful or two of the batter, and drop into the hot oil by the spoonful. Onion is particularly nice this way – maybe you could combine both methods and serve them together.

See also Vegetable stew for couscous, Pineapple fritters, Hummus.

CHICORY
See also **Radicchio**

Not widely used in Britain – though popular in much of Europe, especially in Mediterranean countries – this vegetable looks rather like an over-grown bud, and has a slightly bitter taste. (Confusingly, both the Continentals and Americans calls chicory 'endive' – and the lettuce we call endive they refer to as 'chicory'!) It is also cultivated for its roots which are considered to be nutritious. These are dried, ground, and either added to coffee or used to make a coffee substitute.

Nutrition: Chicory contains some iron and folic acid.

Buying/Storing: A head of chicory should be white to pale green, plump and well formed. If the edges of the leaves are a stronger green, it will probably be more bitter. Such a chicory is better cooked.

How to use: Use whole leaves to line a bowl before filling with a salad mixture, or chop the leaves and add to other vegetables. Add to quiches. Braise the whole heads in butter and lemon juice. Serve in a white or cheese sauce. Goes well with the taste of peppers.

CHICORY SALAD WITH TEMPEH

2 heads chicory, separated and washed
1 small red-tinged lettuce (such as oakleaf or lollo rosso)
1 bunch watercress, washed
115g/4oz radishes, trimmed and halved
115g/4oz/¹/₂ cup tempeh
2 tablespoons vegetable oil for cooking
bread croûtons
vinaigrette dressing

Chop the chicory and lettuce coarsely. In a bowl mix together the chicory, lettuce, watercress sprigs and radishes.

Slice the tempeh as thinly as possible (this is easiest if it is very cold). Heat the oil and fry the tempeh strips, turning them frequently, until a golden brown.

Crumble the tempeh and sprinkle it over the salad with the bread croûtons. Add a small amount of vinaigrette dressing, toss the salad lightly, and serve at once.

See also Radicchio salad with blue cheese dressing.

||||||||||||||||||||| CHILLI PEPPERS |||||||||||||||||||||
See also **Chilli powder**

These fiery members of the capsicum family originated in South America. More shops are now selling them, some being grown in this country though most are imported from abroad. They are still, though, not widely available. If you find them, do try them. Choose from red or green. They will vary enormously in taste, some being sweet and mild, others having more flavour, others being hot as flames.

Buying/Storing: Look out for well formed peppers that are blemish free and have a good colour. The long thin pods are generally hotter than the shorter, rounder variety; the red are generally hotter than the green.

Traditionally they are tied in bunches and hung up to dry, and they keep well this way provided they are in a dry warm spot. Single peppers are best kept in a fridge, but not for too long. As a little goes a long way, wrap any left-over pieces in polythene before storing.

How to use: Be careful when cutting peppers as the vapour that comes from the seeds can cause irritation to the skin. A good way to combat this is to cut the chillies under water. Though the seeds can be used to add flavour, they are even hotter than the flesh! Use fresh chilli peppers to flavour stews, sauces, dips, flan fillings. Can be used in traditional Mexican dishes in much the same way as chilli powder. Adds interest also to Chinese stir-fries and spring rolls. A popular addition to Indian curries.

BURGER RELISH

2 tablespoons vegetable oil
1 clove garlic, crushed
1 small onion, chopped
2 green chillies, trimmed
395g/14oz tin tomatoes*
good pinch of turmeric
salt to taste

Heat the oil and gently fry the garlic and onion for a few minutes.
Cut the chillies in half lengthways and scoop out the seeds (do this under running water if the smell bothers you). Chop the flesh very finely and add to the pan. Cook for 5 minutes, stirring often.
Add the tomatoes, turmeric and salt. Cook briefly then set aside to cool. Purée in a blender.
Pour the relish into a screw-top jar and keep in the fridge until needed.

Note: To make a milder relish use the shorter, rounder variety of chilli. Soaking the cut chillies in cold salted water for an hour before using also removes some of the volatile oils. For a hotter relish include a few of the seeds.
*Though fresh tomatoes contain more nutrients, the tinned variety has a better taste for this particular recipe.

CHILLI POWDER
See also **Chilli peppers**

This powder, made from the dried small red pod of a particular chilli pepper, is especially popular in Mexico where it is an essential ingredient in many traditional dishes. It is burning hot.

Buying/Storing: Best bought in small quantities when fresh, and stored in an airtight container.

How to use: Chilli con carne is a dish with which you may already be familiar. For vegetarians, chilli beans make a good alternative. Even just a pinch of chilli powder will add zing to soups, stews, creamy dips. To begin with, use sparingly.

CHILLI KIDNEY BEANS

340g/³/₄ lb/2 cups red kidney beans, soaked overnight
1 small onion
1 small green pepper
1-2 tablespoons vegetable oil
225g/¹/₂ lb tomatoes, skinned and chopped
3 tablespoons tomato purée
2 tablespoons mixed dried herbs
1 teaspoon chilli powder, or to taste
seasoning to taste

Cook the beans in fresh water, boiling them first for 10 minutes, then lowering the heat and simmering for 50 minutes, or until just tender. Finely chop the onion and pepper and sauté in the oil to soften. Add the tomatoes, purée, herbs, chilli powder and seasoning. Mash most of the beans and stir into the other ingredients. Cover the saucepan and simmer for about 15 minutes. Add the remaining beans to give texture, and cook just long enough to heat through.

Chilli beans cooked this way can be topped with grated cheese or yogurt. Serve them with corn bread and a side salad.

Note: Chilli powder can vary in strength, but is usually strong, so don't use too much until you are sure you like it.

See also Guacamole dip, Mexican flan, Black bean and pumpkin stew, Mushroom and tofu tacos.

▥▥▥▥ CHINESE LEAVES ▥▥▥▥

These large heads of leaves that look rather like a paler version of cos lettuce are only just becoming popular here, though they have been used in China for centuries. Available most of the year – either homegrown or imported – they make an excellent salad ingredient, are sweet and crisp, and are especially useful in the winter. Sometimes called Chinese cabbage.

Buying/Storing: Look out for bruising or broken leaves, or for wilting. Chinese leaves should be firm to the touch and crisp. They will keep well if stored in the polythene sleeve in which you purchase them, and put at the bottom of the fridge.

How to use: Slice across and mix with other salad ingredients – good with fruits such as apricot and banana added too. Cook gently and sprinkle with seeds. Single leaves can be stuffed, rolled up, topped with tomato sauce and then baked (as an alternative to vine leaves). A delicious addition to stir-fried vegetables.

FRUITED LETTUCE LEAVES

1 small head of Chinese leaves, coarsely shredded
1 medium peach
12 strawberries
12 grapes
1 apple
lemon juice
1 tablespoon raisins
55g/2oz/¹/₂ cup hazelnuts, roasted and coarsely chopped
watercress to garnish

dressing:
approx. 70ml/1/8th pint/1/3rd cup vegetable oil
1 tablespoon honey
30g/1oz creamed coconut, grated
1 teaspoon lemon juice
good pinch ground cinnamon

Put the Chinese leaves into a salad bowl. Dice the peach, halve the strawberries and grapes, dice the apple, and toss all the fruit in the lemon juice to prevent discolouring. Add to the Chinese leaves, together with the raisins and nuts. Combine the dressing ingredients in a small screw-top jar and shake very well until thoroughly mixed. The coconut should dissolve completely. Pour a little of the sweet dressing over the salad, toss lightly. Top with sprigs of watercress.

CHIVES

A very common garden herb that grows in a grass-like clump, and has hollow leaves. Particularly popular in Britain. It is a member of the onion family, so not surprisingly has a mild and oniony flavour, though it actually contains an oil similar to that found in garlic.

Buying/Storing: Dried chives can be purchased and keep reasonably well in an airtight jar. However, there is nothing to beat the taste of fresh chives, and as they grow well in this climate – even in pots on window sills! – try to use them fresh whenever possible. Use scissors to snip as many strands as you need from the plant.

How to use: Fresh chives should be snipped or chopped into small pieces before sprinkling over a wide variety of dishes including salads, omelettes, casseroles and savoury pancakes. Good too with cheese dips, especially cottage and curd cheese. Add to mashed potatoes.

OMELETTE AUX FINES HERBES

8 eggs
1 tablespoon fresh chives, chopped
3 tablespoons other fresh herbs as available, chopped
seasoning to taste

55g/2oz/¹/₄ cup butter or margarine

Break 2 eggs into a bowl and whisk well. Add ¹/₂ tablespoon of herbs, salt and freshly-ground pepper. Melt 15g/¹/₂oz fat in a heavy-based pan, pour in the eggs, and cook gently for 2 minutes. Tilt the pan and use a spatula to lift the omelette on one side so that the liquid runs underneath. Repeat this until the eggs are just beginning to set. Add the remaining ¹/₂ tablespoon of herbs, fold and serve at once. Cook three more omelettes in the same way.

Note: Omelette aux fines herbes is traditionally made and served like this, relying on fresh free-range eggs and flavourful herbs like chives, tarragon, parsley and chervil to make it a very special omelette. You can, of course adapt it by adding cheese, strips of pepper, sweetcorn or cream to the eggs as you whisk them.

See also Three bean salad, Turnip and cheese croquettes.

CHO CHO

Though this tropical vegetable is a member of the squash family, the variety most often found in Britain looks more like a pear with ridges. Other varieties can occasionally be found – these can come in many shapes and colours, though all share a firm white flesh and delicate flavour. The cho cho – also called chayote and christophine – is much used in the Caribbean, Southeast Asia, East and West Africa, and Mexico.

If purchased when fresh, and stored in a cool dry place, cho chos will keep for a month or two.

How to use: They can be used in a wide variety of ways. Add them to stir-fries, stuff them with cheese and onion. Good with spiced sauces. Use raw in salads. When cooked the flesh can be mashed and then mixed with sugar and spices and used to make a sweet pie.

CHRISTOPHINE
See **Cho cho**

CHUTNEY

A chutney is a relish made from fruits and vegetables. Some form of acid is added, plus seasoning, spices and other flavourings. Chutneys were originally used as a way of preserving food – especially when there were gluts – to be eaten later. How nutritious they are depends entirely on how they are made. Commercially-made chutneys can be full of chemicals and little else. Those you buy in wholefood and healthfood shops will be made from more wholesome ingredients. You can, of course, make your own. When doing so make sure the jars you use are well sterilised, and seal them carefully when full. In this way your chutney will stay deliciously edible for months – in fact, it is a good idea to store them for a time before eating to enable the flavours to mingle.

How to use: Use chutneys with salads, flans, pasties. A spoonful or two can be stirred into a sauce, or will add interest to a stew. They also go well with Indian food.

PARSNIP AND BANANA CHUTNEY

455g/1 lb parsnips, peeled and sliced
1.4 kilos/3 lb fresh bananas, sliced
850ml/1 1/2 pints/3 3/4 cups cider vinegar
455g/1 lb/2 1/2 cups sugar
225g/1/2 lb/1 1/2 cups dates, chopped
1 tablespoon curry powder
1 teaspoon ground cumin
1 teaspoon ground cinnamon
2 teaspoons salt

Combine all the ingredients in a large, heavy-based saucepan. Bring to the boil then cover the pan, lower the heat and cook gently for 30 minutes.
Remove the lid and continue cooking over a low heat, stirring frequently, until there is no liquid left and the ingredients have become thick and mushy.
Leave to cool completely before pouring into clean hot jars and sealing.

CIDER VINEGAR
See **Vinegar**

CINNAMON

Strips from the bark of a small evergreen tree of the laurel family, native to Sri Lanka. Contains a powerful antiseptic oil though the taste it gives is sweet and rather delicate.

Buying/Storing: Cinnamon can be purchased ready-ground. Buy only a small quantity at a time and store in an airtight container in a cool place. Better still, buy your cinnamon in stick form and grind it yourself as and when you need it.

How to use: Ground cinnamon can be added to all kinds of fruit dishes – especially tasty with rhubarb pie. Use to flavour gingerbread, milk puddings, stuffing for apples. In Eastern cookery sticks of cinnamon are put in with meat dishes. Can be used in savoury dishes where a warm rich flavour is wanted. Nice added to both tea and coffee.

CINNAMON HONEY CAKE

225g/¹/₂ lb /2 cups wholemeal flour
pinch of salt
1-2 teaspoons ground cinnamon
170g/6oz/2/3rd cup margarine or butter
3-4 tablespoons honey
85g/3oz/¹/₂ cup raw cane sugar
85g/3oz/3 tablespoons candied peel
2 eggs
55g/2oz/¹/₂ cup flaked almonds

Sift together the flour, salt and cinnamon. In a small saucepan melt the fat and honey together, and stir in the sugar. Remove from the heat and cool slightly, then add the candied peel and whisked eggs. Combine all the ingredients. Turn the mixture into a greased loaf tin.
Bake at 200°C/400°F (Gas Mark 6) for 15 minutes, then lower the heat to 180°C/350°F (Gas Mark 4), scatter with the flaked nuts, and bake for 30-40 minutes, or until cooked. Transfer to a wire rack to cool.

See also Mulled wine, Spiced mooli, Pecan pumpkin pie, Ginger and melon starter.

CITRUS FRUIT
See also **individual varieties**

In the Middle Ages, the richer you were the more oranges you used in your food. Now, with such a variety of oranges and other citrus fruits being imported from many parts of the world, particularly Florida and Cyprus, they are one of our most popular and inexpensive fruits.

Nutrition: Citrus fruits (so called because they contain citric acid) are a good source of vitamin C. Nowadays the skins are often sprayed to give them a shine, and may even be dyed, so if you want to use the skin in your cooking be sure to scrub it well. Alternatively, buy organically-grown fruits which are now becoming more widely available.

Buying/Storing: Buy only firm fruit that is free from blemishes and bruises, and not wrinkled. The heavier it feels in the hand, the juicier it is likely to be.

How to use: See individual varieties.

CITRUS FRUIT, SOFT

These are the citrus fruits that have loose-fitting skins which makes them easier and less messy to peel. They are usually also smaller than the others, which makes them especially popular as a snack for children.

Varieties: More are coming onto the market all the time. The most popular are clementines, the seedless satsumas, and tangerines.

Buying/Storing: The skins should be shiny, free from bruising or other damage. Watch out too for signs of mould. Heavier fruits will be juicier. Can be kept at room temperature for 3 to 4 days, though do not leave them for too long or they will dry out.

How to use: Best eaten raw or in fruit salads. Can be used in flans or as decoration on special-occasion cakes. For parties, skewer on sticks, alternating with white cheese. The peel can be candied, or added to jams and jellies.

CARAMELLISED SATSUMAS

115g/4oz/2/3rd cup raw cane sugar
8 tablespoons water
6 satsumas
30g/1oz/¹/₄ cup flaked almonds, roasted
natural yogurt or fromage frais to serve – optional

Put the sugar and 4 tablespoons of water into a pan and cook gently, stirring continually, until the sugar has dissolved. Add the rest of the water (be careful it doesn't splash). Boil steadily, without stirring, until the mixture becomes a golden brown caramel.

Use a sharp knife to peel the satsumas and then cut them crossways into thin slices. Divide these between four dishes. Pour the caramel over the tops and leave to cool. Serve sprinkled with flaked almonds and – if liked – a spoonful of yogurt or fromage frais.

Note: This method, more traditionally used with oranges, can be used with any other citrus fruit.

CHOCOLATE
See **Cocoa**

CLINGFILM

Many people have long been concerned about this form of wrapping for food, though it was only in 1990 that such concerns reached the media. Animal tests indicated that such plasticisers may be carcinogenic, and that when allowed to touch food for any length of time, this risk may be passed on to the consumers of the food.

It is, of course, easy for anyone to remove this risk from the home – just avoid using clingfilm. If this seems too extreme you can, it seems, reduce the danger by using it only as a sealer (for example, secured over the top of a dish containing food) rather than as a wrapper that actually touches the food. Many items, however, come ready-wrapped in clingfilm. Two of the most obvious examples are prepared sandwiches, and cheese. To avoid these buy only from shops that do not use clingfilm.

As an alternative, many shops now use polythene bags instead of paper bags – especially when selling loose products – and you can use these again and again. Better than polythene, however, are cellophane bags which are biodegradable. Unfortunately they are a little more expensive than polythene and are therefore less likely to be offered, except by ecologically aware outlets. It might be worth suggesting to the stores you visit regularly that they make the switch?

CLOVES

The dried berries of the clove tree that have a very strong and spicy flavour. They contain oils that really do seem to help relieve toothache.

Buying/Storing: Cloves are usually purchased whole. Provided they are stored in an airtight jar they will keep for ages this way. If you grind them, use them at once.

How to use: Traditionally used in sweet dishes such as mincemeat, apple pies and fruit cakes. Can also be used with vegetable dishes – try sticking whole cloves into an onion and adding to a stew. Cloves add something extra to mulled wine and hot chocolate drinks. Use with caution.

MULLED WINE

1.15 litres/2 pints/5 cups red wine
1 glass brandy
1 tablespoon raw cane sugar
$1/2$-1 teaspoon ground cloves
$1/2$-1 teaspoon ground cinnamon
slices of orange – optional

Put all ingredients into a heavy-based saucepan and heat very gently. Taste and adjust the seasoning just before serving. If you prefer a more potent mulled wine, use a little more brandy.
Serve hot. Float slices of orange on top if liked.

See also Spiced mooli, Pecan pumpkin pie.

COB NUTS
See Hazelnuts

COCOA
See also **Carob**

This is a powder made by grinding the beans of certain small trees that are native to South America. The Aztecs made it into a drink which they called *xocolatl*, from which the word chocolate is derived. Cocoa was brought to Europe by the Spaniards, and arrived in England in 1650 where it soon became very popular – as, of course, it still is. It wasn't, however, until some 200 years later that the Swiss invented a way to turn the powder into chocolate for eating.

Varieties: Cocoa powder is still widely available. Drinking chocolate is the same powder but with sugar added, usually white sugar. There are various kinds of eating chocolate on the market, some plain, others made with dried skimmed milk, some sweetened with white sugar and others with raw cane sugar.

Nutrition: Chocolate contains a few vitamins and minerals (milk chocolate has some calcium). On the reverse side, chocolate is high in fat and calories, eating chocolate being especially so. It also contains small amounts of caffeine, plus theobromine, which has a similar effect to caffeine on the nervous system. Some people find it causes migraines or other allergic reactions.

How to use: In general it is best to avoid or at least limit your use of cocoa and chocolate. Carob makes an excellent and healthy alternative. However, it does have a stronger taste which may not always be suitable for a particular recipe, in which case use unsweetened cocoa powder and – if necessary – add a natural sweetener of your choice. Chocolate cake, for example, can be made this way, as can chocolate drinks and ice cream.

COCONUTS

Coconuts originated in Malaysia, but are now grown throughout the tropics. The coconut palm can grow to 30 metres/100 feet and the whole tree is used, making everything from bristles for brushes to rope, door mats, furniture and fuel. The actual flesh of the fruit is protected by a tough fibrous shell, and the hollow fruit usually contains a milky liquid.

Varieties: Fresh coconuts are now available much of the year. Look out too for 'mini' nuts which are a novelty, though a lot of hard work for a mouthful! In addition you can buy desiccated coconut and dried coconut flakes (look out for the kind that has not been sweetened – usually this contains white sugar). Creamed coconut is made by reducing the nut to a cream; it comes in an airtight pack and can be found at most healthfood and wholefood stores as well as speciality shops. New on the market is an instant coconut milk which comes in powdered form and needs no refrigeration.

Nutrition: Coconuts are low in protein, the highest of all nuts in fibre. They contain saturated fats, which makes it a good idea to restrict their use, though a small amount of coconut gives a delicious flavouring and can do little harm.

Buying/Storing: Shake fresh coconut to be sure there is liquid inside – if not it is stale. Check the shell too for cracks or signs of dampness, which are also not good. Once opened, cover coconut flesh in water and store in the fridge. If the water is changed frequently it will keep well for up to 4 days. All varieties of dried coconut keep for ages if stored in airtight containers. Creamed coconut is best kept in a fridge, especially once the pack has been opened.

How to use: The sweet watery milk that is found inside fresh coconuts is excellent in curries, or as a substitute for water or milk in savoury sauces or sweet dishes, especially with rice. Fresh grated coconut can be added to fruit salads or muesli, or used when making granola. Roasted flaked coconut makes a tasty nibble, or can be sprinkled over dishes. Use desiccated coconut in cakes, biscuits, coconut bread and Indian-style sweets. Creamed coconut adds a subtle and delicious taste to curries, or use it to make a vegan 'cream' and serve with desserts.

COCONUT VEGETABLE RICE

225g/¹/₂ lb/1 cup long grained brown rice
1 small onion, chopped
1 small leek, cleaned and chopped
2 carrots, dried
340ml/2/3rds pint/1¹/₂ cups hot vegetable stock
55g/2oz creamed coconut, grated
1 tablespoon fresh herbs
seasoning to taste
1 banana, peeled, sliced and brushed with lemon

Soak the rice in water for an hour. Drain. Put it in a saucepan with the prepared vegetables and most of the stock. Stir the grated coconut into the remaining stock until it dissolves, then add to the rice and vegetables with herbs and seasoning. Bring to the boil, then cover the pan and cook gently until the liquid is absorbed, the rice and vegetables are cooked.

Set aside for 5 minutes before stirring in the banana gently and serving.

You can use any choice of vegetables in this dish. Or add nuts. For a change, use avocado instead of banana. On special occasions serve the rice in coconut shells. You can actually heat the rice through in these – just cover in aluminium foil first.

See also Mixed grain granola, Coconut cherry slices, Fruited lettuce leaves, Coconut cream pie, Peach and coconut balls, Coconut beans.

COFFEE

See also **Tea, Cash crops**

Coffee is made from the beans of a tropical plant now grown in many countries. Since its introduction to Europe in the 17th century, it has become one of our most popular drinks, second only to tea, and coffee machines are standard equipment in offices, station waiting rooms, cinemas, just about anywhere.

As an instant pick-you-up coffee is undoubtedly effective. But it is a chemical substance called caffeine which stimulates your system, providing a burst of energy, making you alert. As caffeine has no food value, this energy is drawn from the body's emergency supply, the glycogen stored in the liver. As soon as you begin to flag again, you feel the need for more coffee, and the yo-yoing has begun.

But there is more. Drink a cup of coffee and your heart beat will speed up, your stomach produces more acid, the bladder produces twice as much urine, the lungs work harder, the blood vessels expand and muscles tense up. Being a diuretic, coffee puts a strain on your kidneys. Your body has to work twice as hard to get all this activity under control, and the way you feel can only be improved by yet another cup of coffee.

Have no doubts about it: coffee is addictive. If you are addicted to it, consider breaking free for not just the sake of your day-to-day health, but for your life. You may well at first find yourself going through withdrawal symptoms. One way to cope with this is to reduce the number of coffees you drink only gradually, reaching instead – when you need a lift – for some energy-giving food such as raisins, fruit.

Decaffinated coffees are also well worth considering, though do choose them with care. The cheaper varieties may well have had the caffeine removed by a process involving the use of chemicals, some of which could still be there in your cup. Better quality brands remove the caffeine with a water process which is obviously preferable.

You may also find some of the alternative 'coffees' now available worth trying. Made from roasted cereals, beans and chicory roots, they have a similar bitterness and appearance, yet none of the harmful effects.

COLOURINGS, NATURAL
See also **Additives**

There are only a few occasions for which the home cook needs to use food colouring. Sweets are more interesting when coloured in an appropriate way; so is the icing on a birthday cake, especially one for a child. Some dessert dishes – fruit mousse, for example – also benefit from a splash of added colour.

Up until recently the only way you could do this was to add natural ingredients such as fruit juice – fine if you happen to have the right fruit handy – or by using artificial colourings. These are based on chemicals and have been linked with allergies, hypertension in children, and various other health problems. Now, however, there is at least one range of natural food colourings made from vegetable extracts and so also suitable for vegetarians and vegans (not all natural colourings are – cochineal, for example, is made from insects). The colours are not as intense as those obtained with artificial colourings, but are very attractive just the same.

CORIANDER

An annual plant brought to Britain by the Romans, which sometimes grows wild although it is often cultivated in herb gardens. The ripe seeds are used to make the powder which has a mild, sweet, slightly musty flavour.

Buying/Storing: Buy as seeds if possible, and grind them yourself as and when you need them. Or buy ready-powdered coriander in small quantities and store in an airtight jar.

How to use: Often used in curries. Unusual addition to casseroles. Nice in the crumble topping of a fruit dish. Coriander also goes well with Middle Eastern dishes – try it in pilaffs, stuffed vegetables, or sprinkled over a mixture of black olives and potatoes. Good with pea soup. The leaves can be shredded and added to salads and curries.

SPICY CAULIFLOWER

2 tablespoons vegetable oil
1 teaspoon ground coriander
1 teaspoon ground cumin
1 teaspoon turmeric
$^1/_2$ teaspoon ground ginger
$^1/_2$-1 clove garlic, crushed
1 medium cauliflower, cut into florets
2 carrots, peeled and sliced thickly
approx. 200g/1/3rd pint/$^3/_4$ cup vegetable stock
30g/1oz/$^1/_4$ cup flour
85g/3oz/$^1/_2$ cup sultanas
55g/2oz/$^1/_2$ cup cashew nuts
salt
140ml/$^1/_4$ pint/2/3rd cup sour cream or yogurt
chopped parsley

Heat the oil and add the spices and garlic. Cook gently for a few minutes. Stir in the cauliflower, carrots and vegetable stock, cover pan and cook for 10 minutes (take care it doesn't burn).

Mix the flour with a little extra stock and add to the pan, continuing to cook until the sauce thickens. Sprinkle in the sultanas and cashews, add salt to taste.

Off the heat stir in the sour cream or yogurt. Serve sprinkled with chopped parsley.

See also Pakora, Lentil dal, Mattar paneer.

CORN
See **Maize**

CORN CHIPS
See **Maize**

CORN SALAD
See **Lamb's lettuce**

COURGETTES

Courgettes are baby marrows, either specially grown, or actually cut from marrow plants before they have had time to mature. They grow well in Britain, though they are more often used in Mediterranean-style dishes where their subtle flavour is brought out by the addition of herbs. They are also popular in America where they are called 'zucchini'. At their best in the early summer, courgettes should not be too large or the skins will be tough.

Buying/Storing: They should be smooth, brightly coloured and firm to touch. Keep them in a cool place for as short a time as possible.

How to use: Courgettes should not be peeled. Grate them and add raw to salads, or use raw courgette sticks with dips. Include in soups, but add near the end of the cooking time as they quickly over-cook. Slice lengthways and stuff – a lentil mixture is tasty – then bake. Fry in oil, coating each slice first in wheatgerm. Serve in a cheese sauce. Use in vegetable kebabs.

ZUCCHINI BREAD
225g/¹/₂ lb courgettes, washed and trimmed
6 tablespoons vegetable oil
170g/6oz/1 cup raw cane sugar
1 large egg, beaten
170g/6oz/1¹/₂ cups wholemeal flour

¹/₂ teaspoon baking powder
¹/₂ teaspoon bicarbonate of soda
¹/₂-1 teaspoon allspice
55g/2oz/¹/₂ cup pecan nuts (or others), coarsely chopped

Grate the courgettes coarsely into a bowl. Stir in the oil, then the sugar and then the egg, making sure all ingredients are well mixed.

Mix the dry ingredients together. Combine them with the courgettes. Add the nuts, distributing them evenly. The mixture should be thick and moist.

Lightly grease a medium-sized loaf tin and pour in the mixture. Smooth the top. Bake at 180°C/350°F (Gas Mark 4) for about an hour. Test the bread by inserting a sharp knife – it should come out clean.

Set on a wire rack to cool. Good sliced and lightly buttered.

Note: As its name suggests, this is a traditional American recipe that tastes, in fact, more like a cake. Use different nuts or replace them with dried fruit, if liked.

See also Vegetable kebabs with herbs, Fennel ratatouille, Filo parcels, Vegetable stew for couscous.

COUSCOUS

Couscous is a coarse ground semolina usually made from wheat (though it can also be made from millet). It is much used even now by the Arabs, and is traditionally steamed over a stew, the two eventually being served together.

How to use: To cook this properly you need a couscousier. However, you can improvise by putting a steamer or colander lined with muslin over the saucepan in which the stew is cooking, and covering it all with a lid.

OVEN-BAKED COUSCOUS

340g/12oz/1¹/₂ cups couscous grains
2 tablespoons vegetable oil
salt
water

In a heavy-based pan mix the grains and oil and cook gently, stirring continually, until beginning to brown.

Transfer to an ovenproof dish and just cover with boiling water. Heat the oven to 170°C/325°F (Gas Mark 3) and bake the couscous for about 15 minutes, or until the water has been absorbed and the grains are light, separate and just cooked.

Serve with a spicy vegetable and chick pea stew.

See also Vegetable stew for couscous.

CRABAPPLES

These small and rather sour tasting apples can still be found growing wild in hedgerows, though there are fewer of them around than there used to be. Probably all cultivated apples developed from the wild crabapple, and as the larger, sweeter varieties became more popular, crabapple trees are now more likely to be grown for their appearance than their fruit.

How to use: As crabapples are an excellent source of pectin, they are very useful when making jams and jellies.

CRANBERRIES

These are one of the few berries that do not grow in Britain – in fact, they grow in very few places. American Red Indians gave them as gifts to the early settlers, who soon discovered how to make a delicious sauce with these sharp red berries. Up until recently they were hard to find in this country, but now they are being imported from New England (USA) which is where most of the world's cranberries are produced.

Buying/Storing: If possible buy fresh cranberries which should be bright-red and shiny. They will keep for two weeks or so if stored in the fridge, preferably in sealed packaging. A good alternative – when fresh are impossible to find, or simply out of season – is frozen cranberries.

How to use: Cranberries can be used both for sweet sauces (to serve with ice cream or cheesecake) or for more savoury sauces (traditionally served with turkey, but good too with nut roasts).

CRANBERRY SAUCE

30g/1oz/2¹/₂ tablespoons butter or margarine
1 large onion, chopped
30g/1oz/¹/₄ cup wholemeal flour
140ml/¹/₄ pint/2/3rd cup water
140ml/¹/₄ pint/2/3rd cup orange juice
115g/4oz fresh cranberries

Melt the fat and fry the onion briefly, then cover the pan and cook gently for 10 minutes. Stir in the flour and cook for just a minute more before adding the water and orange juice and bringing to the boil. Continue stirring and simmer until the sauce thickens. Add the cranberries and simmer gently for 15 minutes more, or until the cranberries are tender.

If you like you can season the sauce with salt and pepper, or add a little sugar instead. Delicious with croquettes, or nut loaf. If necessary, add a drop more water or orange juice to make the sauce pour easily.

CREAM

Cream consists of the fat of milk together with a decreased proportion of water and other constituents of milk. It is separated from milk by heating and then rotating. Whipping cream may contain sugar and stabilisers. Ultra-heat treated cream and sterilised cream may contain emulsifiers. In Britain, regulations state that single cream must contain not less than 18% fat, whipping cream not less than 35% fat, and double cream not less than 48% fat. A variety not so widely used in Britain is sour cream, though it is popular in America and other parts of the world.

Cream is most widely used in northern countries, as it has always been. Its poor keeping qualities make it unpopular in hot climates. Most of the cream on sale in Britain is home-produced, though tinned creams are sometimes imported from other parts of Europe.

Nutrition: The same as milk, but cream is especially rich in saturated fats, so should be used sparingly. Single cream has approximately 60 calories per ounce, double cream about 128. Sour cream, a single cream that has bacterial culture added, has a fresh taste, is easy to digest, and is less fatty.

Worth looking out for too is the relatively small amount of clotted cream that is sold in summer and has a unique rich flavour, perfect with summer fruits (though even higher in fat than double cream!). In fact, both double and clotted creams are exceptionally high-fat products and should be kept for special occasions only.

Buying/Storing: Check the 'sell-by' date and do not buy any product that is past it. Keep cream in a cool place. Make sure it is covered and well away from strongly-flavoured foods, as it can easily become tainted.

How to use: As with butter, use cream only when you intend to taste it. Two ways to lower the fat content without ruining the flavour are to mix cream with yogurt, or to add a stiffly-beaten egg white. Make an exotically-flavoured cream by soaking rinsed, strongly fragranced rose petals in it for an hour or so – remove them before using.

HOMEMADE SOUR CREAM

570ml/1 pint/2¹/₂ cups single cream
2 tablespoons lemon juice

Pour the cream into a bowl and add the lemon juice, mixing well. Cover the bowl and leave to stand overnight at room temperature. The resulting cream will be thick and have the bite of commercial sour cream. The longer you leave it the thicker and creamier it will become.
Store covered in the fridge for a few days, but no longer. To serve it with fruit salad, stir in a little fresh cream.

See also Gooseberry brulée, Stuffed dates, Brown bread ice cream, Red cabbage with sour cream, Cashew noodles with parsley.

CREAM SUBSTITUTES

Those who want to avoid the high fat content of real cream should look out for the alternatives that – in these cholesterol conscious days – are gradually coming onto the market. Some are made from vegetable ingredients, possibly thickened with gum, and lightly sweetened. They can be poured or whipped. Though certainly lower in saturated fats than cream, they are still a highly processed food.

There are more natural alternatives, though so far they can only be used to replace pouring creams. One you can buy is concentrated soya milk, which has a thick smooth texture and a cream-like taste. Others you can make at home include coconut cream, made from grated coconut and water, or tahini cream made by blending tahini with a sweetener such as honey or maple syrup. Nut creams are also excellent and delicious. They can be made in a variety of ways, though you do need a grinder to make the nuts into a powder. Try using one kind of nut mixed with water, soya milk or fruit juice. Try blends of different nuts. Add spices, rosewater, whatever you fancy.

APRICOT NUT CREAM

115g/4oz/³⁄₄ cup cashew nuts
approx. 6 tablespoons apricot juice
water
pinch of mixed spice – optional

Grind the nuts to a fine powder in a grinder. Stir them together with the apricot juice. Add water to make a thick or thin cream, as desired, and the spice if using it. Chill briefly before serving.

CRESS
See **Mustard and cress**

CRISPBREADS

Once considered only suitable for dieters (they do usually have a low calorie count), crispbreads are now widely available in a variety of forms and flavours. Made from grains and baked hard, they are an excellent alternative to bread as they will keep for some time (if not indefinitely) if stored in an airtight container.

Like bread they *can* be made from white flour, sweetened with white sugar, flavoured with chemicals. Look out for those that are made from the whole grains which are more nutritious and tastier. Many are made from organic grains too. A new idea is puffed rice biscuits, some with sesame seeds added, that are still crisp but thicker and therefore more satisfying.

Many of these crispbreads are imported from abroad, and as they have no preservatives, or only the minimum amount, do buy from a retailer who has a fast turnover, and check the 'sell by' date carefully. It is not unknown to find the packet home to a family of little creatures.

CUCUMBER

Victorians grew white, yellow and blue ones. Today most cucumbers are green. Choose from two different types – the uneven-skinned ridged variety, which looks rather ugly, but has a better taste, or the hothouse cucumber, which has a smooth skin. Though you can get them all year round, they are better in summer.

Buying/Storing: Choose those that are a good colour, round, and not too large. The best way to tell if a cucumber is past its best is to press the stalk end, which should be firm. Store cucumbers in the fridge and eat as quickly as possible.

How to use: This low calorie dieters' favourite is mostly used in salads and sandwiches. Try adding sliced or grated cucumber to natural yogurt to serve with a curry. Layer in a quiche. Make a chilled cucumber soup, or cook and serve in a white sauce.

CUCUMBER AND STRAWBERRY SALAD

1 large cucumber, peeled
225g/¹/₂ lb small firm strawberries
1-2 tablespoons lemon juice
black pepper
approx. 1 tablespoon white wine – optional
sprigs of fresh mint

If you have a scoop to make melon balls, use this to cut cucumber balls out of the cucumber flesh. Otherwise, cut it into thin slices. Sprinkle with lemon juice and add some fresh ground pepper.

If using cucumber balls either leave the strawberries whole or cut them in half, then pile everything into 4 tall glasses and top each with a spoonful of wine and a sprig of mint.

If using slices of cucumber, slice the strawberries too, and arrange both of them in overlapping circles on four small plates. Sprinkle with wine, decorate with mint. Either way you should chill the salad before serving.

See also Moulded salad.

CUMIN

The seed of a plant resembling fennel, though the taste is more like a mild caraway.

Buying/Storing: Best bought in seed form and ground as needed. You can, however, buy it also ready-ground and if doing so should get only a small quantity at a time, and store it in an airtight container.

How to use: Add the powder to cream cheese dips or spreads. Good with egg dishes, lentils and other pulses, vegetables such as cabbage, and in sauerkraut. Use the lightly-crushed seeds in a curry, or sprinkle them over a pizza.

HUMMUS (CHICK PEA DIP)

225g/^{1}/$_2$ lb chick peas, soaked overnight
1-2 cloves garlic, crushed
3 tablespoons tahini
2 tablespoons oil, preferably olive
2 tablespoons lemon juice
^{1}/$_2$ teaspoon ground cumin, or to taste
seasoning to taste
sprig of mint or parsley to garnish

Put the chick peas in a saucepan with fresh water, boil for 10 minutes, then lower the heat and cover the pan. Cook over a medium heat for about 1 hour or until tender. Drain well.

Use a grinder to powder the chick peas, then mix them well with the garlic, tahini, oil, lemon juice, cumin and seasoning. If you have a blender you can simply combine all the ingredients and blend to make a thick, creamy paste. Adjust the taste and texture to suit yourself.

Transfer to a small dish, chill well, and serve topped with sprigs of mint or parsley.

See also Coconut beans, Pakora, Lentil dal.

CURLY KALE
See **Kale**

CURRANTS

Blackcurrants and redcurrants are very small, delicate fruits, both of which can be grown in Britain. Those on sale are usually from this country as the fruits do not travel well. Blackcurrants have a very strong flavour and are the better known of the two. Whitecurrants are a variety of redcurrants that do not have as sharp a taste.

Nutrition: All kinds of currants are especially good sources of vitamin C provided they are eaten when fresh, and preferably raw.

Buying/Storing: Look out for pump smooth fruit with no sign of mould around them. If you get a chance to pick your own, go for those that are even-sized and firm. They should be eaten within 24 hours of buying or picking, and can be stored in the fridge. Do not wash them until just before serving.

How to use: Use either blackcurrants or redcurrants in jams, jellies, sauces, ice creams, sorbets and fools. They are used together in summer puddings.

BLACKCURRANT MOUSSE

570ml/1 pint/2¹/₂ cups blackcurrant juice, sweetened
2 teaspoons agar agar
225g/¹/₂ lb fresh blackcurrants, trimmed
small carton natural yogurt or single cream

Heat the juice and when it reaches boiling point, sprinkle in the agar agar, stirring well so that it dissolves completely. Pour into a dish that has first been washed with cold water. Leave the jelly mixture until just set.

Meanwhile cook the blackcurrants in the minimum of water. If you like your fruit especially sweet add some sugar, though it will detract from the natural taste of the mousse.

Use a whisk to break up the jelly so that it is light and frothy. Mix in the yogurt and most of the blackcurrants. Divide between 4 tall glasses and put into the fridge to chill. Serve decorated with the remaining blackcurrants.

▦ CURRANTS, DRIED ▦

These are dried from a small purple seedless grape called the Corinth grape grown in Greece. They dry very easily and therefore do not always need a preserving solution.

Nutrition: Rich in minerals – potassium in particular – they are at their best when dark and not too tiny.

How to use: Currants are traditionally used in a variety of recipes including spotted dick pudding, Easter biscuits and eccles cakes. They are especially suitable for biscuits because of their size.

See Apple oatmeal biscuits.

▦ CURRIES ▦
See also **Curry powder and paste**

Indian curries have been cooked in much the same way for hundreds of years. They vary from the north of the country – where they are generally milder – to the south, the ingredients depending on what is grown locally, the spices used chosen to compliment those ingredients.

Britain's long association with India has resulted in most of us already being familiar with the taste and smells of curry, though the corner take-away does not always do justice to this unique and fascinating cooking technique. As many Indians are strict Hindus, and are therefore forbidden to eat meat, they have perfected the art of making vegetarian curries, making this kind of food especially appealing to many of those in the West who – having given up meat – are looking for alternative ways to serve plant foods. Even the simplest ingredients can be turned into a feast with the right spices.

Learning how to cook curries can be as simple or professional as you wish it to be. If this is something you are new to, there are numerous books that will help get you started. Do go slowly when you start experimenting, being especially sparing with the chilli powder if you mix your own powders. Contrary to common belief, curry does not have to be fiery hot – some of the most delicious curry sauces have a mild, delicate flavour that allows you to taste the ingredients that are beneath it. The spices are also believed to both stimulate the appetite and help digestion.

All curries benefit from being made a day in advance and being left overnight for the flavours to mingle and mellow.

LENTIL DAL

225g/¹/₂ lb/1 cup split red lentils
2 tablespoons ghee
1 large onion, chopped
2 cloves garlic, crushed
salt and black pepper
1 teaspoon paprika
1 teaspoon ground cumin
1 teaspoon turmeric
1 teaspoon ground coriander
¹/₂ teaspoon garam masala
115g/4oz coconut cream, grated

Cook the lentils in boiling water for about 20 minutes, or until soft.
In a separate pan melt the ghee and fry the onion and garlic until golden. Stir in all the spices and cook a few minutes more. Stir in the lentils and a drop of the water.
Add the coconut cream. Simmer and stir until the mixture is thick and smooth.
Serve with rice and accompaniments such as yogurt, salted peanuts, and banana slices.
You can also add vegetables to the dal to extend it – spinach and potatoes both go especially well with red lentils. Adjust the seasoning if necessary – you might need to use a little more spice.

See also Parsnip curry.

▓ CURRY POWDER AND PASTE ▓
See also **Curries**

Those who do make their own curries in this country tend to rely on ready-made curry powders. The ability to mix different spices together in combinations that work well together is something that needs to be learnt from experience.

By all means use ready-mixed powders if you prefer. When doing so, buy them in small quantities only from retailers who have a fast turnover. Store them in opaque screw-top jars, and check that they are fresh before you use them – stale curry powder will be weak and tasteless.

You can also make up your own mix and store it in much the same way, ready for instant use as and when you need it. Make it from fresh spices and store it correctly, and the flavour should actually improve as time goes by. This will, of course, mean buying individual spices which can work out expensive, especially if you do not intend to make curry very often. On the other hand, a small quantity will go a long way so you do not need to buy vast amounts. You can also, of course, just use individual spices as you go along, varying them each time, experimenting. This also gives you the option of trying recipes from different parts of India, each of which will have an entirely different balance of spices.

Curry pastes are a mixture of spices in an oil base, and come in varying strengths. They can be stirred into a sauce to give an authentic flavour for the minimum work. Another excellent way in which they can be used is as a flavouring – try adding a spoonful of paste to mayonnaise or yogurt, or stir it into a vegetable soup.

Garam masala is a special blend of spices in powder form. Like curry powder, it can be added at the beginning of the cooking period – however, unlike curry powder it can also be added just before a dish is served. This makes it especially useful on those occasions when a final check indicates your curry needs a last minute flavour adjustment.

CURRIED NUTS NIBBLES

2 tablespoons vegetable oil
good pinch of salt
1-2 teaspoons curry powder
50g/2oz/¹/₂ cup cashew nuts
50g/2oz/¹/₂ cup peanuts
50g/2oz/¹/₂ cup almonds

Mix together the oil, salt and curry powder in a shallow ovenproof dish. Add the nuts, stirring well.
Bake at 170°C/325°F (Gas Mark 3) for about 20 minutes, stirring frequently. When they begin to brown, remove from the oven and leave to get completely cold before

storing in an airtight jar. (The amount of curry powder you use will obviously give the nuts a milder or spicier taste.)

See also White sauce (curry).

DAMSONS
See **Plums**

DANDELIONS

The same small yellow-coloured flower that grows wild and is generally considered to be a nuisance. Though not widely used in Britain wild dandelions are eaten in many other parts of the world and are an excellent food. The young leaves have a sharp 'green' taste.

Nutrition: Dandelions contain vitamins A and C, iron and potassium. Dandelion tea may help to relieve liver complaints, and is a mild diuretic, known in France as pissenlit.

How to use: Pick the leaves when they are young and unblemished (and preferably as far as possible away from the road, or from fields growing crops likely to have been sprayed with chemicals!). Wash them and pat dry. Then snip and add to salads, cheese or egg dishes, pulses, or use as a garnish with casseroles, bakes, etc. The flowers can be dipped in batter and deep-fried. You can also make tea with the leaves or the flowers and a coffee substitute from the ground roots. The flowers are also, of course, the key ingredient in dandelion wine.

DANDELION TEA
850ml/1 ¹/₂ pints/3³/₄ cups boiling water
1 good cup fresh dandelion flowers, washed
fresh mint

Use a large jug, warming it first. Pour the water over the flowers, cover the top of the jug, and leave to steep for 5 minutes.

Pour through a sieve into 4 cups, dropping a fresh sprig of mint into each one.

DATES

Usually imported from Middle Eastern countries where they are easy to grow and therefore a staple food, dates are not only a very sweet high energy fruit, but they are also suspected of having aphrodisiac properties.

Varieties: Though fresh dates are finding their way into more and more shops, by far the majority of people know them as a dried fruit that comes packed in boxes or pressed into slabs.

Nutrition: Dates contain iron and potassium, though they have very little vitamin content.

Buying/Storing: When buying fresh dates look out for smooth, plump fruits that are dark-brown in colour. Avoid any that look shrivelled. Can be kept in the refrigerator for several days. Dried dates are best bought loose from a wholefood or healthfood shop.

How to use: Fresh dates can be candied, used in chutneys and cakes. However, they are really too expensive to cook (dried dates, which are cheaper, are the ones to use for cooking). Wash and chop fresh dates and add them to fruit or savoury salads, or split them, remove the stones and stuff them with cream or curd cheese, marzipan, or walnut halves, and serve them as a party nibble.

STUFFED DATES

1-2 boxes dessert dates
almonds
hazelnuts
cream cheese, fromage frais, curd or ricotta cheese
peanut butter
Cheddar cheese, grated, plus mayonnaise
marzipan
glacé cherries
dried apricot pieces
peanut butter

Dessert dates are those that have been left whole and usually come in fancy boxes. Carefully remove the stones first. Try all or a selection of the fillings to stuff the dates.

Use a single nut for some of them, a single spoonful of soft white cheese or peanut butter in others.

A little grated cheese, moistened with mayonnaise and made into a ball, makes an unusual filling.

For those with a sweet tooth fill each date with a sliver of marzipan, a glacé cherry, or a piece of dried apricot.

Serve at parties or with pre-dinner drinks.

See also Parsnip and banana chutney.

DIET

Though the word DIET actually refers to a way of eating, it has been associated with the word SLIMMING for so long that the two are now automatically linked.

Slimming diets are big business in Britain, as they are in most of the affluent countries of the West. Fashion manufacturers, magazines and the media in general have combined to convince most women – especially young ones – that no matter how thin they are they are not thin enough. As proof that the message has struck home, a vast array of medicines, machines, clubs, books and magazines are sold every day to help those that want to be thinner achieve their aim. Probably the most profitable lines, though, are the many specially produced diet foods which sell simply because of their low calorie counts. Most of them are far from nutritious, containing artificial sweeteners and other chemicals to make them palatable. What's more, the calorie count of a wholefood alternative may well be only a fraction higher. Still, though, they sell. Again and again. And the reason is that a dieter rarely follows one diet and then stops. It is a statistical fact that most of those who start a slimming programme will not achieve their desired weight, or if they do, will soon put back the pounds they have lost. Most of them go on to become chronic dieters, suffering restricted eating patterns for weeks, losing control, over-eating until something makes them call a halt and go back onto their diet.

The fact that most dieters fail may have something to do with the fact that many of them do not need to lose weight. Every body is different. The aim should be to have one in which you feel comfortable, that is in good health, a body that suits you and the life you lead. And the best way to achieve this is not to fight it but to work with it. Eating a wide variety of natural and wholesome foods as and when you feel hungry, exercising regularly, and then relaxing and enjoying yourself – these are the keys to success.

DIETARY FIBRE
See also **Bran**

It used to be called roughage, and for many years was considered to be harmful to health. Then, in the 1980s, it did an about turn, was renamed dietary fibre, and became the wonder food of the decade. Dietary fibre, it was realised, did not after all act as an irritant to the system. Instead, it kept it working more efficiently, helping prevent a wide range of health problems including cancer of the bowel and constipation. At the same time it increased the feeling of satiety, making it possible to feel full on less (great for the overweight, who may well have got that way by eating too many low fibre refined foods). Now fibre is widely acknowledged to be something we should all eat more of, though unfortunately the way many people are doing this is not by changing their whole diet but by simply sprinkling everything they eat with bran.

What is natural fibre, and where can you get it? It is, in fact, a substance found only in plants and consists of a carbohydrate material, mostly derived from cell walls, that is not digested by the body. The best sources are grains, fruits, vegetables, nuts and pulses, all of which offer some fibre though the amounts will vary considerably from one to the next.

How they are processed before being passed on to the public also has a bearing on their fibre content. Grains, though an excellent source of fibre in their natural state, often go through considerable processing before we use them. When wheat, for example is refined to make white flour, most of its fibre is stripped away as part of the milling and refining process, and you are left with a grain that is virtually pure starch. It is the bran that has been removed from wheat that is then sold back to you in packets; buy wholemeal flour and you will be saving yourself money if nothing else!

Fruit and vegetables, if purchased in a fresh state, will not have been tampered with in this way. Yet it is traditional to peel many of these before eating them, a habit that means we often discard the part richest in fibre.

Nuts and pulses, also excellent sources of fibre, are not eaten as regularly as they should be, at least, not by most people. Vegetarians and vegans do tend to make better use of them as replacements for meat protein.

Still, though, natural fibre is not hard to come by (and it is important to eat it in its natural and balanced state rather than as yet another processed product like bran, which can easily be taken in amounts that do more harm than good). Many of the grains found in wholefood and healthfood shops will be 'whole', the processing having been kept to only the minimum necessary. Flours, breads and other baked goods made from unrefined grains are now increasingly available. As far as fruit and vegetables go, the choice is yours. Instead of peeling them buy a good brush, scrub them well, and then eat the skin along with the flesh.

Get into the habit of using nuts and pulses as ingredients in savoury dishes such as stews, bakes, soups and crumbles.

If you base your eating habits on wholefoods such as these you will be able to forget altogether about dietary fibre, confident in the knowledge that your body will be getting all it needs.

DILL

A plant originally grown in the Mediterranean, but now cultivated in Britain too. The subtle taste is rather like caraway (it contains the same oils but in a different balance).

Nutrition: It is thought to have a carminative effect, and is often used in children's medicine.

How to use: Chop the mild flavoured feathery leaves and add them to salads and sauces. The seeds go well with pickled vegetables. Add them also to coleslaw, sauerkraut and potato salad. An unusual but delicious apple pie can be made by stirring just a few dill seeds in with the fruit.

CHILLED CUCUMBER DILL SOUP

1 onion
850ml/1 1/2 pints/3 3/4 cups vegetable stock
2 cucumbers
1 clove garlic, crushed
1 bunch dill, chopped
seasoning to taste
pinch of nutmeg
paprika to taste
140ml/1/4 pint/2/3rd cup natural yogurt

Slice the onion and cook for 5 minutes in the stock. Cut the cucumber up and add to the stock with the garlic; cook 10 minutes more. Add the chopped dill, bring to the boil, then simmer the soup for 15 minutes, or until the cucumber is tender. Set aside to cool.

Purée the ingredients, or rub through a sieve. Stir in seasoning, nutmeg and paprika, then gently add the yogurt, mixing it well. Chill the soup before serving. Top with extra dill if liked.

See also Sweet and sour borscht.

DIPS
See **Patés**

DRIED FRUIT
See also **individual varieties**

A wide variety of fruits from the vine and from trees can be dried in order to concentrate the goodness into a form that will keep. The simplest and best way to do this is to lay them in the sun, but nowadays many fruits are dried artificially. Some, especially the pale varieties such as apple rings and sultanas, are treated with sulphur dioxide; others are sprayed with food-grade mineral oil (usually liquid paraffin) in order to stop them sticking together as well as to improve their appearance. As such additives may be harmful to health, and as oil certainly prevents the body absorbing the fruit's fat-soluble vitamins, it is a good idea to wash dried fruit in hot water before using it.

Nutrition: Apart from being an excellent source of fibre, dried fruits contain many minerals, iron in particular, and vitamins, the exact contents depending on the fruit and where it was grown. Though better for us than refined sugar in many ways, it must be remembered that dried fruits eaten in excess can also cause tooth decay!

Buying/Storing: To get them in the most natural condition, dried fruits are best bought in healthfood or wholefood shops. When buying from supermarkets check to see if oil or anything else has been added. Fruits from California and Australia are usually sun-dried. Store in an airtight jar in a cool, dry place.

How to use: Though mostly used in sweet dishes such as muesli, mincemeat, mixed compôtes, Dundee cakes, jams and chutneys, dried fruits can also be added to a number of savoury dishes. Try them with salads, in curries, on pizzas, or with vegetables.

EGGPLANT
See **Aubergine**

EGGS

Eggs are the ova of certain species of birds and animals, usually contained in a shell shaped like an elongated sphere. They have been used for centuries almost everywhere in the world, but though the eggs of almost any bird can be eaten, for most people in the West 'eggs' are synonymous with chickens' eggs. Duck and goose eggs are sometimes available, and have a stronger taste.

Nutrition: An egg in its natural state is one of the most perfect foods of all, containing all the nutrients a chick embryo needs in order to develop.

Unfortunately, in recent years the majority of eggs consumed in this country come from factory farms which means they are far from natural. Chickens in factory farms are cramped together so they can hardly move, they rarely see daylight. These conditions tend to make them aggressive, so they are tranquillised; because they are prone to disease, they are frequently given antibiotics as a matter of course. To make the yolks the bright yellow that customers have come to expect, dye is added to their feed (though this is a natural dye, beta carotene). Thus in order to supply eggs at a lower price, a great deal of the nutritional value of this important food has been lost. Free-range eggs may be a little more expensive, but they are worth it.

Nutrition: Eggs contain a balance of amino acids: 95% of the protein can be used by the human body, and egg white is almost a complete protein. Eggs are also a good source of vitamins and minerals, and at approximately only 70 calories per egg are good for anyone watching their weight. Free-range eggs not only contain fewer chemicals than factory-farmed eggs; they contain more vitamin B12, folic acid, calcium and iron. Some people avoid eggs because of the cholesterol in the yolks, however, this is natural and is counteracted by the lecithin in the egg whites (besides, though the protein is balanced between the yolk and egg white, the vitamins are more abundant in the yolk). What can cause problems is the habit of frying eggs in animal fats or in highly-saturated vegetable oils.

Brown eggs are no different from white ones, except for the colour of their shell. Eggs which contain a tiny red speck have been fertilised, so contain more natural hormones.

Buying/Storing: Avoid factory-farmed or deep-litter eggs. Track down your local supplier of free-range eggs – as demand grows, more and more small-scale farmers are producing eggs from birds which are allowed to move freely and are fed on a natural diet. All eggs are best when fresh. Store them in a cool place (not necessarily in a fridge), with the pointed ends down, and well away from strongly-flavoured foods. Fresh eggs should keep up to 12 days at room temperature, 3 weeks in a fridge. To tell if an egg is fresh, put it into a deep bowl of water; if it sinks it is fresh. A not-so-fresh egg will stand on its end; a stale egg will float.

How to use: Eggs can be used to make dishes in their own right, such as omelettes, soufflés and egg custards. They are also useful as an addition to sauces, or you can hardboil them and sprinkle them over stews, pancakes, pizzas and soups as garnish. Whisked egg white can be added to fruit to make a light dessert dish. Because eggs are easy to digest, they are especially important in children's diets, and for anyone who has problems with heavier food.

CAULIFLOWER CHEESE MERINGUE

170g/6oz/1¹/₂ cups wholemeal flour
pinch of salt
85g/3oz/1/3rd cup margarine
1 medium-sized egg, beaten
approx. 1 tablespoon of water

filling:
1 small cauliflower, trimmed
2 egg whites
55g/2oz/¹/₂ cup Edam cheese, grated
seasoning to taste
pinch of paprika

First make the pastry. Sift together the flour and salt and use fingertips to rub the fat into the flour to form a crumb-like mixture. Use a knife to stir in the egg, then add the water to form a dough.

Knead the dough briefly, adding more flour if it needs it (or extra water if it is too dry). If possible, leave to chill for 30 minutes. Roll out the pastry and use to line a medium-sized flan ring standing on a baking sheet. Bake blind at 190°C/375°F (Gas Mark 5) for 15 minutes.

Meanwhile, break the cauliflower into florets and steam briefly to soften. Drain them well and arrange in the flan case.

Whisk the egg whites until stiff. Fold in the grated cheese, season well, add paprika. Spoon this over the cauliflower. Bake at 170°C/325°F (Gas Mark 3) for 20 minutes or until the meringue is cooked. Serve at once.

See also Quiche au poivre, Bean salad niçoise, Sorrel soufflé, Homemade pasta, Watercress and potato soufflés, Bean sprout omelette, Egg and hazelnut pancakes, Lovage and feta omelette, Zucchini bread, Grapefruit sorbet, Almond biscuits, Egg soup and chervil, Carob cake, Asparagus with hollandaise sauce, Artichoke salad, Omelette aux fines herbes.

EGG SUBSTITUTES

There are many reasons why people choose not to eat eggs. They may have exceptionally high cholesterol levels and wish to avoid all sources of this. They may have moral objections to the way in which eggs are produced, even free-range eggs. A surprisingly large number are allergic to eggs.

For such people there are now at least a couple of egg substitutes on the market, produced not to look and taste like eggs, but to offer their binding and gelling properties. These can be used, for example, in baking (especially useful in sponges), and when making savoury dishes such as nut loaves, pancakes and fritters. At least one can be used to add lightness to mousses and meringues.

Though these products vary in formulation, all of them are based on natural ingredients such as vegetable gums, potato flour, soya. At least one of them is entirely vegan. As they also vary in method of use, be sure to follow the instructions on the packet.

TOFU BALLS

285g/10oz/1¹/₄ cups tofu, drained
1 tablespoon fresh chives
1 large carrot, grated
1 large stick celery, finely chopped
2 tablespoons sesame seeds
approx. 2 tablespoons wholemeal breadcrumbs
soy sauce
seasoning
dried herbs
egg substitute equivalent of 1 large egg
oil for frying

Mash the tofu well. Put it into a bowl with all the other ingredients and use your fingers to mix everything together, squeezing so that a dough is formed.
Shape into small even-sized balls. Shallow- or deep-fry them until golden and firm in texture.
Nice served on rice, or in a tomato sauce with spaghetti.

See also Aubergine fritters.

▌▌▌▌▌▌▌▌▌▌▌ ENDIVE ▌▌▌▌▌▌▌▌▌▌▌

Though often mistaken for a lettuce, endive is actually a member of the chicory family, which explains its slightly bitter taste. Its leaves, which are bright green and crinkly around the edges, look good in a mixed salad. There are various endives now on the market, many being imported though some do also grow in Britain. Curly endives (such as frisée, an especially popular one) are generally available late autumn, whilst those available throughout the winter tend to have less curly and broader leaves.
Buying/Storing: Buy when fresh looking; if the leaves are at all limp it will be past its best. Store for only a day or two in the fridge and wash very carefully before using.
How to use: Wash well then tear into pieces and add to salads. Can also be lightly steamed and served as a vegetable, or added at the last minute to soups or stews.

ENDIVE AND BUTTER BEAN SOUP

225g/¹/₂ lb/1¹/₄ cup butter beans, cooked
1 large leek, chopped
2 sticks celery, chopped
1 large carrot, chopped

850ml/1¹/₂ pints/3³/₄ cups vegetable stock
¹/₂ teaspoon dried parsley
seasoning to taste
2 tablespoons light tahini, or to taste
the outer leaves of a head of endive, shredded
garlic croûtons to serve

Combine the beans, leek, celery, carrot, vegetable stock, parsley and seasoning in a large saucepan. Bring to the boil, then cover the pan, lower the heat and cook for 10-15 minutes, or until the vegetables are just tender.

Pour the soup into a blender and blend it for the shortest possible time. The soup should be thick but not too smooth. Return it to a pan, heat again, stir in tahini to taste and the coarsely shredded endive leaves. Cook just enough to soften the endive.

Serve very hot with a few garlic croûtons sprinkled on top.

See also Radicchio salad with blue cheese dressing.

▦ ESSENCES, NATURAL ▦
See also **Additives**

The best flavourings are those derived from normal constituents of food such as herbs, spices, fruits, nuts and vegetables. However, many of the flavourings that are commercially made on a large scale consist partly or entirely of chemicals that imitate the flavour of the real thing. Though these are tested for safety they are still far from natural products. Not surprisingly, they also rarely have the depth and subtlety of the original.

However, their task is not an easy one. Flavourings can be added to a wide variety of foods – drinks, cakes, biscuits, custards. They can find themselves being frozen, as in ice cream, or boiled to make sweets. Yet they are expected to provide unvarying results in every case.

Happily, there are some excellent quality essences now on the market that are versatile enough to keep their flavour under most circumstances, and yet are based on simple natural ingredients such as essential oil of lemon, orange, peppermint and almond. Some chemicals have to be used, but this is kept to an absolute minimum.

Look for the words 'natural essences'. You may have to pay a little more than you would for artificial flavourings, but they can be used sparingly and will go a long way.

Two other very useful essences that have delicate and rather exotic flavours are orange flower water and rosewater. Buy them from chemists.

See Cardamom and rosewater icing.

FENNEL

This strange bulbous-looking vegetable with its green feathery leaves is not yet well-known here, though it is a popular ingredient in Mediterranean cookery. Though it looks like a root, it is in fact the swollen stembase of the plant. It has a crisp, watery texture, and a mild, sweet taste with a hint of aniseed.

Buying/Storing: Look out for firm, well shaped bulbs, preferably white or pale green. Dark green fennel is likely to be tough. Wrap and store in the refrigerator where it will keep for at least a few days (though fennel is best eaten whilst still moist and fresh).

How to use: Slice and add to salads. Cook with tomatoes and herbs. Goes especially well with mozzarella cheese. Braise and serve with white or orange sauce, or just with butter and lemon. Cut into chunks like an apple (eaten at the end of a meal it will aid digestion). The feathery leaves can be chopped to make an attractive garnish for soups and salads.

FENNEL RATATOUILLE

2 small fennel bulbs, trimmed
3 tablespoons oil, preferably olive
1 onion, peeled and sliced
1 clove garlic, chopped
1 red pepper, sliced
1 green pepper, sliced
2 courgettes, sliced
4 large tomatoes, skinned and chopped
good squeeze of lemon juice
10 green olives
seasoning to taste
fresh parsley

To prepare the fennel, cut it lengthwise and then slice across the bulb.
Heat the oil and add the onion and garlic. Cook for 5 minutes, then add the fennel, cover the pan, and cook gently – stirring occasionally – until the vegetables have just begun to soften.

Add the prepared peppers, courgettes and tomatoes. Stir in the lemon juice. Cover again and continue to simmer for a further 10 minutes, or until all the vegetables are just cooked. You might need to stir them once or twice.
Stone and chop the olives and add to the ratatouille with seasoning to taste. Garnish with parsley.
This ratatouille makes a delicious accompaniment to dry dishes such as burgers or nut loaves. Or serve it with an egg dish. Can also be spooned over rice or another grain, maybe topped with grated cheese or some walnuts.

FENNEL SEEDS

These small mid-brown seeds are taken from the fennel plant and have a taste very similar to the vegetable.
Nutrition: They are especially good as a help for anyone with digestive problems.
How to use: Fennel seeds can be sprinkled over cakes, breads and biscuits. They go well with vegetable dishes and make a good contrast to cream sauces. Try the seeds, slightly crushed, to make a delicious and refreshing tea.

FENUGREEK SEEDS

A tiny dark seed of an annual plant belonging to the bean family, the leaves of which were once used for fodder, hence the name 'Greek hay'. Its bitter-sweet flavour is an essential in curry.
Nutrition: Fenugreek seeds have been used in medicine and healing for thousands of years, and are a good source of protein, iron and vitamin D.
How to use: Use the seeds to make tea, or lightly toast them and sprinkle over dishes. Best sprouted, when they have a spicy curry-like flavour, but be careful – the sprouts can become bitter if cooked for more than 2 or 3 minutes.

FIBRE
See **Dietary fibre**

FIELD BEANS

This is one of the few beans that can be grown in Britain, and is therefore one of the cheapest. Small and brown, it has a rather bland taste which needs livening up, but this also means that the beans are versatile and can be used in more ways than some of the stronger-tasting pulses.
How to use: Allow approximately 1 hour to cook. Add to stews, slow-

cooking casseroles. Mash and make into a paté, or combine with nuts to make a roast. Add to minestrone soup for a change.

MINESTRONE ALLA MILANESE

2 tablespoons olive oil
1 onion, chopped
1 clove garlic, crushed
225g/¹/₂ lb tomatoes, peeled and chopped
115g/4oz/¹/₂ cup field beans, soaked overnight
1.15 litres/2 pints/5 cups vegetable stock
dried basil
fresh parsley
1 carrot, peeled and sliced
1 celery stick, chopped
2 large potatoes, diced
1 large courgette, sliced
55g/2oz/¹/₄ cup brown rice
115g/4oz fresh peas
seasoning to taste
Parmesan cheese to serve – optional

Heat the oil and lightly sauté the onion and garlic for 5 minutes. Add the tomatoes, beans, vegetable stock and herbs, bring to the boil and boil for 10 minutes. Then cover the pan, lower the heat, and cook for about an hour, or until the beans are almost cooked.

Add the prepared vegetables, brown rice and peas. Cook for about 20 minutes more, or until everything is tender. Adjust liquid if necessary, also the seasoning. Serve piping hot. Put Parmesan cheese on the table for those who like it.

Note: All areas in Italy have different kinds of minestrone soup. This one is from the north where rice is eaten more often than the pasta which is so popular in the south. It is also colder in the north, hence the heartiness of this soup!

FIGS

Originally grown in western Asia, figs were well established as far back as Biblical times. They are still a very popular fruit in many parts of the world, if not in Britain. Although some fresh figs can occasionally be found in shops here (usually imported from Mediterranean countries), they are hard to find and tend to be very expensive. This is because they travel badly, and really should be eaten very soon after being picked. Some locally grown ones *can* be found – better still, why not plant a fig tree in a sunny spot and grow your own?

Dried figs can be found in most shops. Usually sun-dried, they have a coating of natural sugar that can be eaten or washed off if you prefer. These are sweeter, rather tough, and better for use in cookery.

Buying/Storing: Fresh figs can be different shapes and come in colours that include red, yellow and dark purple. They should be plump, just soft to the touch, undamaged. Can be stored for a day or two in the fridge, but best eaten at once.

How to use: Fresh figs are delicious just as they are, or maybe topped with honey, nuts and cream. Try stuffing them as a party dish (maybe with cake crumbs in some kind of liqueur?). Can be added to fruit salad. Soak dry figs in fruit juice and then use in similar ways. Or chop and use with apples in a crumble. Nice lightly cooked and flavoured with lemon peel, topped with yogurt and a sprinkling of granola at breakfast time.

MUESLI (FOR ONE)

1 tablespoon rolled oats
1 tablespoon wheatgerm
approx. 6 tablespoons cold water
2 large dried figs
good squeeze of lemon juice
1 tablespoon mixed chopped nuts
1 small apple, chopped
milk, soya milk or yogurt
honey or raw cane sugar – optional

Put the oats, wheatgerm and water in a small bowl. Wash the figs, remove the stalks, chop them and add to the bowl with the lemon juice. Cover and leave overnight.

In the morning add nuts and the apple. Pour on just as much milk or yogurt as you need and, if necessary, sweeten to taste. Eat at once.

This was the way muesli was originally made, and it offers far more nutrients than most of the packet varieties for half the price. If you get the habit, try varying the ingredients with different grains, dried fruit, nuts and seeds. Always add fresh fruit.

FILBERTS
See **Hazelnuts**

FILO PASTRY

This is not a wholefood as it is almost impossible to make out of wholemeal flour. It also requires to be brushed with a fair amount of oil or butter before cooking! However, it is well worth keeping some around for use when you want to make a dish with a difference.

Many countries use it for one or more of their traditional recipes. Greek spinach and feta cheese parcels are made with this fine flaky pastry, so is German apple strudel. It can be cooked in a long strip and then cut into wedges, filled and folded into envelopes, or wrapped around your choice of ingredients and then made into small parcels. As it is unsweetened it can be used with either savoury or sweet recipes.

Buying/Storing: Filo pastry can be found in the freezers of most supermarkets and speciality shops. It comes in different sizes and shapes so choose the most appropriate. Then keep it in the freezer until needed.

How to use: De-frost it, and then keep it covered with a tea towel. Each thin sheet must be brushed from edge to edge with oil or melted butter before use, or it will dry out and burn once in the oven. Whilst working with one sheet be sure to keep the others covered. Make a long savoury slice filled with broccoli in a creamy sauce, then cut into wedges to serve. Fill small envelopes with a purée of beans, onions and spices and serve with yogurt. Use to make an unusual spring roll and fill with a tofu and bean sprouts mixture. At Christmas make a mincemeat strudel instead of mince pies.

FILO PARCELS

2 small courgettes, chopped fine
2 large mushrooms, chopped fine
30g/1oz/2 tablespoons sunflower seeds
55g/2oz/¹/₄ cup curd cheese
seasoning to taste
good pinch of nutmeg
2 rectangular sheets of filo pastry, de-frosted
melted butter or vegetable oil

Combine the first 6 ingredients to make the filling.
Lay one sheet of pastry out and brush it lightly with butter or oil. As filo pastry dries out very quickly, cover any other sheets with a damp tea towel until you need them.
Use a sharp knife to cut it lengthwise into 4 strips.
Place a heaped teaspoon of the vegetable mixture in one corner. Fold the edge to make a triangle, bringing the corner up to meet the other side. Continue folding in this manner to make a small neat triangular parcel.
Repeat this, using remaining pastry and filling. You will eventually have 8 small parcels. Brush the tops carefully with more fat.
Bake them at 200°C/400°F (Gas Mark 6) for about 20 minutes, until golden and nicely crisp.
Serve hot. An unusual starter, also good for buffets.

FISH

As meat loses popularity, the consumption of fish is on the increase in Britain. Publicity about the wisdom of consuming fish oils to help lower blood cholesterol and prevent heart disease has helped the trend. Yet at the same time the Danes, inhabitants of a country surrounded by sea, have been advised to reduce their consumption of fish. And even here in Britain it has been suggested there might be dangers lurking in shellfish.

Certainly there is some truth in the idea that fish oils do have health benefits, but these are outweighed by the state of the environment in which the fish live. The chance of getting food poisoning from eating fish is 25 times greater than that from eating beef and 16 times greater than that from eating poultry or pork. Every day our seas become more polluted. Despite promises that things will improve, chemicals and raw sewage continue to be dumped in the water all around us; it is estimated that some 100,000 man-made substances are now present in the North Sea. Seals die of mysterious viruses. Sea birds starve because of food shortages. The signs are all around us and yet we continue to ignore them.

Over-fishing is also threatening our seas. In the early 1960s fishermen would catch, each year, about a third of the cod in the North Sea. Now they take about two-thirds of the population. More young fish are caught leaving a reduced breeding stock. Pollution takes its toll on them. The time is coming when the seas around us will be empty of fish, which will mean more birds will starve or move on.

Uncontrolled fishing poses yet another threat. For example, the sand eel is too small to be consumed by humans but is caught and fed to factory-farmed chickens and salmon. Many species of birds rely on the sand eel as an important source of food. So do cod. By removing them the whole ecological balance of the sea and surrounding area has been upset.

Of course, much of the fish consumed in Britain does not come from around our island, but from much further away. Around the world fishing vessels comb the oceans daily leaving thousands of miles of plastic netting behind them, entangling and killing marine mammals and birds. Waste dumped from the boats chokes and poisons more of them. Tuna fishermen – catering for the vast demand for this one fish – are responsible for also killing thousands of dolphins each year.

If fish was once a natural food, it is no longer. Nor is it an ecologically sound one.

▧▧▧▧ ■ FLAGEOLET BEANS ▧▧▧▧

A very pretty pale green bean that grows in long slender pods shaped like a flute, which is where the name comes from. The beans are picked when young, and therefore have a delicate taste not unlike the fresh bean. They are expensive. A popular bean in France.

How to use: Allow approximately 45 minutes-1 hour to cook. Flageolet beans can be added to soups, hotpots and casseroles, but do not use with strongly-flavoured ingredients or their effect will be lost. Probably best served as a vegetable on their own, or cold in salads.

FLAGEOLET SALAD

170g/6oz/³/₄ cup flageolet beans, soaked overnight
¹/₂ small cauliflower
¹/₂ red pepper
2 spring onions
115g/4oz/2 cups mushrooms
lettuce
mustard and cress

dressing:
1 small carton natural yogurt or sour cream
squeeze of lemon juice
seasoning to taste
watercress

Drain the beans, put in a saucepan with fresh water, and boil for 10 minutes. Lower heat and cook for about 30 minutes more, or until just tender – do not overcook. Rinse, then drain well.
Wash and trim the cauliflower into florets, and mix with strips of pepper and the finely chopped onions. Slice the cleaned mushrooms and add.
Make up the dressing by mixing together all the ingredients. Add a little finely chopped watercress. Mix enough of the dressing with the beans and prepared vegetables to moisten but not drown them – any extra can be served at the table. Arrange the salad on a lettuce base and garnish with the mustard and cress.

FLAVOURINGS
See **Essences**

FLOUR

A flour is a very finely ground meal, usually made from a grain though sometimes also from pulses and other ingredients. The purpose of grinding it is to make it quicker to use in cooking, more versatile, and also easier to digest. The most widely used flour in Britain is taken from wheat to be used in baking; this is usually white flour, which means the nutritious wheat-germ and fibre-rich bran have both been removed. Flours made from the whole grain are preferable. One reason for removing the wheatgerm, however, is that it contains an oil which will eventually go stale, and will therefore reduce the shelf-life of the flour. This means that when buying flours made from whole grains you should purchase only a small amount at a time, and store it in an airtight container in a cool place.

Soya flour – besides being added to boost the protein content of the recipe – has binding qualities which make it useful as a replacement for eggs.

Those following a gluten-free diet can purchase special flours to use in baking, though the results may well be very different. They usually come with instructions for use and recipe suggestions, so be prepared to do some experimenting before you get the results you want. Look out for sago flour, tapioca flour, gram flour (made from chick peas, mung beans or dried green peas), potato and rice flours.

FRENCH BEANS
See **Beans, fresh**

FRUIT, FRESH
See also **individual varieties**

Fruit is the fleshy seed-bearing part of a wide variety of plants. Tasty, nutritious, it is not surprising that fruit was a very important part of the diet of the first human beings. In Africa, where it is believed the ancestors of the human race first stood on two feet, they would have found an ample variety of fruits within easy reach, just waiting to be picked. Though fruit is becoming more popular in Britain, we have one of the lowest fruit consumptions in the EEC. What is more, we have developed a habit that very few other nationalities follow to the same extent: we cook our fruit. This is fine for special occasions, but do try to eat some fresh raw fruit every day.

Nowadays there is an excellent variety of fruits to choose from, but remember that this is made possible because of relative or absolute poverty elsewhere in the world, so don't overlook your local fruit.

Nutrition: Most fruits contain little protein or fat, but are excellent sources of the mineral salts needed for the correct functioning of the human body, together with vitamins, especially vitamin C, natural sugars and fibre, which is found mostly in their skins (so eat the skins, but wash them first).

Buying/Storing: All fruits should be smooth, undamaged, and have a good colour. Never buy anything that looks stale. Organically-grown fruit is well worth looking out for – this is produced without chemical fertilisers and without spraying, which means that it contains no dangerous additives. If you find a worm in your apple think of it as a good sign! Many fruits can be kept in the fridge. When you take them out to eat, make sure you leave them at room temperature for at least an hour before eating them.

How to use: See individual varieties.

FRUIT SPREADS

Jam, jellies, preserves and fruit spreads are all versions of much the same thing. Originally they were devised as ways of using stocks of over-ripe fruit, as well as preserving fruits to be eaten when fresh supplies were not available. Now they are more of a luxury food, something to make basics such as bread that much more interesting.

Varieties: Preserves are the thickest in texture, jams come next and jellies – as their name implies – are lighter and smoother. All are usually made from fruit and sugar, sometimes with pectin added. Pectin occurs naturally in ripening fruit and reacts to set the jam, though different fruits contain different amounts so it may be necessary to add more pectin. Fruits especially rich in pectin are green apples, gooseberries and redcurrants. Citric acid is also used in making jam, the most obvious source being fresh lemon juice.

Fruit spreads are more like thick fruit purées, the setting qualities being less important. Some are sweetened with honey, maple syrup or molasses instead of sugar, others are not sweetened at all. These need to be stored in the fridge and eaten within a short time.

Nutrition: This depends very much on the kind of product. Mass-produced jams made with a huge amount of white sugar (this bulks them out and reduces the fruit content, which also reduces the costs for the manufacturer) have no nutritional content at all. Many 'reduced sugar' jams are now made, which are better. The varieties you find in wholefood and healthfood stores are more likely to be made with raw cane sugar or none at all. Spreads are obviously the most nutritious, though these are not widely available. You can always, of course, make your own.

Buying/Storing: Buy only those that state on the jar that they contain the minimum sweetening, preferably unrefined. Also try to avoid those that contain colouring and preservatives. Once opened, store them in the fridge.

How to use: Apart from the obvious use of spreading on bread, muffins, scones, try stirring them into yogurt and rice puddings, spooning them over ice cream. Can also be used to sweeten stewed fruit, to sandwich two cake halves, to decorate flans, fill pasties, add interest to cottage cheese.

FRUIT AND HONEY SPREAD

455g/1 lb/3 cups dried pears, soaked overnight
455g/1 lb/1 1/3rd cups honey
1 lemon

Drain the pears and then purée them in a blender. Stir in the honey and mix very well. Add lemon juice and some of the peel of the lemon, finely grated. Store in a screw-top jar in the fridge, and use within a few weeks.
Good on bread, stirred into yogurt, or as a topping for ice cream. Try whisking in an egg white, spooning it into glasses, and topping with nuts for dessert.
If you like you can add spices to this spread, or you can make it in exactly the same way using other dried fruits such as apricots and peaches.

GARAM MASALA
See **Curry powder and paste**

GARBANZOS
See **Chick peas**

GARLIC

One of the earliest herbs used in cooking, garlic has been in use for at least 5,000 years. (In Britain it was worn around the neck to ward off evil spirits, but that is another story!) It is a member of the onion family. Though grown and used throughout much of the world as much for its food and medicinal value as for its taste, the best garlic is said to come from the warmer climates.

Varieties: Without doubt fresh garlic gives the best flavour. If, however, you cannot obtain it, there are other alternatives you might like to try. Garlic salt is the best known. Newer on the market are garlic purée (which is garlic in a thick and creamy form – great for garlic bread), and garlic in an oil base which can be added to stews, sauces and so on at the end of cooking as the flavour penetrates quickly.

Nutrition: Contains some vitamins, but is best known for its ability to not only cleanse the blood but to reduce cholesterol. It is also believed to help prevent colds.

Buying/Storing: The clove or bulb can vary in size or shape, can have a white, pink or mauve skin, but should always be firm to the touch and free from blemishes. The pink skinned variety tends to have a more subtle flavour. If it has green shoots it is not fresh. Store in a cool dry place (not the fridge), allowing air to circulate. A wire basket or string bag is ideal or – if you use garlic a lot – treat yourself to one of the specially-made garlic pots.

How to use: Rub a clove of garlic around the bowl when only a slight flavour is required, as for salads and fondues. Peel, chop, or put through a garlic press for a stronger taste. Garlic can be added to most savoury dishes. Try it with vegetables, cheese and egg recipes, in soups and stews, on pizzas, with pastas, and in sauces. Garlic bread is another popular way to enjoy this herb. To make it easier to peel a garlic clove, drop it into a cup of boiling water and leave for a minute, then cut across the bottom of the clove and the skin will fall away.

SKORDALIA (GARLIC DIP)

2 cloves garlic, crushed
1 teaspoon salt
2 tablespoons lemon juice
3 tablespoons ground almonds
approx. 6 tablespoons olive oil
2 tablespoons flaked almonds, roasted
fresh parsley

Use a mortar and pestle to pound the garlic and salt. Add the lemon juice and ground almonds to make a smooth paste. Add the oil a few drops at a time, mixing well so that it is completely absorbed. Keep stirring so that the sauce is thick and creamy.

Turn into a small dish, top with the flaked almonds and some parsley sprigs.

Note: This sauce makes an excellent dip for fresh vegetables such as celery and carrot sticks. Use it too as a sauce for broccoli, cauliflower or new potatoes, or as a filling for avocado halves. Add some breadcrumbs to thicken it and serve it as a paté.

See also Burger relish, Hummus, Lentil dal, Bulgur stuffed marrow rings, Vegetable stew for couscous, Stir-fried vegetables with seaweed, Sorrel soufflé, Tiger nut loaf.

GHEE

Traditionally, ghee was made by heating butter and then skimming it. Now, however, there is also a ghee made from vegetable oils. It is widely used in Indian cookery, both for sweet and savoury dishes.

Nutrition: Ghee is not as high in fats as butter because the unstable fats have been removed during the clarifying process – it is still, however, a high-fat ingredient. It does not burn as butter does, so can be heated to higher temperatures, making it less likely to be absorbed by the food being cooked in it. Vegetable ghee contains no saturated fats at all.

Buying/Storing: It comes in tins that can be found in delicatessen, ethnic and wholefood shops. Once open the tin should preferably be stored in a cool place, though ghee will keep reasonably well for up to a year under most conditions – it is this ability that makes it especially useful in the hot climate of India.

How to use: Use in cooking as you would use butter. Particularly appropriate with curries.

See Lentil dal, Mattar paneer.

GINGER

Ginger is the root of a tuberous-rooted plant that grows in the hot, wet climate of the tropics. It is most commonly used as a powder which needs to be added to a dish in only small amounts to impart its distinctive hot, spicy flavour. However, you can sometimes buy fresh ginger which can then be peeled, mashed and used in the same way as the powder – the flavour is richer and sweeter. Stem ginger is also available crystallised, covered in sugar, or preserved in white sugar solution (both best avoided) or honey (better).

Nutrition: Ginger is believed to reduce flatulence.

Buying/Storing: Buy the powder in small quantities, store in an airtight container and use as soon as possible. When choosing root ginger look for smooth skin that is a light reddish-brown in colour, and check that the root is firm – a wrinkled, stale looking root will have little flavour. Keeps well until cut, then best used all at once.

How to use: Used in Indian curries, but also in Chinese foods – try it in stir-fried vegetables, or add to the filling for egg rolls. Ginger is also used for beers and cordials, treacle tarts, and cakes such as gingerbread; also ginger biscuits. Try a little sprinkled over melon slices, or added to rice pudding. Crystallised stem ginger is an expensive but delicious addition to fruit salads or stewed apples. Or use it in a ginger cake or rhubarb ginger jam. Always use ginger sparingly.

GINGER AND MELON STARTER

1 medium-sized honeydew melon
approx. 50g/2oz preserved stem ginger, chopped fine
liquid from preserved stem ginger
good pinch of cinnamon

Peel the melon, cut the flesh into even-sized cubes, divide between 4 small bowls or glasses.
Scatter each with some of the ginger, pour on a little of the liquid, sprinkle with spice. If possible chill for an hour or so before serving.

Note: This is best made with stem ginger that has been preserved in honey. Expensive, but worth it.

See also Green tomato chutney, Spicy cauliflower, Dried fruit compôte, Rhubarb orange crumble, Stir-fried vegetables with seaweed.

GLUTEN-FREE

Coeliac disease – or gluten allergy – is more common than people realise. The distended stomach and diarrhoea that can be symptoms can also be symptoms of other problems, and it is only with professional help that an allergy to gluten can be confirmed. For anyone suffering from this, a diet that is gluten-free is very important.

Gluten is found in certain starches. As it is a very stretchy substance and holds air well it is especially useful in breadmaking – which is why wheat grain and bread made with wheat are the first things to be avoided. Rye, barley and oats also contain gluten. For baking, thickening sauces, and so on, use flours such as those made from rice, soya, potato, gram, millet, sorghum, buckwheat and maize. Also now available are sago and tapioca flours. Take care to oil the tins especially well as all these flours have a tendency to stick.

As so many ready-prepared food products contain wheat flour without actually listing it as such (other names can include starch or vegetable protein), buy only those that carry the 'gluten-free' symbol, guaranteeing they are safe. This is a circle containing a head of wheat with a line across it.

GOMASIO

A highly nutritious condiment used in Japan. It has a taste rather like a nutty salt.

Buying/Storing: Can be purchased in most wholefood shops and should be kept in a dark airtight container and used as soon as possible. Better still – make your own as and when you need it.

How to make: Make your own gomasio by grinding lightly-roasted sesame seeds together with sea salt to make a fine powder. Adjust the proportions to suit yourself: the usual ratio is 8 parts sesame seeds to 1 part salt. If you like you can lightly roast the salt as well. Make only a small quantity at a time – gomasio soon loses its taste and goodness.

How to use: Sprinkle over any dish: salads, bakes, casseroles, soups, vegetables, grains, egg and cheese dishes. Best added at the table.

GOOSEBERRIES
See **Berries**

GRAINS
See also **individual varieties**

Also called cereals (from the goddess Ceres, giver of the earth's bounties) grains are the seeds of certain species of grass. Since they were first cultivated some 15,000 years ago they have been a staple food for the majority of the world's population – and they still are, particularly for those who live in non-industrialised societies.

Varieties: Apart from being eaten as whole grains, they can be milled in such a way as to produce quicker-cooking flakes and groats. They are also available as flours – look out for wheat, barley, rye, rice, millet, sorghum, buckwheat and maize flours.

Nutrition: Though small and uninteresting to look at, grains are actually tiny food stores and are packed with nutrients. Their food values are roughly similar; almost completely carbohydrate (70% to 80%) they are an excellent source of energy. They also contain protein, minerals such as calcium, phosphorus, iron and potassium, B vitamins, and sometimes fat. Most important of all, especially as far as people in the affluent West are concerned, is the high fibre content of unrefined grains.

Buying/Storing: Look out for unrefined whole grains in healthfood and wholefood shops – the few that are sold through supermarkets are usually the processed variety. They can be bought in large quantities, as they will keep well in a cool dry place. Flakes also keep quite well (their big advantage is the speed at which they cook). When buying flours, do not get too much at once as they can go off quite quickly. Store flours in an airtight jar, in the fridge if you have room.

How to use: See individual varieties.

GRAM FLOUR
See **Flour**

GRANOLA

This is a popular breakfast cereal from America. What it is, in fact, is a cooked muesli. Grains, either singly or mixed, are coated with oil and a sweetener such as sugar or honey, and are then roasted just long enough to make them crisp and golden. Fruit peel, nuts, spices and dried fruits may be added. In Britain these are often on sale under such names as 'oat crunch' or 'crunchy cereal'. Look out for those made with the minimum added sugar (and if they have been sweetened, make sure it is with raw cane sugar or honey). Granolas made with organically-grown cereals are obviously better.

Another use for granola is to sprinkle it over fruit salads or purées, ice creams and sorbets. Try mixing it too with the crumble ingredients when making a fruit crumble.

See Mixed grain granola.

GRAPEFRUIT

Grown in hot climates, all our grapefruits are imported. Though they are usually yellow, look out for the pink variety which is now becoming more widely available and is especially liked for the sweet taste.

Buying/Storing: Choose fruit with a good colour and clear skin. They should feel heavy to hold, which means they are full of juice. Store in a cool place (not the fridge).

How to use: A quick and easy starter is made by topping grapefruit halves with butter and some cinnamon, and popping under a grill. Try chopping grapefruit and stirring into natural yogurt. Mix with salad ingredients – an unusual but delicious combination is grapefruit and avocado. Make marmalade.

GRAPEFRUIT SORBET

the peel of 1/2 grapefruit, finely grated
285ml/1/2 pint/1 1/3rd cups concentrated grapefruit juice
285ml/1/2 pint/1 1/3rd cup water
approx. 225g/1/2 lb/1 1/3rd cups raw cane sugar
2 egg whites

Combine the peel and juice. In a saucepan stir together the water and sugar until the sugar dissolves, then set aside to cool.

Add the juice and peel, mix well, pour into a freezing tray. Leave in the freezer until the mixture begins to firm up, then stir well again. Repeat this.

Whisk the egg whites until stiff enough to hold a peak. Fold this into the grapefruit mixture. Return to the freezer and freeze again until completely set. Remove from the freezer shortly before needed and serve in chilled glasses or bowls.

You can make lemon or orange sorbets in much the same way. Adjust the amount of sugar according to the sweetness of the fruit you are using.

GRAPES

It was the Romans who first discovered that by making grapes into a syrup and allowing it to ferment you get wine! Since then grapes have spread around the world, and are now widely grown. This means that, by importing from different countries, most of us have access to grapes of one kind or another throughout the year.

Nutrition: Another useful winter source of vitamin C as well as some minerals.

Buying/Storing: Whether they are white or black they should have a bloom on them, be firm and not over-ripe, and preferably still on their branch. Can be kept in the salad drawer of a fridge for a few days if not required for immediate consumption.

How to use: Add a few grapes to a salad or bowl of muesli. Mix tiny seedless grapes with cream or yogurt and use to stuff crêpes. Top a cheesecake with grape halves (they also make an unusual garnish for a savoury quiche).

GRAPES IN WINE

approx. 225g/¹/₂ lb black grapes
approx. 225g/¹/₂ lb white grapes
approx. 285ml/¹/₂ pint/1 1/3rd cup white wine

Make sure the grapes are absolutely clean, dry and undamaged – discard any that are less than perfect.

Put them in a screw-top jar and cover with the wine. Seal, and store in a cool place for a few days, or until needed.

Serve the grapes in small dishes or glasses with the wine poured over them. A few nuts and/or some cream could be added.

See also Fruited lettuce leaves.

GREENGAGES
See **Plums**

GRINDERS

Though the more expensive food processors are obviously excellent at grinding up all sorts of things, you will also find a small coffee grinder just as efficient for half the cost. Buy one with a blender fitment attached and you will be able to make a wide variety of dishes.

The main uses for a grinder in the wholefood kitchen are to chop nuts, to make breadcrumbs, to powder sugar so that it resembles icing sugar. It can also be used to purée cooked chick peas to make hummus, or other beans to make them into burgers or croquettes. You could even use it for grinding decaffeinated coffee beans!

Do make sure that whatever you put into the grinder is as dry as possible, and – when finished with it – clean it carefully. Many wholefoods have strong aromas and they do not always compliment each other.

GROUNDNUTS
See **Peanuts**

GUMBO
See **Okra**

HALVA

Halva is a Middle Eastern sweetmeat that is basically made from honey and sesame seeds, though there are other varieties now available, including pistachio halva and almond halva. Though a natural food, halva is exceptionally sweet, so if you care about your teeth eat it in moderation. It is usually available pre-packed, though some shops sell it loose.

HARICOT BEANS

Also called cannellini, this small white bean is used throughout much of the world, but is probably best known as the one that comes tinned in tomato sauce!

How to use: Allow 1-1½ hours to cook. Good with barbecue and spicy sauces, or make your own homemade version of the tinned variety. Add to stews and casseroles. Nice in salads.

THREE BEAN SALAD
½ small onion, finely chopped
115g/4oz/2/3rd cup haricot beans, cooked
115g/4oz/2/3rd cup kidney beans, cooked
115g/4oz fresh green beans, sliced and cooked
French dressing (oil and lemon)
freshly ground black pepper
1-2 tablespoons chives, snipped

Combine the onion and beans in a bowl, adding just enough French dressing to coat the beans lightly. Add black pepper and chives to taste. Leave the beans in the

fridge for an hour or two, if possible, so that the flavours can be absorbed.
Garnish with extra chives before serving.
If liked you can add some yogurt to the French dressing – a creamy dressing goes
especially well with the beans.

▓▓▓▓▓▓▓▓▓▓▓▓▓ HAZELNUTS ▓▓▓▓▓▓▓▓▓▓▓▓

Though also grown throughout much of the world, hazelnuts are one of the few varieties of nut that grow well in Britain, on an attractive tree bearing catkins that are wind-pollinated. Haesil is the Anglo-Saxon word for 'head-dress', which describes the way the nuts fit into their cap of leaves. They are also called cob nuts and filberts. Fresh cob nuts, on sale in the autumn, have a creamier taste and smoother texture. These are best eaten raw.

Nutrition: They are a particularly good source of vitamin E, and, having a very low calorie count – just 110 per ounce – are an ideal choice for dieters.

How to use: Hazelnuts are one of the most popular varieties of nut with chocolate manufacturers – make your own sweets using raw cane sugar and carob instead of chocolate. As they go so well with sweet foods, try them in cakes and biscuits, sprinkle them over ice cream, stir into yogurt or sprinkle chopped over fruit salad. To bring out the flavour, roast them in a moderate oven for 10-15 minutes (this also makes it easier to remove the skin). Ground roasted hazelnuts mixed with a little oil make a tasty butter.

EGG AND HAZELNUT PANCAKES

pancakes:
115g/4oz/1 cup wholemeal flour
pinch of salt
1 egg, beaten
285ml/¹/₂ pint/1 1/3rd cups half milk, half water

filling:
3 tablespoons mayonnaise
¹/₄ teaspoon ground coriander
seasoning to taste
55g/2oz/¹/₂ cup hazelnuts, coarsely chopped
2 hardboiled eggs, coarsely chopped
2 sticks celery, finely chopped
55g/2oz/¹/₄ cup margarine
55g/2oz/1 cup wholemeal breadcrumbs
parsley to garnish

Make the pancakes following instructions on page 43.
Put the mayonnaise into a bowl and stir in the coriander and seasoning. Add the chopped nuts, eggs and celery.
Divide the filling between the pancakes, roll them up, and lay side by side in a

heatproof dish. Dot with margarine, sprinkle with crumbs, and either put in the oven for 5 minutes, or leave briefly under the grill.
Serve hot, garnished with parsley.

See also Frozen banana yogurt, Fruited lettuce leaves, Apple oatmeal biscuits, Sweet potato dessert, Stuffed dates.

HERBS
See also **individual varieties**

Most of the herbs we use come from the aromatic leaves of plants grown in temperate climates. They are best used when fresh, but because they are not always available – especially in winter – many people also use them dried. When adding dried herbs to a recipe, use between a third and half the quantity of dried herbs as you would fresh, since they are much more concentrated.

Buying/Storing: Buy in small quantities. Fresh herbs are best used the same day as they are either purchased or picked. How you store dried herbs is very important. Though it is traditional to have them in decorative displays on the kitchen wall, they retain their flavour and colour far better if they are stored in a cupboard. A good compromise is to use opaque storage jars. And even though dried herbs keep considerably longer than fresh, they should still be used as soon as possible. An alternative way to keep fresh herbs is to freeze them. This can be done by tying them with cotton, putting into polythene bags and putting directly into the freezer, or by chopping and freezing them in ice cubes. When ready to use, don't defrost but add them directly to the dish you are preparing.

How to dry herbs: Pick them when young, preferably early in the morning when the sun has just dried the dew. Wash if necessary in cool water, then gently shake or pat dry. Hang them in loose bunches, tops downward, in a warm, dry, shaded area. If you prefer, lay the herbs on a flat tray and put in an airing cupboard. When crisp, break off the leaves and store as described above. Crumble them just before using.

How to use: See individual herbs.

HERB TEAS
See **Teas, herb**

HIZIKI
See **Seaweed**

HONEY

A sweet heavy liquid produced by bees from the nectar of flowers, honey has been used for at least 15,000 years, and not only as a food. The prophet Mohammed recommended honey as a remedy for every illness, and the ancient Egyptians used its antiseptic qualities for treating wounds and burns. Many naturopaths nowadays advise the use of honey for these and many other ailments, especially for sore throats, which also encourages people to swallow it and get the benefit of its nutrients.

It should be added that some vegans avoid eating honey, as commercial honey production does undoubtedly involve cruel practices. As with the production of so many foods, responsible bee keepers who are not motivated only by profit can – if they choose – avoid this to a large extent, whilst at the same time offering an undoubtedly superior product.

Varieties: A wide variety of honeys can be bought, some home-produced, others imported. They range from pale cream to a dark golden brown, from very sweet to creamy and mild, in consistencies from liquid to hard-set.

Nutrition: This varies from one honey to the next and depends on the flowers from which the bees fed, the weather and the season. However, all honeys consist of about 25% water, the rest being divided between glucose and fructose about 4:1, which is only very slightly more fructose than is contained in refined sugar. Most honeys contain vitamins B and C as well as traces of minerals. Although honey is better for you than sugar weight for weight, there is not much nutritional evidence to show it to be a particularly health-enhancing food – just the same, many people swear by its beneficial qualities. Best then to still restrict its use, though do by all means enjoy it as a special food. At the very least a switch from sugar to honey will reduce your dependence on a land-hungry cash crop, and thus help the planet in a small way.

Buying/Storing: It is worth paying for the more expensive brands of honey as these will tend to be the tastiest. Many of the cheaper brands contain honey from bees which have been fed on white sugar. Keep honey in a screw-top jar in a dry spot at room temperature. Crystallisation does not affect the quality of the honey, but if you want to make crystallised honey run freely again, stand the pot in a pan of warm water.

How to use: As honey is very concentrated, use it in small amounts, and only if you intend to taste it. Do not overheat it if you are using it in cooking. Honey can be used wherever a recipe asks for sugar – use three quarters of the amount of honey as is asked for in sugar and adjust the liquid accordingly. To make honey more nutritious as a spread, try mixing it with wheatgerm, peanut butter, tahini or ground nuts.

LEMON HONEY SQUARES

115g/4oz/¹/₂ cup margarine
55g/2oz/1/3rd cup raw cane sugar
115g/4oz/1/3rd cup thick honey
1 lemon, juice and grated peel
2 eggs, beaten
55g/2oz/¹/₂ cup sultanas
55g/2oz/¹/₂ cup almonds, chopped
225g/8oz/2 cups wholemeal self-raising flour
1 teaspoon baking powder

Put the margarine, sugar, honey, lemon juice and peel into a small saucepan, and heat gently – stirring continually – until well mixed.

Leave to cool for a few minutes. Add the eggs, sultanas and almonds. Sift together the flour and baking powder and fold into the first mixture, then beat until the batter is smooth.

Grease and line a medium-sized shallow baking tin. Pour in the mixture. Bake at 180°C/350°F (Gas Mark 4) for 30-40 minutes, or until firm. Leave to cool for a few minutes before removing from the tin and leaving on a wire rack to cool completely. Cut into squares.

See also Frozen banana yogurt, Red and white slaw, Fruited lettuce leaves, Marinated beans, Cashew nut butter, Cinnamon honey cake, Fruit and honey spread, Prune flapjacks, Tamari honey salad dressing.

HORSERADISH

Horseradish is another herb which has been used since earliest times. It grows up to 1 metre/3 feet tall and has leaves similar to those of the dock; it is often found growing wild. The roots give a strong, bitter taste.

Nutrition: A natural antibiotic, it also has antiseptic qualities and is a gentle laxative. In fact, weight for weight horseradish is one of the most nutritious vegetables there is!

How to use: The roots are used to make the classic horseradish relish. Can also be added to sauces and dips. Use sparingly.

CHEESE AND HORSERADISH FONDUE

15g/¹/₂oz/1 good tablespoon butter
285ml/¹/₂ pint/1 1/3rd cups dry white wine
455g/1 lb/4 cups Cheddar cheese, grated
seasoning to taste
2 teaspoons dried grated horseradish
1 tablespoon wholemeal flour
1 tablespoon water
wholemeal bread cut into cubes

Use the butter to grease the sides and base of a heatproof casserole.

Pour in the wine, add the grated cheese, seasoning and horseradish. Heat very gently, stirring continually, until the cheese melts.
Blend the flour with the water and stir this into the cheese and horseradish mixture. Continue simmering for 5 minutes, stirring continually.
Transfer to the table and stand the casserole over a candle burner to keep the fondue warm.
Serve with cubes of wholemeal bread, which are put onto a fork and then dipped into the fondue. Other ingredients you can use to dip are cauliflower florets, button mushrooms, slices of carrot, garlic croûtons.

HUMMUS

Very popular in Britain now, this is a cross between a spread and a dip, and comes from the Middle East where it is traditionally served with falaffels and pita bread. Hummus is made from cooked ground chick peas, tahini, lemon juice and olive oil, with spices and herbs added. It can be purchased in delicatessen and many supermarkets as well as wholefood and healthfood stores. However, there is nothing to beat homemade hummus.
Buying/Storing: It is not yet made on a large scale in this country, so when you do find fresh hummus in the shops it has probably been made locally. Store fresh hummus in the fridge and eat within a few days. Frozen hummus is also sometimes available. Or buy it in dry form in packets and hydrate it when you need it. Tinned hummus is nothing like the real thing.
How to use: Hummus can be thinned down with extra oil and/or lemon juice and used as a dip with corn chips and vegetable sticks. Or thicken it with breadcrumbs and make it into a paté. It is also delicious stirred into soups and casseroles. Or for an unusual way with spaghetti, add it to tomato sauce.

See page 77 for recipe.

HYSSOP

An attractive plant that has clusters of sky-blue flowers. To the ancient Greeks it was 'the holy herb', and much valued for its cleansing properties. Aromatic, it has a bitter aftertaste. Also used to flavour chartreuse.
How to use: Add chopped leaves to salads, sauces and bakes. Especially good with pulse dishes such as bean stews and lentil purées.

ICE CREAM

Commercially-made ice creams are generally rich in white sugar, artificial flavouring and colouring. They may also be rich in saturated fats – though from processed oils rather than dairy cream. Natural ice creams can be found in some wholefood and healthfood shops, and delicious they are too. There are also some excellent ones for vegans.

However, ice cream is not as difficult to make as you may think. Make your own and you will be able to use ingredients you know to be wholesome, choose your own flavouring, add in whatever takes your fancy. You'll save money too. And if you make extra and keep some in the freezer you will never be stuck for a quick dessert.

You will need a reasonable size ice-making compartment in your fridge, or better still, a deep freeze. When making ice cream it is important to freeze the ingredients as quickly as possible, so always turn the setting as low as possible when you start making the recipe. Once it has been frozen firm you can turn it back to normal. As homemade ice cream can be a little gritty compared to the commercial kind, it should be beaten or stirred when half set and then frozen again. This breaks down the crystals and adds air to the mixture. Do not, however, reduce the mixture to liquid.

A certain amount of fat is necessary, best in the form of double or whipping cream. You can reduce this slightly, if you like, by replacing part of it with single cream. Other ingredients are up to you. Try carob chips (grated from a carob bar), candied orange peel, roasted hazelnuts chopped coarsely, fresh blackcurrants, mashed bananas, and so on. If adding colour remember that it will tend to be paler when frozen, so adjust accordingly.

Water ices are made in much the same way as ice cream but are made from fruit juices only. Sorbets are water ices with egg white whisked in to them to give them a creamier texture. Neither of these actually need to be broken down half way through freezing, though it will do them no harm.

BROWN BREAD ICE CREAM

115g/4oz/2 cups brown bread (without crusts)
340ml/2/3rd pint/1 1/2 cups whipping cream
140ml/1/4 pint/2/3rd cup single cream
115g/4oz/2/3rd cup raw cane sugar, powdered in grinder
1/2 teaspoon vanilla essence
55g/2oz/1/3rd cup raw cane sugar
4 tablespoons water

Crumble the bread and spread it on a baking sheet. Cook at 130°C/250°F (Gas Mark 1/2) for 30 minutes or until crisp, then buzz it in a blender or roll out to make fine breadcrumbs.

Whip the cream until just thick (do not over-beat it). Fold in the single cream, powdered sugar and vanilla essence, then transfer the mixture to a freezing tray and leave for about an hour, or until it begins to set.

Meanwhile, heat the water and dissolve the remaining sugar in it. Bring to the boil and continue boiling for 2 minutes without stirring. Remove from the heat, add the breadcrumbs and leave to cool.

Tip the semi-frozen ice cream into a bowl, whisk and then stir in the breadcrumb mixture. Return the mixture to the freezing tray and freeze until set.

Note: Always serve ice cream, water ices and sorbets in chilled glasses.

See also Grapefruit sorbet.

IRISH MOSS
See **Carrageen**

IRRADIATION

Irradiation is not new – in fact, it has been around since the turn of the century. For some years now it has been used to sterilise equipment in hospitals, and in Sweden it has been used on strawberries.

Despite the fact that the World Health Organisation has given irradiation the go-ahead, and that it is already in use in some 25 countries, there are still many doubts about not just the safety of this preservation technique but various other side issues.

Irradiated food is food that has been bombarded with gamma rays to kill off bacteria such as those that can cause salmonella and listeria. With foods such as fruit and vegetables – those most likely to benefit from irradiation – the rays also delay ripening which means they have an extended shelf-life and look attractive longer. So far so good. On the down side there is the danger that the toxins irradiation cannot harm may still be alive and active, yet as the food has been treated it will look perfect, giving no clues as to what is going on inside. Vitamins and essential fatty acids will have been damaged. We have no way of knowing how irradiation affects pesticide deposits, how eating treated foods over a long period of time will affect our bodies – nor will we be able to tell for sure if a product has actually been irradiated.

One thing is for sure: irradiated food can never be termed a natural food. And in a world that every day moves further away from nature, this can only be another step in the wrong direction.

Although the government may allow irradiated food to be put on the shelves, it will be up to the individual stores to decide whether or not they stock it. Ultimately, of course, it will be up to the public to make the final choice.

JAMS
See **Fruit spreads**

JAPONICAS
See **Quinces**

JELLIES
See **Fruit spreads**

JUICES

Fruit and vegetable juices contain the concentrated goodness of the ingredients from which they are made, and should be considered a food rather than a drink. They can, of course, be diluted to taste, adding a little lemon juice and some crushed ice if you like. Juices are best made at home with an extractor or juicer, and should be drunk right away while still full of goodness. Such juices are also useful for children who refuse to eat their fruit and vegetables, or for older people whose teeth may not be able to cope with them.

If you want to try frozen and tinned juices, check the labels. Many of those imported from Europe – though much inferior to the fresh variety – do not contain dyes or additives, and are therefore a good alternative when fresh is unavailable. Watch for added sugar; the words to look out for are 'fruit drink' (or worse, 'fruit-flavoured drink') rather than 'fruit juice'. Most fruit juices sold in cartons are reconstituted from concentrated fruit juice, but look out for cartons of pressed English apple juice.

Nutrition: The vitamin content will vary considerably from one to another, though any fruit or vegetable juice should contain at least some vitamin C. More manufacturers are now claiming to have added vitamins and although they will undoubtedly be telling the truth it is likely only the minimum will have been added.

How to use: Apart from making delicious drinks, many juices can be used in cooking. Add fruit juice to cakes and dessert dishes for both flavouring and to replace at least some of the sugar – concentrated apple juice is especially good for this. Use them to make ice creams, sorbets and water ices. The stronger coloured ones can be used to colour sweets and jellies. Vegetable juices can be added to soups and casseroles.

See Cranberry sauce, Candied peel, Tahini custard, Grapefruit sorbet, Apple oatmeal biscuits.

KALE

Though probably eaten by many of our ancestors, kale is no longer very popular in Britain. This may be because it is hard to find, particularly in the south (the Scots eat it more often). Its leaves are dark green, fairly coarse, and crinkle attractively which is why it is sometimes called curly kale. (The other name by which it is known – borecole – is an angelicised version of its Dutch name.) Often grown locally, and available through the winter months, it has a strong flavour that makes it an interesting vegetable even if just lightly steamed and served with a knob of butter. Homegrown kale should not be picked until after a good frost.

Buying/Storing: Leaves should be bright with no signs of damage. Do not buy if they are at all yellow. Store in a cool place and eat preferably within a few days.

How to use: Remove the leaves, wash well, cut away the hard centre stem. Shred the leaves. If young and tender they can be used raw in a salad. Otherwise, steam or boil them lightly to serve as a vegetable. Add to a curry. Combine with white cabbage and a tahini or cream sauce, and use to fill a flan. Layer with potatoes and cheese and bake.

CHINESE STYLE KALE

vegetable oil
1 large carrot, sliced
225g/¹/₂ lb kale, shredded
115g/4oz/1 cup bean sprouts
small tin water chestnuts, drained and sliced
soy sauce

Pour oil into a small pan to a depth of about 12mm (¹/₂ inch), and heat until very hot. Add the prepared carrot and kale, and cook briefly until they begin to crisp up. Add the bean sprouts and water chestnuts and cook for literally a minute more to heat through.

Drain all the vegetables and serve at once sprinkled with soy sauce – good with rice or other grains, plus a handful or two of cashews. Or serve as a side dish with an omelette.

KANTEN
See **Agar agar**

KASHA
See **Buckwheat**

KELP
See **Seaweed**

KIDNEY BEANS

A large, fat, shiny, dried bean with a distinctive red colour and a full flavour. Records indicate that it was used in Mexico 7,000 years ago, and it is still very popular in that part of the world, and throughout Central and South America.

How to use: Allow approximately 1-1¹/₂ hours to cook. Kidney beans are excellent in chilli dishes and thick soups and stews. They go well with rice, and make a good filling for stuffed pancakes. Try them in a sweet and sour sauce, or use them in a salad to add colour and texture.

MEXICAN FLAN

pastry:
55g/2oz/¹/₂ cup wholemeal flour
55g/2oz/just under ¹/₂ cup gram flour
55g/2oz/¹/₄ cup margarine
cold water to mix

filling:
115g/4oz/2/3rd cup kidney beans, cooked
55g/2oz/1/3rd cup sweetcorn, cooked
1 green pepper, sliced
3 tomatoes, sliced
2 eggs, beaten
140ml/¹/₄ pint/2/3rd cup creamy milk
seasoning to taste
good pinch of chilli powder

Sift together the two flours, then use fingertips to rub in the fat. Add just enough water to make a firm dough. Turn out onto a lightly-floured board and knead briefly, then wrap in a polythene bag and chill for 30 minutes.
Roll out the pastry and line a medium-sized flan ring on a baking sheet. Spread the kidney beans and sweetcorn over the base, top with strips of pepper and then the tomato slices.
Beat together the eggs and milk, add seasoning and chilli powder to taste, and pour over the vegetables.
Bake at 200°C/400°F (Gas Mark 6) for 20-30 minutes, or until set. Serve hot or cold.

See also Celeriac salad with mustard, Three bean salad, Chilli kidney beans.

KIWI FRUIT

Though it originated in China, the kiwi is now the national fruit of New Zealand – in fact, it is named after New Zealand's national bird which is also furry and brown! This delicately flavoured fruit is just beginning to become popular here, as a result of which more European countries are growing it on a commercial scale; a sizeable crop is being produced on Guernsey.

Nutrition: A very good source of vitamin C.

Buying/Storing: Avoid buying any fruits that are damaged or over-ripe (they should just yield to gentle pressure). Under-ripe kiwi fruits can be put into a paper bag, preferably with an apple, and left for a few days. Just right fruits should really be eaten at once, but can be stored for a day or so in a cool dark place.

How to use: Lovely in fruit salads. Peeled and sliced kiwi fruits make an attractive topping in fruit flans. Try making ice cream or sorbets, or puréeing and blending with yogurt. Makes an unusual side dish to serve with curry.

KIWI RAITA

285ml/¹/₂ pint/1 1/3rd cups natural yogurt
3-4 kiwi fruit (depending on size)
seeds of 1 cardamom
pinch of ground coriander

Put the yogurt in a bowl. Carefully peel the kiwi fruits and then slice them as finely as possible. Stir them into the yogurt with the cardamom seeds and coriander. Makes a deliciously cool, fresh tasting accompaniment to curry. Can also be sprinkled with raw cane sugar and served as a dessert – try adding a trickle of rosewater to make it really exotic.

KOHLRABI

Though it looks rather like a turnip with leaves, kohlrabi is actually a swollen stem. It is believed to have been developed in the East, and was introduced to Britain in the 17th century.

Buying/Storing: Available during the autumn and winter months, kohlrabi can be white, pale green or purple. Whichever you choose they are best eaten when young (older ones can be tough), so don't buy anything over the size of a small orange. Avoid also any that are discoloured or have holes in them. Keep in a cool place and use as soon as possible.

How to use: Young kohlrabi can be sliced or grated and eaten raw – makes a change in coleslaw with a mayonnaise dressing. Or top slices of kohlrabi with a selection of things to serve at a buffet party. Lightly steam or boil them to dish up as a vegetable accompaniment – nice with a knob of butter. Older kohlrabi can be made quite edible by adding them to stews and casseroles. The leaves make an interesting spinach-like vegetable.

KOHLRABI BAKE

3-4 kohlrabi, well washed, trimmed and peeled
225g/8oz tomatoes, sliced
1 onion, thinly sliced
225g/¹/₂ lb/1 cup tofu, drained and mashed
approx. 6 tablespoons vegetable stock
seasoning to taste
1 teaspoon chopped chives
55g/2oz/¹/₂ cup cheese, grated
30g/1oz/¹/₂ cup wholemeal breadcrumbs
30g/1oz/2 tablespoons margarine

Lightly grease an ovenproof dish. Cut the kohlrabi into thin slices. Layer the kohlrabi, tomatoes, onion and tofu, repeating this until all the ingredients have been used up. Add seasoning and chives to the stock and pour over the prepared ingredients. Sprinkle with grated cheese, the breadcrumbs, and a few knobs of margarine. Cover with a lid or silver foil and bake at 200°C/400°F (Gas Mark 6) for about 45 minutes, or until cooked.

KOMBU
See Seaweed

KUMQUATS

Kumquats look like tiny oranges, with the pitted skin of an orange. They usually contain seeds, and have a taste that is sweet, sharp and bitter all at the same time. The main difference is that you eat the whole thing, peel and all. Native to the Far East, kumquats are now grown in many countries with hot climates. Most of those on sale in Britain come from Sicily or Brazil.

Buying/Storing: They should be firm, full, with shiny skins. If they have patches of green on the skin, they will soon ripen if left at room temperature. If you want to keep them longer, store them in the fridge, but for no more than a week.

How to use: Kumquats can be pickled, made into marmalade, served in a caramel sauce. If preserved in alcohol it is said that vodka suits them best. However, they really are at their best eaten raw.

KUZU

This is a pure white starch powder obtained from the roots of the wild arrowroot that grows on the rocky slopes of volcanic mountains in Japan. It is considered to be an excellent food, rich in trace minerals, and especially easily digested, making it useful for those with bad digestions, or convalescents.

As the production of kuzu is a long process, it is not cheap. Nor, at the moment, is it widely available in Britain. If you can find it, it is well worth trying.

How to use: Use it as a natural thickener for soups and sauces. It can also be made into a glaze for fruit tarts.

LADIES FINGERS
See **Okra**

LAMB'S LETTUCE

Not a lettuce, but an unusual plant that was introduced to Britain from the Netherlands some 400 years ago, yet is still not widely known. It has soft tongue-shaped leaves that have an astringent taste, and makes a useful alternative to lettuce during the winter months. Also called corn salad.

Buying/Storing: Though the leaves should be soft they should not be limp. Look out for lettuces with a good colour. Store in the fridge for a day or two.

How to use: Lamb's lettuce needs careful washing. Add to other salad ingredients and serve with a piquant dressing. Lightly steam and serve as a vegetable (it tastes rather like spinach). Use in flans.

LAVER
See **Seaweed**

LEEKS

A favourite winter vegetable that grows well in Britain's back gardens. The leek was adopted by the Welsh back in 640 AD as their national symbol – and on St. David's Day in Wales people still wear them. A member of the onion family, it is the thick stems of the leek that are eaten.

Buying/Storing: Do not buy if wilted or yellow. The bulb at the base should be firm and white (avoid any that have had the bulbs removed as these will deteriorate quickly). The smaller the leek the sweeter will be its taste.

How to use: Because of the way they grow, leeks can be very dirty – to wash them slit them lengthways and wash well under running water. Then blanch lightly and add to salads, or serve with a vinaigrette dressing. Steam and serve in a white or cheese sauce. Add to stews and soups, put into flans or vegetable crumbles. Leeks combine especially well with tomatoes. Can be used raw if young, but chop very fine and do not use too much – the taste is strong. The tougher green tops are best chopped fine and added to bean hotpots and long-cooking casseroles.

LEEK AND HERB MOUSSE

2 tablespoons lemon juice
2 tablespoons water
1¹/₂ teaspoons carrageen
1 tablespoon fresh chives
1 tablespoon fresh parsley
1 tablespoon fresh tarragon
455g/1 lb/2 cups low fat cream cheese
1 medium leek, cleaned and cooked
seasoning to taste
pinch of cayenne pepper
tomatoes and watercress to garnish
wholemeal toast to serve

Mix together the lemon juice and water, sprinkle in the carrageen, whisk well. Bring the mixture to the boil, then simmer it for 3 minutes before setting aside to cool slightly.
Chop the herbs as finely as possible. Blend them into the cream cheese. Drain the leek well, chop it fine and add to the cheese and herbs. Season generously, add a touch of cayenne pepper.
Blend together the agar agar and cheese mixture. Chill until it starts to set, then stir well before dividing between 4 small dishes.
When ready to serve, turn each mousse out onto a plate and decorate with sliced tomatoes on top, plus a sprig or two of watercress.
Serve with hot wholemeal toast.

See also Aduki and leek roll, Parsnip curry, Artichoke salad.

LEMON BALM
See also **Teas, herb**

This sturdy plant is native to England. Though it looks something like mint, its strong fragrance of lemon makes it unmistakable. Fresh leaves are usually available from early summer to late autumn, and can easily be dried for use in winter.
How to use: Lemon balm is an excellent alternative to fresh lemons. It goes well with a wide variety of dishes, salads, and fruit drinks such as punches. As the flavour is so strong, go sparingly.

LEMON BALM BUTTER

115g/4oz/¹/₂ cup butter
1 good tablespoon fresh lemon balm leaves, finely chopped
seasoning to taste
squeeze of lemon juice

Soften the butter and then blend in the leaves, seasoning and juice. Pile the butter into a carton or dish and chill again. Excellent for topping young and lightly cooked vegetables – or try it in cucumber sandwiches!

LEMONS

This small yellow fruit is used chiefly for its juice. Most of the lemons on sale in this country are imported from the Mediterranean.

Nutrition: Famed for their vitamin C content, though the fruit must be fresh – stale lemons have little nutritional value.

Buying/Storing: Plump lemons that feel heavy will have the most juice. A stale lemon will look shrivelled and tired, its skin matt. Lemons keep well in cool, dry conditions. If using the peel look out for lemons that have not been sprayed – the wax that is added to make the skins of lemons shine can be toxic.

How to use: To get maximum juice from a lemon first warm it slightly then press and roll gently on a firm top before cutting. The tang of lemon can be added to just about any dish, sweet or savoury. It goes well in cakes, sweets, sauces, gravies, casseroles – and what would pancakes be without it? A squeeze of lemon juice makes an excellent alternative to vinegar in salad dressing, and it will also stop other fruits discolouring once cut. Slices of lemon can be used as a garnish, added to drinks. The peel, either raw or candied, is added to cakes and desserts.

LEMON CURD (WITHOUT EGGS)

2 large lemons
55g/2oz/¹/₄ cup margarine or butter
170g/6oz/1 cup raw cane sugar
approx. 55g/2oz/1/3rd cup arrowroot

Warm the lemons and then squeeze them to obtain as much of the juice as possible. Grate some of the peel.
Melt the fat together with the sugar, stirring continually. Add the lemon juice and peel. Stir in the arrowroot, and heat gently until the curd thickens.
Leave to cool and then transfer to a screw-top jar. Keep in the fridge.

See also Guacamole dip, Skordalia, Lemon honey squares, Baked pears.

LENTILS

A small leguminous bean about half the size of a pea, that was one of the very first cultivated crops in the East.

Varieties: Lentils are available in various colours depending on whether they come from Egypt and Turkey (generally orange), or China and India (more likely to be green or brown).

Nutrition: They are richer in protein than any other pulse except soya beans, and are also a good source of vitamins, iron and calcium. One of the quickest-cooking varieties, they are easy to digest, making them especially useful.

How to use: Allow approximately 30-45 minutes to cook brown or green lentils, up to 30 minutes for split red lentils to cook to a mush. Lentils are good in curries, stews and soups. Add nuts and shape into croquettes to be fried. Split lentils can be used to thicken liquid. You can also make them into a sauce to serve with spaghetti, or use as a base for vegetarian shepherd's pie.

SPANISH LENTIL SOUP

225g/¹/₂ lb/1 cup whole lentils, soaked overnight
2 tablespoons vegetable oil
1 onion
1 green pepper
1 clove garlic
1 stick celery
225g/¹/₂ lb tomatoes, peeled and chopped
850ml/1¹/₂ pints/3³/₄ cups vegetable stock
1-2 teaspoons dried oregano
seasoning to taste
parsley to garnish

Put lentils into a pan of fresh water, bring to the boil and continue boiling for 10 minutes. Lower heat and simmer for 20 minutes, or until beginning to soften.
Heat the oil in another pan and add the chopped onion, pepper, garlic and celery. Cook gently for 10 minutes. Add the tomatoes, drained lentils and vegetable stock. Flavour to taste. Cook gently for 10-20 minutes more, or until all the ingredients are tender. Purée or push them through a sieve, reserving 2 or 3 tablespoons of the lentils to add texture to the soup. Reheat. Serve garnished generously with parsley.

See also Swedish shepherd's pie.

LETTUCES
See also **Lamb's lettuce**

One variety or another is available at any time of year in Britain, usually a selection, most of them now homegrown though they may have originated in other countries.

Varieties: Look out for the softer round lettuces, cos, the crisp webbs wonder and the increasingly popular iceberg lettuce. Little gems have a sweet taste. Especially good for improving the appearance of a salad are the attractive pink-tinged oakleaf, or lollo rosso that is more of a bronze colour around its edges. Laitves monet has long curly leaves that are reminiscent of endive. Quatro stagioni and batavia are other continental lettuces worth trying.

Nutrition: Lettuces contain some vitamin A, especially in the outer leaves. They also contain slight traces of sleep-inducing substances!

Buying/Storing: All lettuces should be firm and crisp with no sign of discolouration. Store them in the fridge, preferably in an airtight bag. The softer summer lettuces will only keep a day or so, while some of the crisp varieties will keep up to a week.

How to use: Lettuces should be broken or torn, not cut (except for the crisp lettuces such as iceberg which can be sliced into chunks). Use them in salads – a combination of different types of lettuce not only looks pretty but gives taste and texture contrast. Though best eaten raw lettuces can also be cooked. Try using lettuce leaves instead of vine leaves when making dolmas. Add them to soufflé, make a cream of lettuce soup. Cook with onion to make an alternative vegetable.

LETTUCE DOLMAS

1 cos lettuce
1-2 tablespoons vegetable oil
1 small onion, sliced
2 carrots, grated
55g/2oz/1 cup mushrooms, sliced
1 stick celery, chopped
55g/2oz/¹/₂ cup walnuts, coarsely chopped
approx. 55g/2oz/1 cup wholemeal breadcrumbs
seasoning to taste
a little vegetable stock
approx. 285ml/¹/₂ pint/1 1/3rd cups tomato sauce

Wash 12 large outer leaves of lettuce, pat dry and set aside.

Heat the oil and fry the onion to soften. Add the carrots, mushrooms and celery, and cook for literally a few minutes more. Stir in the nuts and breadcrumbs and use a few spoonfuls of vegetable stock to bind the ingredients loosely. Season to taste and mix well.

Lay the lettuce leaves out as flat as possible and place a tablespoon of mixture on each. Roll up into small parcels, tucking in the edges as you do so to keep the filling in place.

Arrange the rolls close together in a greased ovenproof dish and pour the tomato sauce over them, spreading it as evenly as possible.

Bake at 190°C/375°F (Gas Mark 5) for 20-30 minutes. Serve piping hot.

See also Bean salad niçoise, Scorzonera salad, Celeriac salad with mustard, Fruited lettuce leaves, Chicory salad with tempeh.

LIMA BEANS
See **Butter beans**

LIMES

The most hardy member of the citrus family. Limes have a stronger flavour than lemons and are less widely used here, though they are becoming more available.

Nutrition: Lime juice is high in vitamin C, which is why limes used to be taken on long sea voyages to help prevent sailors getting scurvy.

Buying/Storing: Buy heavy fruits with brightly coloured undamaged skin. Will keep well, though as the skins are less thick than with lemons, do handle them carefully.

How to use: As with lemons, warm the fruit then roll gently on a firm surface before cutting – this releases more juice. Lime juice can be used in much the same way as that of lemons, though remember it is a little stronger. Especially refreshing as a long cool summer drink.

KEY LIME PIE

pastry:
55g/2oz/¹/₄ cup margarine
30g/1oz/2 tablespoons raw cane sugar
115g/4oz/1 cup wholemeal flour
1 egg yolk, lightly beaten
water to mix

filling:
3 eggs, separated
140ml/¹/₄ pint/2/3rd cup fresh lime juice
1 tablespoon lime peel, finely grated
395g/14oz tin condensed milk

Cream together the margarine and sugar. Use a wooden spoon to gradually add the flour and then the egg yolk. Sprinkle in just enough cold water to make a firm dough. Set aside briefly then roll out and use to line a medium-sized flan ring standing on a baking tray. Bake blind at 200°C/400°F (Gas Mark 6) for 20 minutes.

To make the filling, put the egg yolks into a small warm bowl and whisk or beat them for a few minutes until thick. You can also use a blender for this. Slowly beat in the condensed milk, and then the lime juice and peel.

In a separate bowl whisk the egg whites until they form soft peaks (do not over-beat – they should not be stiff for this recipe). Fold them gently into the egg yolk mixture and spoon this into the partially cooked case.

Bake at 180°C/350°F (Gas Mark 4) for 15-20 minutes, or until the filling is set.
Serve at room temperature or cold.

See also Tropical cream dessert.

LOGANBERRIES
See **Berries**

LOVAGE

A tall umbelliferous perennial plant that grows well in southern Europe. It
dies back in winter but grows well again in spring. The leaves and stalks
can both be used in stews, soups and sauces, though lovage does have a
strong taste, so use it sparingly until you know you like it. The stems can be
candied.

LOVAGE AND FETA OMELETTE

8 eggs
seasoning to taste
drop of creamy milk
approx. 2 tablespoons fresh lovage, chopped
170g/6oz/1¹/₂ cups feta cheese, crumbled
margarine to cook
extra lovage to garnish

Whisk 4 eggs, season, add a drop of milk and a tablespoon of lovage (or to taste).
Heat a knob of margarine in an omelette pan, then pour in the egg mixture and cook
over a moderate heat, tipping the pan occasionally to allow the mixture to run
underneath. When set underneath (but still soft on top) add half the cheese and cook
for just a minute or two longer.
Fold the omelette, set aside on a covered plate over a pan of hot water, and use the
remaining ingredients to make another omelette.
Cut each one in half to serve. Add lovage leaves as a garnish.

LYCHEES

This small brown brittle-skinned fruit comes from the Orient. It is often
tinned and exported, but as the syrup is usually made from white sugar, the
delicate taste of the fruit is swamped, so buy the fresh fruit if you can get it.
Buying/Storing: Look out for fruits that are just tender, the skin undamaged. Lychees can be stored at room temperature for up to 4 days.
How to use: Remove the large stone – the pinky flesh is crisp and sweet
and best eaten just as it is. Can be added to fruit salad or used as decoration

on a special flan. Or try them in sweet and sour dishes, add them to savoury salads. Can be frozen until needed.

See Tropical fruit salad.

MACADAMIA NUTS

These are native to Australia, having been brought with them by the early settlers. Most imports, though, now come from Hawaii where they are cultivated on a much larger scale. A medium-sized nut that looks something like a hazelnut when it has been extracted from its shell, macadamias have a smooth texture and sweet taste. If they cost more than many nuts it is because they are especially difficult to reach – an outer fibrous husk has to first be removed, and then the shell itself, which can be up to 12mm ($\frac{1}{2}$ inch) thick. Macadamias are not well-known in Britain, though they can be found if you look hard enough.

WILD RICE AND MACADAMIA STUFFING

85g/3oz/1/3rd cup wild rice
2 tablespoons vegetable oil
$\frac{1}{2}$ small onion, chopped
$\frac{1}{2}$ red pepper, chopped
1 stick celery, chopped
55g/2oz/1 cup mushrooms, chopped
55g/2oz/$\frac{1}{2}$ cup macadamia nuts, chopped
$\frac{1}{2}$-1 teaspoon dried mixed herbs
seasoning to taste
1 egg – optional

Cook the rice in plenty of water for approximately 45 minutes (follow instructions on packet). Drain well.

Heat the oil and gently fry the onion, pepper and celery to soften. Add the mushrooms and cook for a few minutes more. Stir in the rice, nuts, herbs and seasoning. Cook briefly, then use to fill vegetables of your choice. Peppers go especially well with this stuffing, but you could also use it with courgette boats, aubergine or tomatoes. For a firmer filling, add a beaten egg.

MACE

Both mace and nutmeg are the products of a tree that grows in the East and West Indies. During its average lifespan of 60 years it will drop some 1,000 fruits a year. These split open to reveal the nutmeg, the outer coating of which is like a webbing, and which – when removed, dried and ground – becomes mace. Though its taste is similar to that of nutmeg, it is fuller and sweeter, hence it is also more expensive.

How to use: Use whenever you would use nutmeg. Good in fruit cakes or added to whipped cream, also with stewed fruit such as plums and cherries. Add a pinch to a creamy vegetable sauce.

MACROBIOTICS

The word 'macrobiotic' was coined by George Ohsawa, a modern follower of an ancient Oriental medicine and philosophy that originated in Japan. It is based on a concept that divides all aspects of the universe into two polarities, yin and yang, which need to be balanced for mental and physical development.

Foods are also classified as yin and yang. Those that grow in a hot, dry yang environment (such as summer, or tropical countries) are more yin. Those that grow in cold and wet places, which are compacted, harder and drier, are yang. Knowing this, anyone can change themselves – indeed, their whole lives – by choosing their foods with care. Basing our choice on wholefoods, on grains and vegetables (the bulk of them preferably locally grown and in season), we can find the right balance for our own individual needs at any given time in our lives. By doing that we can make a positive contribution to the world around us.

The philosophy needs to be studied to be understood and followed. Many who have done so have found themselves to be more energetic, to feel mentally clear and alert.

MAIZE

This popular yellow grain (more commonly known as corn) was first used in South America some 10,000 years ago, since when it has been a staple food to generations of Americans, including the great Inca and Aztec civilisations. The native peoples of both North and South America wor-shipped it, performing fertility dances in its honour. Though the corn used today is very different from the wild corn of those times, it still plays an important role in the diet of many people in South and Central America, as well as parts of southern and eastern Africa. In fact, after wheat and rice it is the world's largest crop. The USA is one of the biggest producers of corn today, but it is mostly used for cattle feed, which is also the case in Britain.

Varieties: The easiest way to use maize is as corn flour, the best kind being the stoneground variety from which the germ has not been removed. Two popular snack foods that are made of corn flour are corn chips (often flavoured with cheese), and tortilla chips which are crisp and very spicy. When buying the flour make sure it is the real thing and not processed corn flour which is pure, white and nutritionally dead. Polenta is Italian corn meal. Look out too for maize flakes. Popping corn is an inferior grade, but still makes a nutritious snack for children (preferable to sweets!).

How to use: Apart from using the flour to thicken sauces, it can be used to make tacos (Mexican pancakes), flatbreads and corn muffins. Make polenta cakes, add cheese or nuts, serve with a vegetable sauce. Maize flakes can be added to stews, casseroles and soups. Popcorn can be flavoured with honey or a little salt instead of white sugar.

POLENTA BAKE

850ml/1 1/2 pints/3 3/4 cups water
pinch of salt
225g/1/2 lb/1 1/2 cups polenta
55g/2oz/1/4 cup margarine
55g/1oz/1/4 cup wholemeal flour
570ml/1 pint/2 1/2 cups milk
seasoning to taste
pinch of nutmeg
1 large carrot
170g/6oz/3 cups mushrooms
55g/2oz/1/2 cup grated Parmesan cheese

Bring the water to the boil, add salt and sprinkle in the polenta, stirring continuously until thick. Pour into a shallow, lightly-greased tin and leave to cool.

Melt 45g/1 1/2oz of the margarine and add the flour. Cook briefly, then stir in the milk, seasoning and nutmeg. Heat the remaining fat in another pan and gently sauté the grated carrot for a few minutes, add the chopped mushrooms, and cook until just soft. Stir into the white sauce.

Use a cutter or glass to cut the polenta into small circles, and put half of them in the base of a greased ovenproof dish. Cover with half the sauce. Repeat this to use up the rest of the ingredients and top with the grated cheese. Bake at 180°C/350°F (Gas Mark 4) for 20-30 minutes.

See also Mushroom and tofu tacos, Tahini custard, Popcorn nut crunch.

MALT EXTRACT
See **Barley**

MANGETOUT
See **Peas**

MANGOES

A large orange fruit from India, where it is considered to be the king of fruits! The subtle and yet distinctive taste is a cross between a melon and a peach, with ginger undertones.

Nutrition: Rich in vitamin A and a good source of vitamin C.

Buying/Storing: Mangoes should be heavy and unblemished, and are ready to eat when still firm, but will yield slightly to pressure. Though best eaten as soon as possible after purchasing, they can be kept in the fridge for a few days if necessary. Under-ripe fruit will ripen if kept in a warm temperature.

How to use: Usually eaten raw cut into slices or diced. Can also be made into chutney to serve with curry. For something really exotic try making ice cream or sorbet with mangoes.

TROPICAL FRUIT SALAD

1 small mango, peeled, stoned and cubed
1 star fruit, trimmed and sliced
6 lychees, peeled, stoned and sliced
2 bananas, sliced
2 slices pineapple, cubed
a few red berries
orange juice
kirsch – optional
good pinch mixed spice
coconut flakes, roasted

Combine all the prepared fruit, mixing them gently so as not to damage them. Mix together the orange juice, kirsch and spice and pour over the mixed fruit. If possible leave in a cool place for an hour or two for the flavours to mingle.
Serve sprinkled with coconut flakes.

MAPLE SYRUP

A natural syrup taken from various species of maple tree that grow only in North America. It is collected in much the same way as it has been for hundreds of years. The trees are tapped in the spring, and the fluid is either allowed to evaporate, or is boiled away, leaving a concentrated syrup 30 to 50 times stronger than the sap.

Nutrition: Maple syrup contains natural sugars and some minerals, but it is used not so much as a food but as a very special sweetener with a distinctive mellow taste and smooth quality. As with honey, maple syrup is better for you than refined sugar, but it is still a sugar, and not for consumption in large quantities.

Buying/Storing: Look out for 100% pure maple syrup. As it is in short supply it is also expensive, but far superior to the artificially-produced varieties that are now available. Keep in a sealed bottle in a cool place.

How to use: Pour over pancakes, French toast and ice cream, stir into yogurt, mash with bananas, or use as a sweetener when baking. Goes well with rice dishes. Use instead of sugar on pancakes or waffles. Trickle over fresh fruit (blackberries, for example) and top with whipped cream. Can make an interesting sauce for carrots.

FRENCH TOAST WITH MAPLE SYRUP

6 slices wholemeal bread
2 eggs
3 tablespoons milk
vegetable oil for frying
maple syrup

Halve the bread slices. Whisk together the eggs and milk and pour into a wide, shallow dish. Dip the slices of bread briefly into the mixture, making sure that both sides are covered with the egg mixture. Heat the oil and fry the bread until it begins to colour, then cook the other side. Serve while still hot with maple syrup poured over the top.

See also Popcorn nut crunch, Sunflower maple biscuits.

MARGARINE

Margarine was invented by a Frenchman, Mège-Mouries, in 1869, as an alternative to butter. It was made from animal fats and, though it proved reasonably acceptable – especially in Holland where the product was further developed – margarine still retained its reputation as an inferior product to butter.

Varieties: Nowadays there are a large number of margarines on the market from which to choose. They can be hard or soft, come in a tub or in block form, and be made from animal fat, a blend of animal and vegetable fats, or from vegetable oil only.

Nutrition: Soft margarines which say on the packet that they are made from oils like soya or sunflower are a fairly recent innovation; these are often, but not always, low in cholesterol and high in polyunsaturates. Margarines high in polyunsaturates are preferable to others, since instead of clogging the arteries as saturated fats tend to do, they may actually help clear cholesterol. However – because of the way they are produced – just about all margarines contain some saturated fats, and replacing butter with margarine will not automatically protect you from an overdose. Almost all margarines also contain salt, some colouring, and added vitamins A and D which are insisted on by law.

Vegans can find a growing range of margarines that have been produced using no animal-derived ingredients whatsoever (most soft margarines contain whey which is a by-product of cheese production). Like other margarines these can be soft or hard in texture, the harder variety generally being better for baking. Though it has been necessary, up until recently, to go to a wholefood or healthfood store to find such margarines – and these are still your best bet if you want a choice – most supermarkets now offer at least one, usually soya.

Buying/Storing: Decide which kind is best for your needs by reading the pack. Buy small quantities frequently from a retailer who has a fast turnover. Keep margarines in a cool place, preferably in a fridge.

How to use: Margarines can be used for both spreading and cooking (though some are better at one thing or the other – again, check the pack!). Use in sandwiches when taste is not of primary importance. Soft margarines can also be used for frying and baking, and on vegetables and baked potatoes instead of butter.

MARJORAM

There are various kinds of marjoram, though the one we know best is sweet marjoram. This is much used in Mediterranean cuisine, it also grows easily in Britain, and is a half-hardy annual herb of the mint family. It was once strewn on the floor to freshen the air, though now it is used as much for its delicate yet slightly bitter flavour as its aroma.

How to use: Good in soups, casseroles and stuffings. Excellent with egg dishes – try it in a soufflé. Add to scones and bread for a change. Does something special to a fruit salad. Marjoram mixes well with other herbs.

TOMATO AND TOFU SOUP

30g/1oz/2¹/₂ tablespoons margarine
1 small onion, finely chopped
1 stick celery, finely chopped
6 large tomatoes or 395g/14oz tin tomatoes
570ml/1 pint/2¹/₂ cups vegetable stock
285g/10oz/1¹/₄ cups firm tofu, rinsed and drained
seasoning to taste
1 teaspoon fresh marjoram, chopped fine or ¹/₂ teaspoon dried marjoram
extra marjoram to garnish

croûtons:
2 slices thick wholemeal bread
2 teaspoons vegetable oil
30g/1oz/2¹/₂ tablespoons margarine

Melt the margarine and gently fry the chopped onion and celery for a few minutes. Peel and chop the tomatoes, add to the pan, and cook 2 minutes more. Add the stock and simmer briefly.

Pour the vegetable mixture into a blender, add the cubed tofu, and blend to make a smooth purée. Season to taste, add marjoram. Either re-heat the soup gently before serving, or chill and serve cold. Garnish with extra marjoram and croûtons.

To make croûtons, cut the bread into small even-sized cubes and fry them in the oil and margarine. Stir continually so that they are crisp and brown on all sides. Drain and serve warm or cold. For garlic flavoured croûtons, add a crushed garlic clove to the pan and cook briefly before adding the bread cubes.

See also Marinated beans, Glazed carrots almondine.

MARROWS
See also **Courgettes**

Marrows, like courgettes, are summer squashes, though they are particularly plentiful in autumn. These long, heavy vegetables can grow huge and are one of the categories for which gardening enthusiasts can win prizes (though when they reach record size they tend to have watery, rather bitter tasting flesh!).

Buying/Storing: They should be smooth, unblemished, and not too big. When ripe the skin can be easily pierced with a thumbnail. Marrows keep well if stored in the fridge, or you can put an under-ripe marrow in a warm spot.

How to use: This is a very watery vegetable. If you like you can cut your marrow, sprinkle the flesh with salt, leave for half an hour and then put under a running tap before using – this will remove some of the excess moisture. Then cube, steam lightly, chill and serve with yogurt and herbs. Or make ratatouille using marrow instead of courgettes. Serve in a white or cheese sauce. Make into soup. Stuff small whole marrows, or cut larger ones into rings and stuff them. Add at the last minute to stir-fries. Older marrows make good jams and chutneys – marrow and ginger jam is a traditional favourite.

BULGUR STUFFED MARROW RINGS
1 large marrow
2 tablespoons vegetable oil
1 small onion, chopped
¹/₂-1 clove garlic, crushed

115g/4oz/¹/₂ cup bulgur
approx. 285ml/¹/₂ pint/1 1/3rd cups water or vegetable stock
3 tomatoes, peeled and chopped
1 tablespoon parsley, chopped
seasoning to taste
115g/4oz/¹/₂ cup Gouda cheese, grated

Use a sharp knife to cut the marrow into thick rings and cut out the seeds. Drop the marrow rings into a large pan of boiling salted water and cook for 2 minutes. Remove and drain them.

In another pan heat the oil and fry the onion and garlic to soften. Add the bulgur, stir, pour on the stock or water. Bring to the boil, then lower the heat, cover the pan and simmer for about 10 minutes. The bulgur should be cooked, but not mushy.

Drain the bulgur and mix with the tomatoes, parsley and seasoning. Arrange the marrow rings close together in a greased ovenproof dish, and divide the mixture between them. Top each one with grated cheese. Bake at 180°C/350°F (Gas Mark 4) for 20-30 minutes. Serve hot.

Note: Any other grain can be used instead of bulgur in this recipe. It is also an ideal way to use up left-overs.

MAYONNAISE

Mayonnaise is a classic salad dressing generally made with oil and eggs (though vegan versions are now available, most of them using soya flour or tofu to replace the eggs). Commercially-made mayonnaise is nowhere near as nutritious as the kind you can buy in wholefood and healthfood stores. You can, of course, make your own – this is best done with a blender.

Mayonnaise can be flavoured with onions, garlic, herbs, tomato purée. All mayonnaise is best stored in the fridge and used within a reasonable time.

CUCUMBER MAYONNAISE

4 eggs
1 teaspoon dry mustard powder
good pinch of salt
good pinch cayenne pepper
1 tablespoon cider vinegar
oil, preferably olive
¹/₂ small cucumber, finely chopped

The eggs should be at room temperature. Crack them and drop into the blender together with the spices, vinegar, and a couple of spoonfuls of oil. Work the blender at a low speed, very gradually trickling in more oil until the mayonnaise begins to thicken. It is up to you at what point you stop adding oil. Early on you will have a thinner mayonnaise that can be poured over salad. Add more oil and it will thicken up to a creamier mayonnaise, ideal for dips. Whisk in more oil by hand to make it heavier still.

If it curdles, empty the blender and add another egg, then gradually pour the first mixture back in again.
Drain any excess liquid from the cucumber and then stir it into the mayonnaise.
Transfer to a screw-top jar and store in the fridge.

MEAT

There may be doubts about the feasibility of a world that is entirely vegetarian, especially if we are to have organically-grown crops. Many of those on sale today are produced with the aid of manure and slaughter-house waste such as blood and bones. This, however, is surely irrelevant. The world will never be entirely vegetarian.

What is important right now is for those who feel concern about our planet to understand just how much harm is being caused by the production of meat.

In Britain, most of our meat-producing animals are raised on factory farms. (Sheep are the main exception.) One of the biggest problems they present to the farmer is how to dispose of the vast quantities of waste they produce. Though farmyard manure, with its high straw content, can be spread on soil to enrich it, the slurry from these farms – particularly that from pigs, but also cattle – is too concentrated and liquid to be very useful. Vast slurry lagoons dot the countryside. Many leak or burst their banks, the slurry – like the small amount that *is* used on fields – finding its way into rivers where it poses a threat to fishes and plants alike. There is also evidence to suggest that ammonia that is released by slurry contributes to acid rain, so helping to destroy trees.

Slurry can also get into our drinking water. There have been some 9,000 cases of illness caused by cryptosporidium, a parasite which is almost certainly passed from farm animals to humans via slurry-contaminated drinking water.

Britain is not alone with the slurry problem. In some parts of Holland, the massive amounts produced by pig and poultry farms have led to estimates that within 10-20 years there will be no water available for drinking.

Slaughterhouses must also take some responsibility for polluting the countryside. Despite treatment plants, they are frequently taken to court for breaching waste discharge levels. On at least one occasion, a river had turned red with blood.

Then there is the significant contribution cattle and sheep make to greenhouse gases through flatulence! Methane is second only to carbon dioxide in its impact on global warming; it has been estimated that cattle account for up to 15% of all methane emissions.

Such things aside, it is obvious that if we are to feed a growing population, meat is a wasteful and inefficient way of obtaining food. In this country more than 70% of our agricultural land is used to grow animal feed. Worldwide, more than one third of all food grains are fed to livestock. Much of this is imported by western countries from the Third World; our factory-farmed animals eat whilst people starve to death.

With climatic changes not only forecast but actually happening, water becomes increasingly valuable. Yet it takes 2,500 gallons of water to produce one pound of meat compared with 25 gallons for one pound of wheat.

Tomorrow's world may not be completely vegetarian, but undoubtedly plant protein will be one of the main foods whilst meat – for those who want it – will be little more than a garnish.

Today, however, there is another option for those who need their pound of flesh. In Britain there is a range of shops now selling meat guaranteed to be from animals raised on small farms in natural, traditional conditions. No growth promoters are used on them, no drugs. Undoubtedly they are a healthier food than their factory-farmed relatives. Whether that makes them an ecologically sound food is up to you to decide.

MEAT SUBSTITUTES
See also **TVP**

For all those who want to cut out or cut back on meat, there is now a variety of products that claim to taste and have the texture of the real thing. Some are dry mixes that need to be hydrated, others come in vacuum packs or are frozen and need nothing more than to be heated through. They come in the form of sausages and burgers usually, and are made from pulses and/or grains with natural flavourings added. Though they would not, of course, fool anyone, they are just the same a nutritious, relatively inexpensive and often tasty alternative.

MELONS

These are also members of the squash family, and there are a number of varieties, all crisp and sweet. Most of them were cultivated originally in Egypt and were introduced to Europe during the Renaissance. Water-melons, however, are native to Africa.

Varieties: Look out for canteloupe melons (which include charentais and ogen), galia, honeydew and watermelons.

Nutrition: Most melons contain up to 95% water, so are excellent for slimmers. They offer some vitamins and minerals, depending on variety.

Buying/Storing: To check if a melon is ready to eat, press your thumb into the end opposite the calyx, which should give slightly. Most melons are best eaten as soon as ripe, though honeydews will keep for some time if stored in a cool spot.

How to use: Traditionally all melons are best eaten raw, especially watermelons which – with their crisp and sweet red flesh – are very refreshing. Melon cubes go well in both fruit salads and savoury mixtures. The flesh can be made into a sorbet. Cream cheese goes well with melon. For a quick and attractive starter or dessert, slice off the top of a large melon, scoop out the flesh and shape into balls, mix with juice, orange segments and grapes, and pile everything back into the shell to serve.

See Ginger and melon starter, California salad.

MICROWAVE OVENS

Though these have been on the market for some time, it is only in the past few years that they have become almost standard equipment in the modern kitchen. They are also useful for anyone with limited space, or who cooks regularly just for one.

Though there are many models now available – from basic to those with luxuries such as a revolving turntable – they all work in the same way. When a microwave oven is switched on, something called a magnetron generates waves which pass through a channel into the cavity, these waves oscillating at great speed. As they enter the food the molecules that make up that food are agitated, and this produces the heat that cooks it. When the oven stops or is turned off, the microwaves also stop.

Controlled by time switches, microwaves are used in a completely different way from conventional ovens, and need to be studied carefully if they are to be put to full use. There is a tendency to use them just for defrosting foods from the freezer; this they do well, but they can also cope with just about any cooking requirement. If they have one failing it is that microwaves do not brown food. This can be done quickly – once the food is cooked – by using a conventional grill, and the newer microwave ovens come with built-in grills for just this purpose.

If the general public was at first dubious about the safety of cooking in such a scientific way, it was with good reason. Many of the scare stories that hit the papers were more fiction than fact, but even the manufacturers had to admit that they needed to look again at some of the features. Whilst problems were being ironed out, regulations were being tightened up. Now all models come fitted with a number of safety devices, and full instructions as to how to use them. They are probably as safe as they can ever be.

But is microwave cookery Green cookery? There are arguments for and against. Certainly it is very fuel efficient. Food can be cooked in glass, china or ceramic dishes which avoids the risks associated with traditional cookware such as – for example – aluminium or non-stick pans.

Just the same there are many who are concerned about the way in which food molecules are affected by the microwaves, pointing out that we cannot be sure just what this does to them. And that if it does have any kind of sinister effect, it may well take some time for this to show up. Such things have happened before when we moved too far away from nature; they could, say these warning voices, happen again.

The choice is yours.

MILK

Milk is a highly-concentrated liquid produced by animals for their young, and is very rich in nutrients. It comes from a wide variety of animals, and until recently was drunk while still fresh. Milk has always been used as part of the human diet, starting of course with the breast milk that traditionally sustained the newborn baby. In many parts of the world, milk is still the chief source of protein, supplemented by cereals and vegetables.

Varieties: Most dairies now offer not just full fat milk, but semi-skimmed and skimmed also. Though most of the milk consumed in this country comes from cows, there is a growing interest in goat's milk (which is easier to digest). Both organic goat's and ewe's milk are being produced on a small scale from animals fed on natural diets; these are especially popular with the growing number of people suffering from allergies or milk intolerance. Powdered milk is also available and popular for its keeping qualities. Condensed milk comes in tins and is useful, especially for cooking, though it sometimes contains white sugar; use it only occasionally. Long-life milk – which can be skimmed, semi-skimmed or whole – has been heat-treated so that it will stay fresh until opened.

Nutrients: Milk is very high in protein, and is a good source of calcium. It is also rich in saturated fats, which are the kind suspected of contributing to many illnesses prevalent in the western world. Many nutritionists believe that we drink too much milk, using it as a drink when it should really be considered as a highly concentrated food. On average, British people each drink two thirds of a pint of milk a day, most of it a highly processed product. It is true that pasteurisation kills most bacteria and prolongs the life of milk, but it also destroys some of the nutrients. At the same time, today's dairy farming methods involve over-use of drugs and artificial feed supplements which many nutritionalists and doctors consider suspect, and a possible risk to health. Dioxin levels and their possible effects on children are also giving cause for concern in some areas.

Buying/Storing: Many people have their milk delivered to the door on a daily basis. All milk should be drunk as soon as possible after purchase, and should be kept meanwhile in a cool place, preferably in a fridge.

How to use: Think of milk as a food. Use it to make a white sauce to go with vegetables and rice and you have a completely balanced meal. Make egg custards or sweet puddings. Give milk to children, invalids and old people – anyone who is reluctant to eat. Instead of drinking surplus milk simply because it will go off if you do not, turn it into yogurt which will keep longer and is easier to digest. Most importantly, remember that you do not need a lot of milk in anything.

SOFT CHEESE

1.15 litres/2 pints/5 cups milk (whole or skimmed, cow's or goat's)
juice of 1 lemon
salt
freshly ground black pepper
flavouring of your choice (i.e. finely chopped onion, garlic, fresh herbs, caraway seeds, crushed pineapple, nuts, etc.)
a drop of single cream – optional

Take a heavy medium-sized saucepan and make sure it is absolutely clean (using a sterilising solution if necessary). Pour the milk into the pan and heat until warm (approx. 38°C/100°F). Add the lemon juice, stir well, then set aside to cool.

Put the mixture into a piece of muslin and tie the corners to make a bag. Then suspend this over a bowl (not touching) and leave until all the whey has drained off, which can take anything from 12 to 24 hours.

You will be left with a soft curd cheese which you can flavour as you wish; make sure the added ingredients are well mixed in. Turn the cheese into a small carton (such as the kind in which soft margarine is sold), prick the bottom just in case there is any moisture remaining, and store in the fridge. It should keep for up to a week though is best eaten when deliciously fresh.

See also Butterscotch cream, Polenta bake, Peppermint milk, Swiss cheese and poppy seed scones, Key lime pie, Homemade yogurt, Banana milkshake.

MILLET

A very small, beige-coloured grain that has been hulled as the outer casing is extremely tough. Millet was a staple food in China before rice was introduced, and is still eaten in parts of Africa, Asia and India, and in Russia, where athletes are said to train on a diet of millet. It is also a staple for the Hunza, the long-lived Himalayan people whose diet is thought to be responsible for their excellent health.

Nutrition: Millet is a balanced source of the essential amino acids, and contains more iron than any other cereal. As it is gluten-free, it can be used by anyone who wants to avoid gluten in their diet.

How to use: Dry-roast millet first to give it more flavour. Cook with 4 parts water to 1 part millet – a small amount expands to feed many! Use as a base with bean or vegetable dishes, or make into croquettes. Shape into balls and deep-fry. Millet is also nice with fresh or stewed fruit, nuts and yogurt as a dessert.

MILLET AND SUNFLOWER CROQUETTES

115g/4oz/¹/₂ cup millet, cooked
115g/4oz/³/₄ cup sunflower seeds, coarsely ground
1 small stick celery, finely chopped
1 small carrot, peeled and grated
2 tablespoons chopped parsley
seasoning to taste
soy sauce
wholemeal flour
sesame seeds to coat

In a bowl mix together the millet, sunflower seeds, celery, carrot, parsley, seasoning and soy sauce. Make sure it is thoroughly blended – this is easiest to do if you use your fingers. The mixture should be thick and moist. If it seems too wet, add a little flour.
Divide into 8 equal-sized pieces and shape them into croquettes. Roll each one in sesame seeds.
Shallow-fry in hot oil, turning them every so often so that they brown evenly. Drain before serving.

MINT

There are a number of mints in common use, the most popular being peppermint, spearmint and pennyroyal. All belong to the same family and have a fresh, sharp taste, though some are sweeter than others. Apart from adding flavour to food, mint is widely considered to have a beneficial effect on the digestion. Mint can also be used to help alleviate feelings of nausea.
How to use: Whole or chopped leaves are good with new potatoes, in mint sauce, and mixed with other vegetables, especially young peas. Use as a garnish for cold soups and cold drinks. Mint tea is also easy to make, and delicious. Add chopped mint to yogurt with garlic or onion and pour over a cucumber salad. Use to flavour a Waldorf salad or a fruit salad. Nice with grain dishes, especially when serving them cold.

PEPPERMINT MILK (FOR ONE)

1 mug milk
1-2 tablespoons fresh mint, shredded

Put the milk and leaves into a saucepan, bring gently to the boil. Turn off the heat.

Leave to stand for just a minute or two, then strain to remove the leaves and drink whilst still hot.

This drink is said to be both soothing and helpful for anyone with poor digestion or tummy troubles. It can also be drunk cold.

See also Bazargan, Dandelion tea.

MISO

A thick soya bean paste produced by lactic fermentation, and used to add a rich and salty flavour to savoury foods. It has been used in Japan for over 2,000 years, where a variety of different misos are produced, some light and mild, others darker and more concentrated.

Nutrition: Miso contains all the many nutrients of the soya bean, and is a good vegetable source of vitamin B12.

How to use: Dissolve a small quantity of paste in liquid and add to soups, gravies, stews and casseroles. Do not use too much, as the flavour is strong and will overpower more subtle tastes. As it is very salty, adjust other seasonings accordingly. Make a sandwich spread by mixing miso with tahini and a drop of water.

WINTER HOTPOT WITH MISO

30g/1oz/2^1/$_2$ tablespoons miso
570ml/1 pint/2^1/$_2$ cups vegetable stock or water
2 tablespoons vegetable oil
3 carrots
1 large onion
1 large turnip
115g/4oz Brussels sprouts
115g/4oz peas, fresh or frozen
watercress to garnish

Stir the miso into a drop of the vegetable stock and set aside. Heat the vegetable oil in a large pan and gently sauté the peeled and chopped carrots, onion and turnip for 5 minutes, stirring frequently. Add the trimmed and halved Brussels sprouts, the peas (if fresh) and the vegetable stock. Bring to the boil, then cover the pan, lower the heat, and cook gently for 20 minutes. Add the peas (if frozen). Cook 5 minutes more, then check if vegetables are cooked. When tender, stir in the miso and cook for literally a minute more. Serve garnished with watercress. Good with a grain such as rice or wholewheat berries.

See also Sorghum and green bean stew.

MOLASSES

The introduction of molasses dates from the beginning of commercial sugar refining some 200 years ago. This thick, dark treacle is a by-product of the sugar-refining industry. When the sugar cane is crushed and processed it loses all its valuable minerals and vitamins, and it is these that make molasses such a highly nutritious sweetener. Surprising, then, that many people still think of molasses as the poor relation to white sugar. Just the same, molasses are still widely used in the sugar-plantation area of the USA, where many of the traditional molasses-based dishes come from.

Nutrition: Molasses is an extremely nutritious product, with the darker varieties being the best. After yeast, molasses is the richest source of the B vitamins, especially vitamin B6. Weight for weight it contains more iron than liver, together with considerable amounts of copper, calcium, phosphorus and potassium. Molasses has fewer calories than other natural sweeteners – 59 per ounce for blackstrap molasses compared with 80-90 for honey and 112 for sugar.

Buying/Storing: Buy pure molasses from your local wholefood or healthfood store. If kept covered in a cool dry place, molasses keeps well for a long time.

How to use: In savoury dishes molasses goes well with beans (as in Boston baked beans), and sweet and sour sauces. Can also be used on bread, stirred into drinks, or used to flavour chutney. Use in baking for such favourites as flapjacks and gingerbread. As it has a strong and distinctive flavour, go slowly until you are used to it, adding quantities to suit your own taste.

BANANA MILKSHAKE

850ml/1 ¹/₂ pints/3³/₄ cups milk, cow's or soya
3 large ripe bananas
squeeze lemon juice
2 tablespoons molasses, or to taste

Blend or whisk together the milk, bananas and lemon juice. When thick and creamy add the molasses to taste. Chill briefly before serving.

See also Molasses toffee apples.

MONKEY NUTS
See **Peanuts**

MOOLI

These look rather like a white carrot though they're smoother and usually larger. Their taste is similar to that of a mild red radish with a touch more bitterness. Most of them are imported from Kenya and Holland, and they are available in speciality shops as well as a growing number of greengrocers.

Nutrition: A reasonable source of vitamin C, provided they are fresh.

Buying/Storing: Buy only those that look firm, smooth and undamaged. The larger they are the tougher the flesh will be. Mooli will keep well in a cool dry spot.

How to use: Peel and slice then steam and serve with a white or tomato sauce. Unusual in stir-fries. Young ones can be grated and added raw to salad in small amounts.

SPICED MOOLI

approx. 1 kilo/2 lbs mooli
2 tablespoons vegetable oil
½ teaspoon ground cinnamon
¼ teaspoon ground cloves
¼ teaspoon ground nutmeg
30g/1oz/3 tablespoons walnuts, coarsely chopped
parsley

Peel and dice the mooli, and cook in a pan of boiling water for about 10 minutes, or until just tender.
Meanwhile, use another pan to heat the oil and gently fry the spices and walnuts for a few minutes. When the mooli is ready, drain it and add to the spices. Cook for literally a minute or two more, stirring constantly.
Serve garnished with parsley.

MUESLI

The man who originated muesli was Dr. Bircher-Benner who dished it up to his patients at his famous clinic in Zurich, Switzerland. His 'Swiss Breakfast', as it was originally called, contained a small amount of whole grain cereals mixed with a few nuts and lots of fresh fruit. He probably wouldn't recognise many of today's mueslis as having anything to do with his invention. Those you buy in supermarkets *can* contain refined grains, white sugar, chemical flavourings. However, as the general public demands healthier foods even supermarkets are trying harder to get it right. Better still, go to your local wholefood or healthfood shop where you should find a range of pre-packed cereals made from natural ingredients only. You will save money, though, by making your own muesli. Buy a few pounds of mixed organic grains (these usually include flakes of oat, wheat, barley and rye). Add a small amount of dried fruit such as raisins, chopped dates, dried apricots or pears. Sprinkle in some seeds – sunflower are especially good for you – and a few nuts. Roast a few handfuls of coconut flakes until golden and add them. Add the minimum of sugar if you must, though this is best done at the table as everyone has different tastes. Store the whole lot in an airtight container.

Though many people just add milk and eat, the way to make the grains especially easy to digest is to soak them overnight. Use water and they will be creamy enough in the morning to eat just as they are, though you can of course add milk, soya milk, or fruit juice if you have a sweet tooth. On cold winter mornings cook your muesli for literally a few minutes so that it is hot and yet still not mushy.

See recipe on page 94.

MULBERRIES

No longer very well-known, but grown in Britain on a small scale. A large firm red berry something like a raspberry, but with a spicier taste.

Buying/Storing: Look for firm brightly-coloured fruit. Avoid any that look dull or damaged. Store for no more than a day in the fridge; best eaten at once.

How to use: Mulberries are delicious eaten raw with yogurt, cream or nut cream, and maybe a little sugar. Go well in a fruit salad, and make an attractive garnish for flans and tarts.

RED FRUIT SALAD

455g/1 lb mulberries
225g/¹/₂ lb strawberries
225g/¹/₂ lb black cherries
225g/¹/₂ lb raspberries
2 tablespoons honey

Clean all the fruit. Put the mulberries, strawberries (halved if they are large) and cherries into a bowl.

In a saucepan gently cook the raspberries, honey and a drop of water, for 10 minutes. Cool slightly then press through a sieve to make a thick purée. Gently heat this again and pour over the fruits in the bowl. Stir carefully. Leave to cool.

Serve with cream, yogurt or concentrated soya milk, plus crisp golden biscuits.

MUNG BEANS

A small round bean that is usually green when found in British shops, though other colours are also grown. Mung beans are part of the cuisine of both India and China (where they are usually sprouted).

Varieties: Buy the beans themselves, or flour (called gram) which is usually imported from India where it is widely used.

Nutrition: They are easy to digest, and when sprouted are an especially good source of nutrients, particularly vitamin C.

How to use: Allow approximately 30-40 minutes for the beans to cook. Use in casseroles, stews and soups. If you cannot buy gram flour, grind the beans yourself and use as a quick way of adding protein to any dish. Mung beans go well with brown rice, also in curries. Try sprouting mung beans and add them to salads or stir-fried vegetables.

BEAN SPROUT OMELETTE

8 eggs
pinch of salt
115g/4oz/2 cups mung bean sprouts
2 spring onions, finely chopped
2 large tomatoes, peeled and chopped
oil for frying
tomato sauce to serve – optional

Beat 2 eggs together lightly. Pour a little of the oil into a pan, spread it evenly, add the eggs. Cook them over a gentle heat until golden brown underneath and just beginning to set on top. Add some bean sprouts, onion and tomato and continue cooking for a few minutes more. Fold.

Keep this warm whilst using the remaining ingredients to make 3 more omelettes. Serve them at once.

An interesting addition is a spoonful or two of hot tomato sauce spread over the top of each omelette.

MUSHROOMS

Mushrooms are fungi, of which there are literally thousands of varieties – though many of them can be not only unappetising but also dangerous to eat. For the best flavour you should get up early, go in search of field mushrooms, and cook them for breakfast! However, commercially-grown mushrooms are less flavoursome but easier to obtain. Nowadays they are an all-year-round vegetable that is inexpensive and versatile.

Varieties: More become available every day. Choose from cultivated flat or button mushrooms (which are the same, the button ones being younger and not yet opened out). Or try the more exotic chanterelles and oyster mushrooms. Some speciality stores even sell the famous porcini mushrooms. If picking your own wild mushrooms do make sure you know which are safe to eat – when in doubt, don't! Dried mushrooms are an important ingredient in Oriental cookery and can be purchased at speciality stores.

Buying/Storing: In general choose only mushrooms that are firm and free from blemishes or damage. They should also look plump and a good colour. Mushrooms are best eaten within a day or two of purchase as they dehydrate quickly. Store them in a cool place such as the fridge, preferably in a paper bag tucked inside a polythene one (do not fasten the top).

How to use: Nice raw in salads, or cook them in egg dishes such as quiches, omelettes or soufflés. Dip in flour and then batter, deep-fry, and serve with hollandaise sauce. Cook with garlic, wine and tomatoes in Greek style. Add to pizzas, or make into a sauce for pasta, or simply fry or grill.

MUSHROOM AND TOFU TACOS

taco shells:
55g/2oz/1/3rd cup maize meal
55g/2oz/¹/₂ cup wholemeal flour
2 tablespoons vegetable oil
2 tablespoons warm water
vegetable oil to cook

filling:
2 tablespoons vegetable oil
1 onion, sliced
1 red pepper, sliced
115g/4oz/2 cups mushrooms, chopped
115g/4oz/¹/₂ cup tofu, drained and mashed
seasoning to taste
chilli powder to taste
lettuce

Combine the flours, add the oil and water, and knead the dough until smooth. Roll it out on a floured board, making it as thin as possible. Cut into circles about the size of a saucer. Deep-fry them in hot oil for barely a minute, then flip them over and cook the other side for half that time. Remove them from the oil and leave folded over a wooden handle so that, when cold, they form shells that can be stuffed.

Heat the oil, fry the onion and pepper for a few minutes, add the mushrooms and tofu and cook for a few minutes more. Season to taste, add chilli powder.

Tuck some finely shredded lettuce into each shell, add a spoonful or two of the filling. Serve as they are, or bake them for 10 minutes to heat up. Tacos are a popular snack food from Mexico. Traditional accompaniments include guacamole, burger relish, sour cream and chilli tomato sauce.

See also Aduki and leek roll, Stuffed mushrooms, Vegetable kebabs with herbs, Sunflower and celery paté, Mushrooms à la Grècque, Chestnut paté, Polenta bake, Stuffed globe artichokes.

MUSTARD AND CRESS

A combination of mustard and cress seeds are grown together to produce tiny leaves that have a strong peppery taste. It used to be grown at home on damp blotting paper or muslin and was popular for many years. Now, however, it seems to have faded from fashion, though it can still be found in some greengrocers. You buy a small box with the seeds still growing, and snip off as much as you want (with scissors) when needed. Like bean sprouts, mustard and cress is especially useful in winter when supplies of fresh green ingredients may be more scarce. If you cannot find it in the shops, why not grow your own?

How to use: Mustard and cress is used as a garnish – the flavour goes well with most savoury dishes, soups and salads. It is also useful in sandwiches where it adds moisture as well as taste.

See Yogurt rarebit.

MUSTARD SEED

The seeds of the dazzling yellow mustard plant, which grows well in temperate climates and is found in many countries. Black seeds have a stronger smell, white ones are more pungent, and it is the way in which they are combined that gives each commercially-made mustard its individual flavour.

Varieties: You can buy the seeds, or a ready ground powder that is much hotter as it is more concentrated. Alternatively, of course, you can use made-up mustard; the colouring in this usually comes from saffron or turmeric.

How to use: Use mustard seeds or powder whenever you want to liven up a dish, as mustard goes well with most ingredients, but use it sparingly. Ideal in pickles, coleslaw, sauerkraut, cheese dishes and soufflés. Add a pinch of powder to salad dressings and mayonnaise.

YOGURT RAREBIT

30g/1oz/2¹/₂ tablespoons margarine
1 tablespoon wholemeal flour
225g/¹/₂ lb/2 cups Cheddar cheese, grated
140ml/¹/₄ pint/2/3rd cup natural yogurt
¹/₄ teaspoon ground mustard, or to taste
seasoning to taste
4 thick slices wholemeal bread
mustard and cress

Melt the margarine in a pan, stir in the flour, and cook gently for a few minutes. Add the cheese, yogurt, mustard and seasoning. Cook over a low heat, stirring continually with a wooden spoon. The sauce will become thick and creamy. At the same time, lightly toast the bread. Spoon a good amount of the sauce onto each slice and sprinkle generously with mustard and cress. Serve piping hot.

Note: The flour stops the yogurt curdling, but do heat the sauce gently and only for the minimum time. A handful of bean sprouts would make a delicious addition, or a sprinkling of chopped nuts.

See also Celeriac salad with mustard, Parsnip curry, Stir-fried vegetables with seaweed.

NECTARINES
See **Peaches**

NORI
See **Seaweed**

NUTMEG

This is the inner part of the fruit of an evergreen tree that grows up to 8 metres (25 feet) tall, and from which mace is also derived. Ground nutmeg has a sweet and spicy taste.

How to use: Good in sweet dishes such as custards, rice puddings and stewed fruit. Essential to mulled wine. Try a pinch in savoury recipes such as cheese sauces, rice dishes and vegetable casseroles. The Italians add nutmeg to ricotta cheese and spinach which they then use to stuff ravioli or pancakes, and it is an essential ingredient in many Middle Eastern dishes. Use nutmeg sparingly.

TAHINI CUSTARD
55g/2oz/1/3rd cup maize meal
285ml/¹/₂ pint/1 1/3rd cups water
2 tablespoons light tahini
2 tablespoons apple juice concentrate or honey
¹/₂ teaspoon ground nutmeg, or to taste

Put the maize meal into a saucepan and gradually whisk in the water. Bring to the boil gently, stirring continually. Add the tahini and apple juice or honey. Flavour to taste with nutmeg.

Serve hot or cold. Can be poured into dishes or glasses and served as it is, maybe topped with nuts or granola. Or pour it hot over such dessert dishes as baked apple, fruit crumble. It is delicious in trifles.

If you cannot get maize meal, try using arrowroot instead.

See also Ricotta cheese and spinach pasties, Peach and coconut balls, Spiced mooli, Baked pears, Butternut au gratin.

NUTS
See also **individual varieties**

Nuts are the dried fruit of various trees, and come encased in a protective shell. Like fresh fruit, nuts were among the first foods to be eaten by human beings (a combination that is still considered to be one of the best and most natural). Nuts of one variety or another grow in most countries, whatever the weather and soil conditions, and as they are easy to collect and store they are a perfect food.

Nutrition: They are one of the most concentrated sources of protein available, some offering considerably more protein than meat at a much lower price. Nuts are also rich in other nutrients including vitamins B1, B2 and B6, nicotinic acid, vitamin E and several important minerals. Their fibre content is high. Nuts are a fatty food but, apart from coconuts and brazils, the fat is mostly polyunsaturated and thus not a danger to health. Unfortunately, mass production has resulted in many nuts being treated with preservatives and dyes, and the biggest-selling nuts in Britain are those that have been salted and fried (usually in saturated fats) making them unhealthy whilst stripping them of most of their goodness.

Buying/Storing: All nuts are best bought as fresh as possible, preferably still in their shells. To avoid additives shop from a reputable outlet – and if you have any doubts, ask. Ready-shelled nuts should be bought in small quantities only and stored in an airtight jar, preferably in the dark. Do not chop or grind nuts until just before you intend to use them.

OATS

An easy to grow cereal, even in cold and harsh climates, though surprisingly few countries use them on a large scale. Even in Scotland, where they were once a staple, they now feature less frequently at the table. However, recent awareness of the nutritional qualities of this inexpensive grain are helping to bring it back into fashion, and slowly its popularity is growing.

Varieties: Oats are sold in the form of whole grain, as rolled oats or oat flakes (which are made from pinhead oatmeal). Instant or quick-cooking oats have been partially cooked. Jumbo oats are slower-cooking but have a better texture. Oatmeal bran is paler and finer than wheat bran.

Nutrition: Oats are an exceptionally nutritious grain, rich in minerals and vitamins including E. They have one of the highest protein contents of all grains, and by far the largest fat content of any grain, this fat being polyunsaturated and therefore beneficial to health. Oats are also gluten-free, and considered to be especially easy to digest.

How to use: Muesli, granola (try mixing with other flaked grains), cakes, bread, porridge. Sweet and savoury biscuits such as oatcakes and flapjacks – or substitute oats for just a part of the flour to give a crunchy texture to any biscuits. Use oats to make a delicious crumble topping. Stir into a casserole or soup to thicken it.

APPLE OATMEAL BISCUITS

85g/3oz/³/₄ cup wholemeal flour
1¹/₂ teaspoons baking powder
¹/₂ teaspoon mixed spice
¹/₂ teaspoon ground ginger
55g/2oz/¹/₂ cup hazelnuts, chopped
55g/2oz/1/3rd cup currants
170g/6oz/1¹/₂ cups rolled oats
6 tablespoons apple juice
1 egg white, beaten
1 teaspoon vanilla essence

2 tablespoons honey
1 eating apple, peeled and coarsely grated

Mix together the flour, baking powder and spices. Stir in the nuts and currants. In another bowl stir together the oats and apple juice, then add the stiffly beaten egg white, vanilla and honey. Combine the two mixtures. Add the apple, making sure it is evenly distributed.
The mixture should be thick and moist, so if it is too dry add a drop more apple juice or a tablespoon of oil.
Drop from a teaspoon onto a greased baking sheet, allowing room between each one to allow for spreading.
Bake at 190°C/375°F (Gas Mark 5) for about 20 minutes. Loosen from the tray with a knife, but let cool completely before removing and storing in an airtight container.

See also Mixed grain granola, Oatcakes with thyme, Muesli, Sesame crackers, Prune flapjacks, Almond vegetable crumble, Borlotti bean burgers.

OILS

Smooth and viscous substances which are lighter than, and insoluble in, water, and are generally liquid at room temperature. Oils used to cook with are usually of vegetable origin; most animal products which are oils at high temperatures are actually fats at room temperature. Although some vegetable oils are fairly highly saturated, several pure vegetable oils are high in polyunsaturates, which tend to help clear the arteries of fats rather than clog them.

Varieties: Vegetable oils are extracted from seeds or nuts in one of three ways. In cold-pressed oils, the seeds are pressed in hydraulic presses, no heat or chemicals being used. In semi-refined oils, the seeds are heated and pressed at the same time. Various processes are used to make refined oils, the most common being to dissolve the seeds in petroleum-based materials, then to purify the oil with caustic soda and Fullers earth. This process gets most oil from the seeds and is therefore the most profitable. Vegetable oils are made from a variety of different plants, most of them being polyunsaturated (the chief exception to this is olive oil which is monosaturated); look out for safflower, sunflower, soya, peanut. Sesame is particularly popular in hot climates because it does not go rancid. New on the market is an unrefined pumpkin seed oil, an especially good source of vitamin E. Rapeseed is the only oilseed crop grown in Britain, which makes this one of the cheapest oils (it also gives us those dazzling yellow fields in early summer!). Two delicious oils to use with salad are walnut and hazelnut.

Nutrition: As well as the fat content (safflower, with its high linoleic acid content, is the richest of all in polyunsaturates), all vegetable oils also contain vitamins, particularly A, D and E, and minerals.

Buying/Storing: If you can afford the higher price, buy cold-pressed oils which contain more nutrients. It is also better to buy oil from a single source rather than one that has been blended. Apart from the fact that these often contain cheaper and inferior oils, the blending process detracts also from the nutrients. All oils should be stored in a cool, dark place in a sealed bottle.

How to use: Most vegetable oils can be used in salad dressings, though the best is undoubtedly olive oil. The golden liquid from the first crushing (called virgin oil) has the finest taste. As it has a low smoking point, however, olive oil is not suitable for deep-frying; if you must use it try mixing it with one of the lighter oils such as safflower. A spoonful of oil added to cooking water will help stop pasta or rice sticking.

See Skordalia, Cucumber mayonnaise.

OKRA

An unusual small dark-green finger-shaped vegetable that is much used in Africa and the West Indies. It is imported to Britain now mostly from Kenya and is usually available on and off throughout the year. Okra is also an important ingredient in the Creole cookery of the southern states of America (where it is called gumbo).

Buying/Storing: Do not buy if tired-looking, and preferably not over 10cm (4 inches) long, or they are likely to be tough. Slightly under-ripe okra are best. Do not keep for more than a couple of days and store them in the fridge.

How to use: The delicate flavour of okra is best appreciated if they are simply trimmed top and bottom and then steamed whole until just tender. Can also be added to soups and stews. The seeds inside, when cooked, have thickening qualities that are useful in casseroles and sauces. Serve okra with onion, celery and peppers in a tomato sauce. Batter it and deep-fry. Especially good in curry or other spiced dishes.

VEGETABLE STEW FOR COUSCOUS

225g/^{1}/$_2$ lb/1 1/3rd cup chick peas, cooked
2 tablespoons vegetable oil
1 onion, sliced
2 cloves garlic, crushed
1 red pepper, sliced
2 courgettes, sliced
small head of cauliflower, broken into florets
2 potatoes, cut into large cubes
225g/^{1}/$_2$ lb okra, with tops and tails removed
850ml/1 ^{1}/$_2$ pints/3^3/$_4$ cups water

55g/2oz/1/3rd cup raisins
1 teaspoon cayenne pepper
1 teaspoon paprika
1 teaspoon ground cumin
seasoning to taste
3 tomatoes, quartered
oven-baked couscous (see page 72)
4 hardboiled eggs, quartered – optional

Drain the chick peas. In a large saucepan, or a couscousier, heat the oil and gently fry the onion, garlic and pepper to soften. Add the courgettes, cauliflower, potatoes and okra, and pour on the water. Bring to the boil, reduce the heat, cover the pan and simmer for 15 minutes. Stir in the well drained chick peas, raisins and spices and seasoning. Bring back to the boil, lower the heat again and continue cooking for about 15 minutes, or until everything is cooked. Add the tomatoes to the stew. Put the couscous in a large serving dish and spoon the vegetables into the centre. Arrange the eggs on top, if using them.

Note: In Morocco it is possible to buy a special spice for use with couscous. It contains 35 different spices and has a unique flavour. Buy it if ever you get the chance.

See also Corn and peanut gumbo.

▉▉▉▉▉▉▉ OLIVES ▉▉▉▉▉▉▉

These are picked when ripe and added immediately to either brine or oil, both of which act as preservatives and stop them drying out. Olives can be large or small, black or green, and will vary considerably in taste, depending on where they were grown. All are good sources of the oil for which they are famous. Some come ready stuffed either with pimentos (red peppers) or whole almonds.

Once opened store them in the liquid in which they were preserved, preferably in a screw-top jar in the fridge.

Nutrition: They can have an oil content of up to 50%, this being monosaturated and therefore free of the problems associated with saturated fats. They are also a good source of potassium.

How to use: Olives go well with pre-dinner drinks. Add them to pasta dishes and pizzas. Great with salads. Finely ground olives can make a delicious paté.

BEAN SALAD NIÇOISE

340g/³/₄ lb green beans
¹/₂ small crisp lettuce
¹/₂ small onion, finely chopped
4 tomatoes, quartered
1 tablespoon capers

approx. 6 tablespoons French dressing
4 hardboiled eggs, shelled and quartered
16 black olives

Trim, chop and steam the green beans until just tender, then drain well and cool.
Shred the lettuce coarsely and arrange on 4 small dishes.
In a bowl gently toss the onion, tomatoes, capers and beans in the dressing. Divide
the mixture between the dishes. Decorate with the egg quarters and olives.

See also Vegetable kebabs with herbs, Fennel ratatouille, Sunflower and celery
paté, Radicchio salad with blue cheese dressing, Pita pizzas.

ONIONS

Onions were one of the very first cultivated foods, and have been a basic in
the cookery of many cultures for centuries. In Britain there is a choice of
varieties available throughout the year, most of them homegrown.

Varieties: Look out for tiny pickling onions (sometimes called shallots),
the milder red-skinned onions, and spring onions to add to salads. Larger
varieties include Spanish onions which – because they have plenty of sun –
tend to be sweeter, and the British main crop which have a stronger flavour
and are best cooked.

Buying/Storing: When buying onions, avoid any that are bruised or
damaged, or sprouting. If they have skin on this should be dry and rustling.
Keep onions in a cool, dark spot and they should last for some time.

How to use: Use to give flavour to stews and casseroles. Onions go well
with eggs, so add to omelettes and soufflés. Make French onion soup. Use
in curries. Stuff whole onions with breadcrumbs, cheese and herbs. Use
spring onions or Spanish onions in salads. Shallots are also good in creamy
sauces.

PICKLED ONIONS

1 kilo/2 lb small pickling onions
salt
425ml/³/₄ pint/2 cups white wine vinegar
1 tablespoon pickling spices

Drop the onions into boiling water and bring it back to the boil, then remove them at
once and drop into cold water. Peel with a sharp knife. Put them into a bowl, sprinkle
well with salt, stir so that they are evenly coated. Cover the bowl and set aside for 24
hours, stirring every so often.
Rinse the onions and dry them.
Combine the vinegar and pickling spices in a saucepan and boil them for 10
minutes. Strain the vinegar then leave to cool. Divide the onions between sterilised
glass jars and cover with vinegar. Seal and store in a cool place. Best left for at least
2 months before serving, when the onions should be crisp and quite strongly
flavoured.

Note: Pickling spices are ready-mixed specially for the purpose. If, however, you prefer to mix your own, use a combination of cloves, cinnamon, allspice, chilli, black pepper, coriander. Experience will show you how much of each you need to get the flavour you like best.

See also Spanish lentil soup, Vegetable kebabs with herbs, Sorrel soufflé, Cranberry sauce, Tempeh in sweet and sour sauce, Bean sprout omelette.

ORANGE FLOWER WATER
See Essences, natural

ORANGES

These popular fruits take their name from the French town of Orange which was a major growing area for them during the Middle Ages. Now they are grown throughout the world and are available in British greengrocers all year round. Not only are they used for their juice and flesh, but candied orange peel is a favourite sweet.

Varieties: Though all oranges look much alike some will have more flavour, others will be almost sharp to taste. New varieties include some that are pip-free. Blood oranges, with their bright red juice, are probably the sweetest. Bitter Seville oranges can be made into marmalade.

How to use: An obvious in fruit salads, orange segments also make an attractive topping for fruit flan or cheesecake. The juice can be used to make sauces, to flavour cakes and can be added to salad dressing. If using the peel in cakes or sweets, make sure it has not been sprayed or waxed. Organically-grown oranges are probably the least likely to have been adulterated in this way.

CANDIED PEEL

2 oranges
2 lemons
concentrated apple juice

Scrub the fruit very well, then dry it. Quarter the fruit and carefully remove the peel trying to avoid the pith.

Put the sliced peel into a bowl with just enough apple juice to cover, and leave it in the fridge for a few days. Move the peel around every so often to make sure it is well covered.

Transfer the peel and apple juice to a small saucepan and add a drop of water. Bring to the boil. Keep cooking on a fairly high heat for as long as it takes for the fruit to absorb all of the liquid.

Drain the peel and place it on a flat dish. Leave to dry before storing it in an airtight jar in the fridge.

Note: Obviously this peel will not keep as well as commercially-made candied peel. Try making it using other fruit peel.

See also Gooseberry brulée, Carob cake, Sesame soya fudge, Rhubarb orange crumble, Fruit and nut bran muffins.

▌▌▌▌▌▌▌▌▌▌ OREGANO ▌▌▌▌▌▌▌▌▌▌

A member of the marjoram family, sometimes called wild or common marjoram. It does, in fact, have a similar taste to that of marjoram, but stronger and with bitter undertones.

How to use: Oregano is traditionally used in Italian cookery and is essential in such dishes as pastas and pizzas. It also goes well with hotter Mexican dishes, Greek dishes, and tomatoes cooked Spanish-style with onions. Try adding it to mushrooms, also lentils. It also works well in combination with other herbs, but be careful not to use too much.

GORGONZOLA PIZZAS

15g/^{1}/$_2$oz/good tablespoon fresh yeast, or 7g/^{1}/$_4$oz dried yeast
pinch of raw cane sugar
140ml/^{1}/$_4$ pint/2/3rd cup warm water
225g/^{1}/$_2$ lb/2 cups wholemeal flour
pinch of salt
3 tablespoons olive oil

topping:
340g/^{3}/$_4$ lb tomatoes
170g/6oz gorgonzola cheese
1 small green pepper
115g/4oz/2 cups mushrooms
12 black olives
2 teaspoons oregano
seasoning to taste
olive oil

Dissolve the yeast and sugar in half the water, and set aside in a warm place for 10 minutes, or until it begins to froth. Sift the flour and salt into a warm bowl and add the yeast mixture, the rest of the water, and the oil. Mix well until it comes away from the sides of the bowl, adding a drop more water if necessary to bind. Turn onto a floured board and knead for 5 minutes. Put into a clean, floured bowl, cover with a damp cloth, and leave in a warm spot until doubled in volume. Punch the dough down, divide into four and roll out to make medium-sized circles no thicker than ^{1}/$_4$ inch (6mm). Arrange on greased floured baking trays.
Brush the tops with a little oil. Slice the tomatoes and arrange on the pizzas. Cover with crumbled cheese. Cut the pepper into rings and divide between the four. Top with a sprinkling of sliced mushrooms. Add the olives, oregano and seasoning, and trickle a little oil over each pizza.
Bake at 200°C/400°F (Gas Mark 6) for 20-30 minutes, or until dough is crisp.

ORGANIC

See also **Meat**

It wasn't so long ago that farmming was about understanding ecology rather than having a good knowledge of chemisstry. Farming, after all, iis one of the oldest professions in the world, the early farmers having to learn about the interplay of sun, rain, wind and soil if they were to feed themselves and their families. The foods they produced may have been simple, varying little from year to year, but they were tasty, healthy, nutritious.

More recently, the sudden population explosion, plus a move away from plant foods to animal products, has meant that farmers have been forced to increase their yields. The development of technology based on petroleum has given them fertilisers, herbicides, pesticides, fungicides, petrol and diesel to run their tractors and harvesters, heating for their greenhouses. Nature is no longer of importance. Tropical plants can be grown in cold climates, summer plants in winter, even bad soil can yield a good crop. Food is abundant.

But is it safe food? And what about the soil? And the planet?

Though tests are continually being run to assure us our food contains nothing that can harm us, there are a growing number of people who would question their accuracy. Tests on animals have little validity in that their bodies are not the same as ours. The only test is that of time, and already there are indications that the chemicals in our food are *not* safe, that they may be the direct cause of a wide range of health problems, from allergies to stomach cancer.

What they do to the soil is easier to see. By forcing the soil to yield unnaturally abundant crops, chemical farming has many damaging side effects including pollution, breakdown of soil structure, destruction of the countryside and its wildlife. Insects may become even more of a pest; they have a fast breeding cycle and soon build up resistance to pesticides, may even thrive on them. Chemical residues are not only inevitable in the actual crops, but may seep down to contaminate water supplies.

Such a method of farming also affects the future of the planet. Based on petroleum, it consumes a great deal of energy, requiring far more to be put into it than the food energy produced at the end. Petroleum is also a non-renewable resource, one that is fast dwindling. The fear of losing access to it results in aggression, in the exploitation of remote and until-now unexploited corners of the world, in national budgets having to be continually raised to pay for it.

Not surprisingly, there is a surge of interest in organic farming.

Organic farming is not simply a return to old-fashioned farming methods, but a system that combines a true understanding of ecology, plant physiology and biochemistry with an awareness of current research and development. It includes such methods as using crop wastes to enrich the soil rather than burning them off, controlling pests with intercropping or physical barriers. Food produced organically has lower levels of pesticides and nitrates (in this day and age pesticide contamination is so universal that it is virtually impossible to say any food is completely free of it). It is free of artificial additives, has been processed only as much as is absolutely necessary. What this food does have is a higher level of the natural trace elements we need for health.

At the moment organic farms are still few and far between. They are usually small, and may be anywhere in the country. Hence such products cost more than those produced on a large scale where the costs are cut accordingly. As more people buy organic foods, however, it is to be hoped that increased production and better distribution methods will enable the prices to drop. Even so, the extra you may be asked to pay for organic food is the extra you would expect to pay for any high quality product, and when it is one that so directly affects your health and the environment in which you live, it is surely worth the price.

At this time there is no one organisation governing standards of organic agriculture. The Soil Association is, however, considered to be the premier organisation promoting this way of farming, and they have a symbol that they award to farmers and growers, food processors and distributors, and industrial manufacturers who follow the standards set by them. A scheme for retailers is to be launched. Look out for their symbol on products.

PAK CHOI

This is a leafy green vegetable with thick white stalks. It was introduced to the Caribbean by the Chinese and is now widely used as a vegetable. Always cook it before eating.

Buying/Storing: Look out for the small yellow flowers that can sometimes be found growing on pak choi – these show that it is at its very best. The leaves should be tightly furled and crisp. Keep in the fridge for a few days if necessary.

How to use: Detach the leaves from the stalk, trim, slice or shred. Then cook it in the minimum water (when it will go bright green in colour). Use as a vegetable accompaniment, add to stir-fries, use in savoury flans and crumbles. The stalk can be boiled, steamed or stir-fried.

PANEER

Paneer is a vegetarian cheese that is widely used in India. Made from whole milk that has been treated with acetic acid, it comes in the form of a soft block rather like tofu, and – because of its very mild flavour – can be used in a variety of different dishes. Up until recently it was only found in restaurants, but it is now on sale in some speciality shops and will hopefully soon be available in many more.

How to use: Paneer can be added to sweet dishes, pies, used as a stuffing for vegetables. It is obviously especially suited to curries, the best known of which is mattar paneer.

MATTAR PANEER

455g/1 lb fresh peas, cooked
6 tablespoons ghee
225g/¹/₂ lb/1 cup paneer
1 teaspoon ground cinnamon
1 teaspoon ground turmeric
good pinch chilli powder
2 tablespoons fresh coriander leaves, chopped
salt to taste

Melt the ghee in a heavy frying pan. Sprinkle in the spices, stir, cook for a few minutes.

Add the peas. Cut the paneer into small cubes and add this also to the pan, stirring so that everything is coated in the spices. Cook gently for 5 minutes, still stirring occasionally. Sprinkle with the coriander, add salt, continue cooking for 5 minutes more or until everything is tender.

Serve with rice.

Note: Although coriander leaves are more authentic in this recipe, parsley makes an acceptable substitute.

PAPAYAS
See **Paw paws**

PAPRIKA

A powder made from dried, ground peppers called Hungarian red peppers which are, appropriately, bright red in colour. It has a mild sweet taste.

How to use: Traditionally used in popular Hungarian dishes such as goulash, or a coriander and paprika cheese spread. Try too paprika sauce, in egg dishes, with rice and other grain recipes. It is often just sprinkled over the top of pale dishes to add colour.

RED CABBAGE WITH SOUR CREAM

455g/1 lb red cabbage, coarsely shredded
1 small onion, finely chopped
1 apple, chopped
approx. 6 tablespoons vegetable stock
1 tablespoon cider vinegar
good pinch of garlic salt
seasoning to taste
200ml/1/3rd pint/³/₄ cup sour cream
1-2 teaspoons paprika
parsley to garnish

Lightly grease an ovenproof dish. Mix together the cabbage, onion and apple and put into the dish. Combine the vegetable stock, cider vinegar, salt and seasoning and pour over the cabbage.

Cover the dish and bake at 180°C/350°F (Gas Mark 4) for about 30 minutes, or until the cabbage is just cooked, but still crisp.

Serve with the cream poured over the top, the paprika sprinkled over that and a generous garnish of fresh parsley sprigs.

See also Guacamole dip.

PARSLEY

One of the most popular herbs in Britain, its mild aromatic taste having been a distinctive addition to traditional dishes for centuries. It also featured in many legends and folk tales.

Varieties: Two types of parsley are available, the traditional crinkly variety and a flat-leaved parsley.

Nutrition: Parsley is especially rich in vitamins A and C, also iron, iodine and calcium. It is said that chewing a sprig helps freshen the breath, especially after eating garlic.

How to use: It is most popular as a garnish, which means that it is often pushed uneaten to the side of the plate! Add it instead whilst cooking such dishes as sauces, stews, casseroles and bean bakes. Try parsley soufflé, or add a generous handful to scrambled eggs. Mix into dips such as hummus, cheese or tahini. Put parsley butter on new potatoes. Add to grain dishes.

CASHEW NOODLES WITH PARSLEY

225g/¹/₂ lb/1³/₄ cups noodles
30g/1oz/2¹/₂ tablespoons butter
1 clove garlic, finely chopped
1 spring onion, finely chopped
good pinch cayenne pepper
seasoning to taste
55g/2oz/¹/₂ cup cashews, coarsely chopped
115g/4oz/¹/₂ cup cottage cheese
200ml/1/3rd pint/³/₄ cup sour cream
2 tablespoons parsley, chopped
15g/¹/₂oz/1 tablespoon Parmesan cheese

Cook the noodles in a pan of boiling water until just tender. Drain well.
In a bowl gently mix together the noodles and all the other ingredients, except the Parmesan cheese. Transfer the mixture to a greased ovenproof dish. Sprinkle with Parmesan.
Bake at 180°C/350°F (Gas Mark 4) for 20-30 minutes, or until heated through and bubbly.

PARSNIPS

The parsnip is native to Britain. It has been around since Roman times and has been used not just as a vegetable, but as an ingredient in cakes, jams, and also as a kind of flour.

Buying/Storing: Look for vegetables that are white, firm, and free from knobbles or damage. Shrivelled, dry-looking parsnips are also best avoided. Store them in a cool, dry place where they should keep for some time.

How to use: The slightly sweet taste of parsnip goes well with a wide variety of ingredients. Steam or boil parsnips, add butter and serve as a vegetable. Cut into thin slices and fry. Make into a purée, mix with eggs and herbs, and use the mixture to fill a flan or as the base for a savoury crumble. To get the maximum food value, grate young raw parsnips and add to a salad – delicious combined with apple and raisins.

PARSNIP CURRY

455g/1 lb parsnips
225g/¹/₂ lb leeks
2 large carrots
85g/3oz/³/₄ cup cashew nuts

sauce:
2 tablespoons vegetable oil
1 onion, chopped
1 clove garlic, crushed

1 teaspoon ground turmeric
1 teaspoon ground cumin
2 teaspoons ground coriander
$^1/_2$ teaspoon ground ginger
1 teaspoon mustard seed
seasoning to taste

Peel and cube the parsnip, clean and chop the leeks, slice the carrots. Parboil all the vegetables for 5 minutes until just beginning to soften. Drain and reserve water. Heat the oil and add the chopped onion and garlic. Cook for 5 minutes or until they begin to colour, then add the spices and cook for a few minutes more. Season to taste, and add about 285ml/$^1/_2$ pint of the reserved water. Bring to the boil, then cover and simmer for 15 minutes. Remove the lid and cook gently until sauce thickens. Stir in the vegetables and nuts and cook for 5-10 minutes more.

Curry sauce improves in flavour if made a day or two before needed and then reheated.

See also Parsnip and banana chutney.

PASSION FRUITS

Native to South America, it is the purply brown variety of these small wrinkled fruits that is most often found in Britain, though yellow and orange varieties can sometimes be purchased. A tropical vine fruit, passion fruits are now grown in Australia, Africa and the southeast of the USA as well as in Mediterranean countries. Though unappetising to look at, inside the hard outer skin is a rosy jelly-like pulp dotted with tiny seeds that has a deliciously sweet flavour. The wrinkled skin – far from indicating that the fruit is stale – tells you that it is in fact just ripe for eating.

How to use: Cut in half with a sharp knife and use a small spoon to scoop out the flesh. Though best eaten raw, just as it is, passion fruit can also be used to flavour sorbets, ice cream, yogurt and sweet mousses.

PASTA

Pasta is a paste from durum wheat, an especially hard wheat grown mainly in Italy and North America, which has a high gluten content, and therefore the dough holds together when cooking. No one knows quite where pasta originated, though Marco Polo is said to have introduced it to Italy after visiting China. By the Middle Ages it was a staple in the Italian diet – and it still is today, especially in the south of the country.

Varieties: The wheat is ground, sometimes egg is added, and the resulting paste is shaped into some 150 varieties of pasta. The best known include spaghetti, macaroni, lasagne, tagliatelle, shells and noodles. You can buy pasta made from refined flour, wholewheat pasta, and a new product on the market is high-fibre pasta which is made from refined flour with bran added. Green pasta has usually been coloured by adding a little spinach. With less than 100 calories per dry ounce it is far from the fattening food it was once thought to be, though if calories concern you, watch out for the sauces!

Nutrition: Most dried pasta on sale in supermarkets is made from refined white flour, though a growing demand for wholewheat varieties means that more are being introduced, and they are in any case available at healthfood and wholefood shops. Like wholemeal bread, wholemeal pasta contains the important wheatgerm and bran. Freshly-made pasta is also sold through speciality shops – and you can make your own with far less effort than is usually imagined.

Buying/Storing: Store dry pasta carefully and it will keep for years. You can buy special storage jars for spaghetti, though any cool, dry place will do. Freshly-made pasta should be eaten the same day.

How to use: Pasta cooks very quickly and is filling, so makes an excellent food. It can be served in countless ways, both in savoury and sweet recipes. Be adventurous and make up sauces of your own. For a change, serve noodles instead of rice with Chinese food. Allow 55-80g/2-3oz of pasta per person.

HOMEMADE PASTA

225g/¹/₂ lb/2 cups wholemeal flour
pinch of salt
2 eggs
1 tablespoon vegetable oil
cold water to mix

Sift together the flour and the salt. Make a well in the centre and add the eggs lightly beaten with the oil. Mix, adding just enough water to bind. Knead lightly until the dough is smooth and glossy. Wrap in a polythene bag and set aside in a cool place for 30 minutes.

Divide into two and roll out on a floured board. The pastry should be as fine as possible. Cut into thin strips to make tagliatelle; into oblongs for lasagne, or to be rolled up to make cannelloni.

Homemade pasta is best used the same day, but if put in an airtight container and stored in the fridge will keep for a day or two.

When cooking it in boiling water, test after literally 2 or 3 minutes – it is ready when tender but still firm.

See also Spaghetti with caper sauce, Egg soup and chervil, Cashew noodles with parsley, Spinach lasagne.

PASTRY

See also **Raising agents, Filo pastry**

Pastry is a mixture of flour, fat, water and sometimes salt. Some pastries also include eggs, sugar, cheese and herbs. Though there are many different kinds, the most widely used is shortcrust, probably because it is one of the most versatile being ideal for both sweet and savoury flans, pies and pasties. Flaky pastry is softer in texture, as is rough puff pastry (which is made not by rubbing in the fat, but by mixing it in as small lumps). One of the most complicated pastries to make is puff pastry, which is folded time and again so that air is trapped between the layers, this air making the pastry rise as it cooks. Vol-au-vents are made with puff pastry. Choux pastry is made by cooking the ingredients in a saucepan before baking them. The result is a very light pastry such as is used for eclairs.

There are a number of general rules it is worth remembering when making pastry. Keep everything as cool as possible – ingredients, working surface, and your hands. Introduce as much air into the mixture as possible, either by sieving the flour, or by lifting it and letting it fall back into the bowl a few times before you start. Handle and roll the dough with a light touch. Use the minimum amount of water necessary to make the dough. When rolling the dough never stretch it – it will shrink when cooking. If you have time to leave the dough in a cool place for a short while before cooking, do so. And finally, always heat the oven to the required temperature before you put the pastry into it.

Many cooks have difficulty with making pastry, especially when they first start using wholemeal flour. It is the bran that makes the pastry drier, meaning water content has to be adjusted carefully or it may be difficult to roll out (or, worse still, may cook to the texture of cardboard!). To start with it might be best to sift out the bran, or to use an unbleached white flour. Another tip is to roll out the pastry on aluminium foil and then to use this to lift it across to the dish or flan case, so reducing the risk of it breaking up. When making flans you intend to fill, the recipe often calls for you to bake the case 'blind' first for a short time. With white flour pastry this means filling the case with something such as rice or beans to weigh it down. Because it is heavier in texture, you do not need to do this with wholemeal pastry – though you can, of course, if you prefer. Otherwise, simply prick the base with a fork and cook it as instructed.

Once you are used to making the basic pastries, try adding other ingredients to ring the changes. You can also use different flours either in combination with wheat, or alone. Anyone suffering from gluten or other allergies will find pastry can be made from such flours as gram, potato, sago, tapioca. The resulting pastry will not be the same as that made with wheat flour, but will be very tasty.

See Aduki and leek roll, Butter bean pie, Ricotta cheese and spinach pasties, Cauliflower cheese meringue, Mexican flan, Quiche au poivre, Pecan pumpkin pie.

PATECHOI
See **Pak choi**

PATÉS

Patés originated in France where they are still popular. (The word itself came from the pastry case in which patés were originally served.) They are a combination of ingredients blended until smooth and then set to a medium-soft consistency. Sometimes they are cooked, though they can also be made without cooking. Traditionally patés are enriched with lashings of cream and butter, making them not exactly a healthy food. Up until recently they have also usually been based on meat products. Paté de foie gras is maybe one of the best known; it is made from the livers of geese which are force-fed until they are so huge their legs can no longer support them, and they are in danger of dying from heart attacks.

Nowadays patés are made from a wide variety of ingredients including nuts, grains, cheeses, eggs. They are an ideal food in that they can be served as part of a light meal, as a starter for a main meal, as a late night snack. They go especially well with French bread, though crunchier bases such as crispbreads and melba toast make a good contrast to their smooth texture. Patés can also be thinned down and used as a dip to put on the table with raw vegetable sticks, crisps, corn and tortilla chips. (Dips, of course, can also be thickened up and used as patés!)

Many wholefood and healthfood shops have fresh patés made up specially for them which they keep in the chilled section. They may also stock the few patés now being commercially made, these coming in tubes, jars or rolls. Such patés tend to have a softer texture than most – adjust this, if you like, by adding a few breadcrumbs, then putting the paté in a small dish and chilling it before using.

It is, however, easy to make our own patés, especially if you have a grinder. You need one ingredient that will hold all the others together (such as curd cheese), or use oil and vegetable stock to achieve much the same effect. Remember that all ingredients should be chopped as small as possible so that the mixture does not break up.

How to use: Besides using in the usual way, patés can be used to fill raw vegetables, or mixed with other ingredients and made into a stuffing for cooked vegetables. The same kind of mixture can be added to pancakes or pasties. Stir some into sauces and stews to add flavour and thickening. Or use your paté as a spread in sandwiches.

SUNFLOWER AND CELERY PATÉ

115g/4oz/³/₄ cup sunflower seeds
2 large sticks celery, finely chopped
55g/2oz/1 cup mushrooms, finely chopped
6 green olives, chopped
approx. 4 tablespoons oil
celery salt
freshly ground black pepper
celery leaves to garnish – optional

Grind the seeds to a fine powder. If liked you can dry roast them first. Mix together the seeds, celery, mushrooms, olives and the oil, stirring continually. The mixture should be thick and smooth. Season to taste.

Spoon the mixture into a small bowl, smooth the top. Garnish with celery leaves and maybe an olive in the centre. Chill before serving. Nice with warm wholemeal baps.

See also Guacamole dip, Brussels sprouts paté, Cauliflower paté, Chestnut paté, Split pea spread, Stuffed eggs.

▌▌▌▌▌▌▌▌▌▌▌ PAW PAWS ▌▌▌▌▌▌▌▌▌▌▌

A large greeny-yellow pear-shaped fruit that is grown throughout the tropics, Central and South America. It is filled with small dark seeds that should be discarded. The flesh is orange and something like that of apricots though it has a firmer texture. If you find dried paw paws in the shops do try them – good added to muesli or granola, or made into a jam.

Nutrition: A good source of vitamin A. Said to be good for the digestion.

Buying/Storing: Buy when just beginning to soften, and eat as soon as possible. Store in the fridge for a day or two if necessary.

How to use: Best served rather like melon – chill it well, then cut into wedges and serve with a squeeze of lemon juice and maybe a sprinkling of spice. Also excellent in fruit salads. Can also be filled with a savoury stuffing, baked, and served as a main course.

TROPICAL CREAM DESSERT

2 medium paw paws
juice of 1 lime
1 tablespoon lime peel, grated
225g/¹/₂ lb/1 cup soft white cheese (i.e. fromage frais, ricotta, quark)
30g-55g/1-2oz/2-4 tablespoons raw cane sugar, powdered in a grinder
ginger biscuits to serve

Peel the paw paws, remove the seeds, reserve a quarter of one of the two fruits.

Mash or blend the rest of the fruit with the lime juice and peel. Add the cheese and sugar to taste.
Divide this cream between 4 glasses. Decorate each one with a few slices of paw paw. Serve chilled, with ginger biscuits.

PEACHES

Like nectarines, these are members of the rose family. Though they originated in China they reached Europe some 2,000 years ago, and it is from the Mediterranean countries that they are now mostly imported to Britain. Unfortunately they are usually picked before they are ripe and are left to ripen en route, which means that they taste nothing like peaches eaten fresh from the trees.

Varieties: Peaches can be pink or yellow, large or small, depending on the country of origin. Nectarines are classed as a fuzzless peach, and they are usually smaller. Hard to find though worth looking out for too are dried nectarines and peaches; the nectarines have a more delicate flavour.

Buying/Storing: To choose a peach or nectarine, look for a firm unblemished skin and a heavy fruit. Be careful too of any that have signs of mould or soft spots. Eat at once if the flesh gives a little when pressed gently. Otherwise they should be kept at room temperature for a few days to ripen.

How to use: Mix chopped fruit with sugar and nuts to fill a crêpe. Peel and mash an over-ripe peach and mix with whipped egg white to make a fool. Make a purée and use as a natural sauce, or add mineral water or another fruit juice for a long drink. Stuff halves with a sweet crumb mixture and bake to make a hot dessert. Fill a sweet omelette with sliced nectarine. Dried peaches make a delicious chutney. Or try them in a sweet and sour sauce with almonds and serve with a grain such as bulgur.

PEACH AND COCONUT BALLS

225g/¹/₂ lb dried peaches
honey or syrup to taste
approx. 85g/3oz/1 cup desiccated coconut
3 tablespoons almonds, finely chopped
¹/₂ teaspoon ground nutmeg
approx. 2 tablespoons orange juice
extra desiccated coconut

Cook the peaches in water until soft, adding a little sweetener if necessary. Drain well and chop as fine as possible. Put the peaches into a bowl and stir in all the ingredients except the extra coconut, mixing well. The mixture should be fairly firm so adjust it as necessary. If it is too wet, add extra coconut, nuts or some bread or cake crumbs.

Divide the mixture into even-sized portions, shape into balls and roll in coconut to coat. Chill before serving.

See also California salad, Fruited lettuce leaves.

PEANUTS

Probably the best-known nut in the world, though peanuts are in fact not nuts at all, but the pod of a leguminous plant which grows underground on long tendrils. Records of the use of peanuts as early as 950 BC have been found in South American tombs. The USA is now one of the largest producers of peanuts. Also known as groundnuts and monkey nuts.

Varieties: Peanuts are available whole, flaked, and ground into a flour.

Nutrition: Peanuts rate with almonds as the nuts richest in protein. They also contain the eight essential amino acids, and are rich in linoleic acid. Fairly high in calories, they should be eaten sparingly, though if used in main dishes rather than as a between-meal snack, they are no more fattening than meat, and equally nutritious.

How to use: Mix roasted ground peanuts with oil and a little yeast extract to make a tasty butter. Use with curries, Chinese dishes and salads. Make into patties, or mix with spinach and egg to make a loaf. Blend with dried fruit and honey, roll in carob powder, and serve as an alternative to sweets.

CORN AND PEANUT GUMBO

30g/1oz/2¹/₂ tablespoons margarine or butter
1 small onion, sliced
1 small green pepper, sliced
225g/¹/₂ lb okra, trimmed
2 sticks celery, chopped
2 tablespoons peanut butter
4 tomatoes, peeled and coarsely chopped
approx. 285ml/¹/₂ pint/1 1/3rd cups vegetable stock
170g/6oz/1 cup sweetcorn kernels, cooked
1 tablespoon chopped parsley
Worcester sauce
seasoning to taste
pinch of garlic salt
55g/2oz/¹/₂ cup raw peanuts

Melt the margarine and cook the onion and pepper gently for a few minutes. Stir in the okra and celery and cook 5 minutes more, then add the peanut butter and continue stirring until it melts. Add the tomatoes and stock. bring to a boil then simmer for 15 minutes, adding a drop more liquid if necessary.
Add the sweetcorn, parsley, Worcester sauce and seasoning to taste, garlic and peanuts. Simmer for 10 minutes more.
Traditionally gumbo is served over hot rice in deep soup bowls. Try it also with other

grains (corn meal goes especially well), or simply accompanied by buttered oatcakes.

See also Autumn salad, Brussels sprouts paté, Gado-gado, red and white slaw, Curried nuts nibbles, Scorzonera salad, Sorghum and green bean stew.

PEARS

Pears were referred to in Homer's *Odyssey* as a gift from the Gods. They are still very popular in all their varieties, many of which are grown in Britain. With more varieties now being imported from around the world, it is possible to eat pears most of the year.

Buying/Storing: Do not buy damaged or bruised fruit. This may mean buying pears that are not quite ripe as once they are, the skin damages easily. If you want to ripen them quickly leave in a warm spot. Otherwise, can be kept in the fridge for up to two weeks. Dried pears are sometimes available – they are usually sold in halves and have a sweet and delicate flavour.

How to use: Crisp pears can be cut up and added to salad, but pears tend to work better in sweet combinations. Try them in a chilled soup, or cooked in red wine with cinnamon and served with cream. Layer pear halves in a flan and, when cooked, top with flaked chocolate. Also nice with sweet rice dishes. Make a quick dessert by adding chopped dried pears and a small piece of crystallised ginger to a thick yogurt, or use with nuts and raisins as a pancake filling.

BAKED PEARS

4 large pears
lemon juice
30g/1oz/2 tablespoons raw cane sugar
30g/1oz/¹/₄ cup wholemeal flour
30g/1oz/2¹/₂ tablespoons margarine
¹/₂ teaspoon ground cinnamon
¹/₄ teaspoon ground nutmeg
¹/₄ teaspoon ground ginger
grated lemon rind
coconut cream
concentrated soya milk

Halve and core the pears. Brush surface with lemon juice, then arrange close together in an ovenproof dish, cut side up. Make a crumble by rubbing together the sugar, flour and margarine, so that you have a crumb-like mixture. Stir in the spices and lemon rind and sprinkle over the pears. Bake at 190°C/375°F (Gas Mark 5) for 30-40 minutes, or until the pears are cooked.

Serve with a topping made by mixing grated coconut cream with a drop of hot water, concentrated soya milk, adding some sugar if you like it sweet.

See also Fruit and honey spread.

‖‖‖‖‖‖‖ PEAS, DRIED ‖‖‖‖‖‖‖
See also **Peas, fresh**

These are the usual maincrop peas that have been dried and are either left whole, or split. The outer skins are removed from split peas, making them even quicker to cook. Also available in speciality shops is a flour made from ground split peas and called gram.

How to use: Allow approximately 1-1½ hours for whole dried peas, 30 minutes for split peas. Yellow split peas are used to make pease pudding, but are also good in dal, a spiced purée from India. Use mashed split peas to make loaves, add them to soups, or cook and then shape them into patties that can be fried. Whole peas can be added to stews and casseroles.

SPLIT PEA SPREAD
30g/1oz/2½ tablespoons margarine
2 spring onions, finely chopped
115g/4oz/2 cups mushrooms, finely chopped
115g/4oz/½ cup split peas, cooked and drained
1 teaspoon yeast extract, or to taste
1 teaspoon tomato purée
seasoning to taste
chopped parsley or chives

Melt the margarine and gently fry the onions for a few minutes, then add the mushrooms and cook 5 minutes more, stirring occasionally.

Add split peas, stir, heat gently. Stir in the yeast extract, tomato purée and seasoning and stir energetically (using a wooden spoon), until you have a thick paste. If it is too moist, add a few spoonsful of oats or breadcrumbs. Add a generous amount of parsley or chives.

Turn into a small dish or jar and store in the fridge until needed. Can also be thickened and served as a paté. Or add some more tomato purée or a drop of vegetable stock and make it into a dip.

Note: As you need only a small quantity of split peas for this, you could use up some left over from when cooking a previous recipe (or cook more than you need and save the extra for a future occasion). Vary the recipe with other pulses and vegetables too.

PEAS, FRESH
See also **Peas, dried**

These are best when grown locally and picked when young – which is usually late spring and early summer. Peas are one of the most popular vegetables in Britain, though it is the tinned and frozen varieties that people tend to prefer. The word 'pease' is of Sanskrit origin.

Varieties: Apart from maincrop peas there are two speciality varieties that are usually imported, but well worth trying. These are petits pois, which are tiny and very sweet, and the flat mangetout which is eaten whole.

Nutrition: Peas are an excellent source of protein, folic acid and vitamin C. They are also rich in natural sugars.

Buying/Storing: Maincrop peas should be brightly-coloured, smooth and undamaged. Do not buy if they are wrinkled. Mangetout peas should also look fresh and juicy. A row of little peas should just be visible down one side – if they are too large the mangetout may be tough. Store for the minimum time in the fridge, preferably in an airtight bag which will stop them drying out.

How to use: Use maincrop peas in pea soup, add them to casseroles and stews. Good in cream sauces. Use to add colour and protein to all sorts of dishes, including omelettes, flans, tomato sauces for pasta, macaroni cheese, pizza topping, and stir-fried vegetables. Petits pois are best served as a side vegetable, maybe with a knob of butter, so that their flavour can be appreciated. Mangetout pods should be topped and tailed, then steam or boil for approximately 5 minutes until tender but still crisp. They also go well in stir-fries, and can also be eaten raw in a vinaigrette dressing.

PEA AND CARROT LOAF

115g/¹/₂ lb/1 1/3rd cup peas, shelled
2 large carrots, peeled and diced
115g/4oz/³/₄ cup walnuts, coarsely chopped
¹/₂ small onion, chopped
2 slices fresh wholemeal bread, made into crumbs
6 tablespoons milk
2 eggs, beaten
1 tablespoon margarine or butter, melted
seasoning to taste

The peas need to be lightly cooked first, and then well drained.
In a bowl mix together all the ingredients and season them generously. Grease a small loaf tin, pile in the mixture, smooth the top.
Bake at 180°C/350°F (Gas Mark 4) for about 50-60 minutes, or until set.
Good with a spicy tomato sauce.

See also Minestrone alla Milanese, Winter hotpot with miso, Mattar paneer, Chinese fried vegetables with eggs.

PECANS

These nuts, from the southern part of North America, were once the staple diet of many native peoples. They are smooth, creamy nuts that come in a brittle pink or red shell, and are only just finding their way into British greengrocers. They are best purchased in their shells, but you can also usually buy them ready-shelled from healthfood and wholefood shops.

How to use: Pecans are especially good with sweet dishes. Try them in biscuits, fruit cakes, flans, or layered with cream between two rounds of sponge cake. In the USA, two popular ways of using pecans are in maple pecan fondants, which are sweets made with maple syrup, and in pecan pie. Try them too with savoury salads and vegetable dishes.

POPCORN NUT CRUNCH

55g/2oz/¹/₄ cup margarine
approx. 4 tablespoons maple syrup or honey
55g/2oz/¹/₂ cup pecan nuts, coarsely chopped
225g/¹/₂ lb popping corn, ready popped

Melt the margarine and maple syrup or honey, stirring as you do so. Combine the chopped nuts and corn, and mix this into the first mixture.
Spread it on a baking tray. Bake at 180°C/350°F (Gas Mark 4) for about 15 minutes, or until crisp.

See also California salad, Zucchini bread, Pecan pumpkin pie.

PECTIN
See **Fruit spreads**

PEPPER

There are two kinds of pepper in general use, black and white. In fact both come from the same tropical fruit, the black berries coming from the unripe fruit, while white peppers have been allowed to ripen, then have been dried and skinned. Though both have a strong spicy taste, black pepper is stronger and has a fuller flavour. Pepper is thought to stimulate digestion and circulation.

Buying/Storing: Can be purchased ready-ground in which case buy only a small quantity at a time and store in a dark airtight jar. Black pepper is best bought as peppercorns and ground in a pepper mill as needed at the table.

How to use: Freshly-ground black pepper brings out the flavour of all foods and can be added to savoury dishes as required. Quiche au poivre is a classic pepper dish. For an unusual sweet, try cottage cheese with honey, peel and spices – and a light sprinkling of black pepper. Whole peppers can be added to pickles. Use white pepper when black would spoil the appearance of a dish. Fresh green pepper corns make an attractive garnish for such dishes as paté.

QUICHE AU POIVRE

225g/¹/₂ lb/2 cups wholemeal flour
pinch of salt
140g/5oz/just under 2/3rd cup margarine
approx. 2 tablespoons cold water
1 tablespoon black peppercorns, crushed
30g/1oz/2¹/₂ tablespoons butter
285ml/¹/₂ pint/1 1/3rd cups single cream or creamy milk
3 egg yolks
salt to taste
115g/4oz/¹/₂ cup curd or cream cheese
55g/2oz/¹/₂ cup grated Parmesan cheese – optional

To make the pastry, put half of the flour, the salt, margarine and water into a bowl, and use a fork to mix them. Gradually work in the rest of the flour to form a firm dough. Knead this lightly on a floured board, then wrap in polythene and chill for 30 minutes.

Roll out the pastry, use to line a medium-sized flan dish, prick the base and bake blind at 200°C/400°F (Gas Mark 6) for 10 minutes.

Meanwhile, fry the peppercorns in the melted butter for a few minutes – watch that the butter does not go black. Remove pan from the heat and let cool a few minutes before adding the cream and egg yolks. Salt to taste. Stir in the cheese so that it melts to form a thick sauce.

Pour the sauce into the partially cooked flan case. Sprinkle with Parmesan cheese if using it. Return to the oven and continue cooking at the same temperature for a further 30 minutes, or until set.

PEPPERS, CHILLI
See **Chilli peppers**

PEPPERS, SWEET
See **Sweet peppers**

PERSIMMON

An unusual fruit, not widely available, but well worth buying if you can find it. In America it is called Sharon fruit. Like large peach-coloured tomatoes to look at, persimmons must be eaten when they are ripe – not before or the taste is bitter. They are usually imported from Italy or Israel.
Buying/Storing: Buy when just soft enough to yield when pressed. They do not always ripen, though if you find some that are almost ready to eat they can be left at room temperature for a few days, and will probably be delicious.
How to use: Best eaten raw as a fruit – just slice off the top and spoon out the exotic tasting flesh. Try also making persimmon ice cream or water ice. Good too in a fruit fool with yogurt or cream.

PICKLES
See also **Preserving methods for home use**

Pickling has long been used as a way of preserving food, and it is still used in many parts of the world. In northern Europe sauerkraut and gherkins are widely eaten even today when there are plentiful supplies of cabbage and cucumbers most of the year.

In pickling, salt stops the action of undesirable micro-organisms and allows the development of lactic acid which gives pickles their distinctive sour taste, and also aids digestion. There are many recipes, each different, so if you want to have a go at pickling your own vegetables, be prepared to experiment.

You will find a number of pickled products in wholefood and healthfood shops, but one of the very best is the umeboshi plum. These have, for centuries, been given pride of place in the Japanese diet, and it is only with the interest in macrobiotics that they have become available here. Pickled in a traditional way that takes a whole year, they have a sweet yet salty taste, plus a number of beneficial medicinal properties. Use to add flavour to grain dishes or vegetables, or boil to make a refreshing drink.

See Pickled onions.

PINEAPPLE

Imported from a variety of tropical countries, pineapples are now easy to find in the shops, especially during the winter. They were once used as table decorations at royal banquets and became a symbol of both hospitality and social standing; they can still be seen carved in stone outside manor houses.

Nutrition: Pineapples are rich in vitamin C. When eaten after a meal they are said to help digestion.

Buying/Storing: Though tinned pineapple is a favourite with the British, the delicious acid yet sweet taste of the fresh fruit bears little comparison with the tinned and sweetened variety. A pineapple is ready to eat when it is soft at the opposite end from the leaves, or when the leaves pull out easily. An under-ripe fruit can be kept at room temperature for a few days to ripen. Dried pineapple may be sugar coated.

How to use: Nice eaten just as it is. Try adding pineapple cubes to a beetroot salad, or to cream cheese; or thread them onto kebabs with vegetables and cheese. Pineapple upside-down cake is a traditional way to bake with fruit, but try crushed pineapple in biscuits too, maybe with some walnut pieces. Fresh pineapple sorbet is delicious, as is pineapple jelly.

PINEAPPLE FRITTERS

1 small pineapple (or tin of pineapple slices in unsweetened juice)
approx. 115g/4oz/³/₄ cup gram flour
1 teaspoon baking powder
pineapple or apple juice
oil to cook

Peel the pineapple and cut into slices. If using tinned pineapple, drain the liquid but reserve it. Dip the rings into the flour to coat very lightly and set aside.

Mix the remaining flour with the baking powder. Add just enough juice (or reserved liquid) to the flour to make a smooth batter, beating it well. It should be thick enough to coat a spoon.

Heat the oil. Dip the pineapple rings in the batter, then drop them into the oil straight away. Cook over a medium heat until they are crisp and golden, turning so that both sides are cooked. This should take no longer than 5 minutes. Drain well and serve hot.

See also Tropical fruit salad.

PINE NUTS

A tiny white oily nut that is taken from the cone of certain species of pine trees. Most of those on sale in Britain are imported from Italy. As the nuts are hard to remove from the tough casing, they are expensive, but worth it for the distinctive taste and texture they add to dishes, even when used in small amounts.

Nutrition: They are a good source of protein.

How to use: Excellent with Middle Eastern dishes, especially those containing aubergines and tomatoes. Use in sweet and sour sauces and rice stuffings, and to make Italian pesto sauce. Sprinkle a few lightly-roasted pine nuts over fruit salads or use them to make sweets.

PESTO SAUCE

1-2 cloves garlic, peeled and chopped
1 good tablespoon fresh basil leaves
salt to taste
115g/4oz/1 cup grated Parmesan cheese
115g/4oz/1 cup pine nuts
1 tablespoon lemon juice
140ml/¹/₄ pint/2/3rd cup olive oil

Use a mortar and pestle to grind together the garlic, basil and salt so that you have a smooth paste. Gradually add the cheese and pine nuts, stir in the lemon juice. The mixture should be thick and smooth. Now add the olive oil, drop by drop, stirring well, so that the sauce is the consistency of a thin cream. Adjust seasoning to taste.
Serve with pasta, or stir into a vegetable soup. Also makes an unusual alternative to sour cream as a filling for jacket potatoes.

PINTO BEANS

These look very much like borlotti beans, are also speckled, but are more of a beige colour. Pinto beans have been cultivated for centuries by the native peoples of North and South America, and are still grown mostly in those continents. They are available here as dried beans. When cooked they turn pink.

How to use: Allow 45 minutes-1 hour to cook. Especially good in loaves and rissoles, also casseroles and stews. Can be added to salads for a change.

MEAL-IN-A-SALAD

115g/4oz/2/3rd cup pinto beans, cooked and drained
225g/¹/₂ lb potatoes, cooked and drained
4 tomatoes, quartered
115g/4oz/2 cups bean sprouts
115g/4oz/1 cup hard cheese, cubed
mayonnaise
seasoning to taste
crisp green lettuce
4 hardboiled eggs, halved
watercress

In a large bowl mix together the beans, potatoes, tomatoes, bean sprouts and cheese. Carefully stir in just enough mayonnaise to moisten everything – most of these ingredients are fragile, so do be gentle. Season generously.
Line a salad bowl with coarsely shredded lettuce, spoon the mixture into the centre. Make a pattern around the edge with the halved eggs and garnish with watercress.
Serve at once.

PISTACHIOS

A small green nut that comes originally from a tree native to Syria, though it is now grown in Turkey, Israel, Greece and Italy, and on a large scale in California and Texas. Pistachios are not widely used in Britain because of their high price, though they are becoming more popular.

Buying/Storing: Pistachios can be purchased both shelled and unshelled. If they are not protected by their shells they should be stored in a dark, airtight container and used as soon as possible.

How to use: Pistachios combine well with sweet ingredients and are used traditionally in such foods as halva, Turkish delight, and pistachio ice cream. Sprinkle them over any fruit salad or sorbet, or add honey and pistachios to low-fat ricotta cheese and top with grated chocolate for a quick dessert. Pistachios are superb in a special-occasion nut roast. Roasted salted pistachios make a good accompaniment for drinks.

CREAMY POTATO SOUP WITH PISTACHIOS

1 tablespoon oil
1 leek, cleaned and chopped
455g/1 lb potatoes, peeled and cubed
850ml/1 1/2 pints/3 3/4 cups vegetable stock
bouquet garni
285ml/1/2 pint/1 1/3rd cups soya milk
seasoning to taste
55g/2oz/1/2 cup pistachios, chopped
chives to garnish

Heat the oil in a large saucepan and fry the leek for 5 minutes. Add the potatoes, vegetable stock and bouquet garni. Bring to the boil, then cover the pan and simmer for about 30 minutes, or until the potatoes are cooked. Mash, sieve or purée the potatoes and leeks in a blender, and return to a clean saucepan with the stock in which they were cooked and the milk. Season to taste. Reheat gently.
Pour the soup into 4 bowls and sprinkle with nuts and chives. Serve at once.

Note: Though excellent made with soya milk (and therefore suitable for vegans), this soup can of course be made with cow's milk.

PLANTAINS
See **Bananas**

PLUMS

These are grown in Britain in a number of shapes and colours – look out for red, golden and purple ones. Many plums are imported too. They vary in sweetness, some being good to eat as they are, others better for cooking.

Damsons are the smallest sharpest plum. Greengages, as their name implies, are a kind of green plum, and can be sweet or rather sour.

Buying/Storing: When buying for eating raw avoid any fruit that is too hard, has a dull colour or has been damaged. Fruit for cooking can be under-ripe, in which case it should be left for a day or two (or, if you wish to use it straight away, add more sugar). All types of plums are best consumed fairly quickly once ripe, though they can be kept in a cool place for a few days.

How to use: Usually cooked and used in pies, crumbles, flans and other dessert dishes. They make excellent jams. A plum sauce can be made to serve with stir-fried vegetables Chinese-style. Try a sweet chilled plum soup.

SPICY PLUM CRUMBLE

455g/1 lb fresh plums, washed
approx. 55g/2oz/1/3rd cup raw cane sugar
approx. 200ml/1/3rd pint/^{3}/₄ cup water

crumble:
55g/2oz/^{1}/₂ cup wholemeal flour
85g/3oz/^{1}/₂ cup raw cane sugar
good pinch of salt
^{1}/₄ teaspoon nutmeg
^{1}/₄ teaspoon cinnamon
55g/2oz/^{1}/₄ cup margarine
55g/2oz/^{1}/₂ cup brazil nuts, chopped

Cook the plums with a little sugar and water, keeping the saucepan covered and cooking gently until just tender. Adjust sweetening as necessary.
Meanwhile combine the flour, sugar, salt and spices. Use fingers to rub in the margarine to make a mixture like breadcrumbs. Stir in the nuts.
Transfer the cooked fruit to a shallow ovenproof dish, sprinkle with the crumble mixture. Bake at 190°C/375°F (Gas Mark 5) for about 30 minutes, or until crisp and golden.

▨▨▨▨▨▨ POMEGRANATES ▨▨▨▨▨▨

Looking rather like a pinky-yellow apple with a tufted calyx, pomegranates are one of the few exotic fruits that have been imported to Britain for many years, though they are still not widely used. The leathery skin covers an inner skin that goes right through the fruit, dividing it into many seed-filled compartments. The seeds can be eaten but are bitter (in India they are dried and used as a spice). Originating in Iran, pomegranates are now grown in many parts of the world, but most imports come from Spain.

Buying/Storing: Look for firm undamaged fruits with a good blush. You can keep them in the fridge for up to a week.

How to use: The flavour of the flesh is best appreciated if the fruit is eaten raw. To do this, cut and peel away the skin and inner skin with a sharp knife. The juice is used to flavour fruit salads, sorbets, tropical drinks. To obtain the juice warm the fruit then roll it gently to soften, then make a hole in the skin and squeeze gently.

POMELOS

This, the largest of all citrus fruits – it can measure up to 300mm (12 inches) across – originated in Malaysia and Thailand where it is still widely grown. It is a rainforest fruit, and hopefully more imports will be coming from such areas, bringing money to the local people whilst preserving the trees. A very thick green to yellow skin covers flesh that looks and tastes like the flesh of grapefruit, though it is less bitter. Some pomelos are seedless.

Buying/Storing: Avoid any pomelos that have been damaged, or have soft patches. If kept in a cool dry place they should stay fresh for several weeks.

How to use: The thick peel is ideal for candying. Use the flesh much as you would grapefruit. Good with avocado in a salad, or make it into marmalade.

POPCORN
See **Maize**

POPPY SEEDS

These tiny blue seeds are taken from the opium poppy, which is indigenous to some parts of the Mediterranean and to Asia. However, they are best known in the cuisine of such countries as Hungary and Poland. Though much of the plant has narcotic properties, the seeds are drug-free. They have a mild and nutty taste.

How to use: Sprinkle over bread, rolls and cakes. Add to cottage cheese or other soft cheeses, or to mashed potatoes. Nice in salad dressings. Try too with pasta when served with a creamy sauce.

SWISS CHEESE AND POPPY SEED SCONES

225g/^{1}/$_2$ lb/2 cups self-raising wholemeal flour
good pinch of salt
30g/1oz/2^1/$_2$ tablespoons margarine
55g/2oz/^{1}/$_2$ cup Swiss cheese, grated

1 good tablespoon poppy seeds
approx. 200ml/1/3rd pint/³/₄ cup milk or sour cream
extra cheese and poppy seeds to top

Sift together the flour and salt, then use fingertips to rub the fat into the flour. Add the cheese and poppy seeds, and enough milk or sour cream to form a stiff dough.
Turn the dough onto a lightly-floured board, knead briefly, then roll out to a thickness of about 12mm (¹/₂ inch) and cut into small rounds.
Place these on a greased baking sheet, sprinkle with some more poppy seeds and cheese, and bake at 220°C/425°F (Gas Mark 7) for 10 to 15 minutes, or until just firming up.

See also Sesame crackers.

POTATOES

Originally grown in South America, potatoes did not reach Europe until the 16th century, and only really became popular in the 19th. By then they were a staple food in Ireland, and much used throughout Europe.

Nutrition: They contribute about a third of the vitamin C in the diets of people who eat little fruit or fresh vegetables other than potatoes. (Though they are, in fact, quite low in vitamin C, people do eat a lot of them!) They also contain some protein – especially new potatoes – and at 80 calories per 100g are low in calories. If you can find organic potatoes in the shops (or have somewhere to grow your own), do snatch them up. They will be more nutritious, and also free from the many chemicals that are now used to both grow and preserve commercially-produced crops. Potato flour is especially useful for anyone with an allergy to gluten.

Buying/Storing: New potatoes should feel slightly damp, and the skins should rub off easily. Old potatoes should be firm and free from mould or bruising. The best part of potatoes is their skin and just beneath it, so try to eat them unpeeled (having checked first that the skins have not been sprayed to stop the potatoes sprouting). Store potatoes in a cool, dark, dry place, and they will keep for a long time.

How to use: Cook new potatoes lightly and serve with mint or garlic; make into a potato salad. Add mashed potatoes to soups to thicken them or make them into curries, flans and stews. Contrary to what is believed, chips can be a healthy food, providing they are cooked in a very hot good quality vegetable oil for the minimum time, and drained well. Make bubble and squeak, or shepherd's pie with a vegetable or lentil base. Jacket potato served with a choice of toppings is one of the quickest and easiest meals to prepare.

POTATO SNACK

2 large potatoes
salt – optional

Scrub the potatoes well, then pat them dry. Cut into thin lengthwise strips about an inch wide.
Arrange these on lightly-greased baking trays. Bake in a very hot oven –
240°C/475°F (Gas Mark 9) for just 3 to 5 minutes, or until puffed up and golden.
Serve hot sprinkled – if liked – with salt.

See also Minestrone alla Milanese, Vegetable stew for couscous, Creamy potato
soup with pistachios, Watercress and potato soufflés, Meal-in-a-salad.

PRESERVING METHODS, COMMERCIAL

See also **Additives, Irradiation**

Apart from using chemical additives, there are other ways in which manufacturers preserve their foods so that they stay fresh whilst being transported across the country – or across the world. Of the three most widely used, probably freezing is the best.

Food frozen shortly after it has been picked may well contain more nutrients than some of the 'fresh' foods found at the greengrocers, weary specimens that would be way past their sell-by date, should they have to show one.

It may also, however, contain other things too. Frozen peas, which account for some 25% of all frozen food sales in Britain, can contain sugar, colouring, even artificial mint flavouring. The way to avoid such foods is to read the pack. And if you cannot see what you need to know, ask. Or write to the manufacturer. It is only when the public insists on better quality foods that manufacturers are going to supply them.

Having said that, there are a growing number of frozen foods that are free from additives, and these are undoubtedly useful for those occasions when no fresh alternative is available.

Another way in which manufacturers preserve foods is to seal them into tins. This does seem to be a very hygienic way, and most certainly tinned foods will last forever. Where they fall down is on their vitamin and mineral content. The heat process used destroys most if not all of them – it also does terrible things to the flavour! Then there is the problem of disposing of the tin, one that is a long way from being resolved. All in all, it might well be wisest to throw away your tin opener.

Dried foods can be good or bad. Some contain a reasonable amount of nutrients, have been naturally dried, are free from colouring and flavouring, and it is certainly worth keeping some of these tucked in a cupboard for emergencies. Others contain little more nourishment than the box in which they are packed. As the manufacturers of such products are obliged by law to list ingredients, read them. If you don't know what half of them are, you do probably best to forget it. Your local wholefood and healthfood stores will probably stock a variety of the better dried foods.

▨▨▨▨▨ PRESERVING METHODS ▨▨▨▨▨ FOR HOME USE

Preserving food at home used to be a matter of life and death. With the growth of the food industry, and the implied promise that there would always be enough, such skills faded away.

If, however, you grow your own fruits and vegetables, you will know that there are inevitably gaps between the gluts. And if you have the time to preserve some of your surpluses, you will be able to enjoy homegrown produce throughout the year. They should never, of course, be used as an alternative to eating the food fresh – fresh foods are live whereas preserved foods, even those preserved by natural methods, will have lost at least some of their nutrients and taste.

There are many books giving detailed advice on preserving methods, but just so that you are aware of your options, here are a few simple facts about the most popular methods.

Freezing For this you obviously need a freezer, the bigger the better. Freezing is an excellent way to preserve food as nothing need be added. Only freeze good quality produce, and do so as soon as possible after picking. Some items may need to be blanched and then dropped at once into iced water (even quick blanching can destroy a lot of vitamin C, so only do this if absolutely necessary). Fruits are best frozen in a sweetened juice to prevent the growth of enzymes; over-ripe fruit can be puréed and then frozen. Pack in small quantities or you may have to defrost a large amount when you only want enough for one or two portions.

Drying One of the oldest methods of preservation – best suited, of course, to countries that have a lot of sunshine. Still, you may be able to dry some fruits outside. Others can be dried in an airing cupboard or cool oven.

Bottling This is a more complicated procedure that also requires equipment such as a preserving pan and jars, a rack and a thermometer. It involves filling sterilised jars with either fruit or vegetables, sealing them, and lowering them into water and boiling them for a certain time.

Pickling Pickles are an acquired taste, and making them involves the use of salt and spices, which do not agree with everyone. However, pickling is a relatively easy thing to do, and is a useful way to use up small amounts of fruits and vegetables.

PRESSURE COOKERS
See **Utensils, cooking**

PROTEIN

One of the main things that worries people about the idea of giving up flesh foods is that they are going to run short of protein. Nothing could be more wrong. Nutritionalists and doctors alike stress that we actually need far less protein than used to be thought to stay healthy. The figure quoted for adults is 35g a day. Most of us – vegetarians included – consume at least twice that amount, and often substantially more.

Until recently, two-thirds of the protein eaten in Britain came from animals and one-third from plants. That is now changing.

All protein foods contain amino acids, but in general only animal proteins contain the eight essential amino acids without which our bodies cannot make the others we need. Soya beans are a complete protein but most plant foods contain only some of the essential amino acids and are therefore considered to be incomplete. However, by combining foods from different plants, or plant foods with other non-meat animal proteins, you can often actually increase the protein content so that the whole is greater than the sum of the parts!

What this means is that you will be getting more protein from sources which make better ecological sense, are more wholesome, put less strain on your digestive system, and cost nothing like as much as the so-called complete proteins.

Some examples of protein mixes to try:

> Muesli (grains, seeds, maybe milk)
> Rice and curried lentils (grain, pulse)
> Minestrone (grain, pulse)
> Beans on toast (grain, pulse)
> Gado-gado (nuts, grain)
> Hummus and pita bread (grain, pulse)
> Cheese sandwich (grain, milk)

PRUNES

One of the most widely-used dried fruits, prunes are made from specially-grown plums. Most of the prunes sold in Britain come from the USA, where they are dried with blasts of hot air (though Californian prunes may be sun-dried). The fruits are sold whole, usually with the stone inside.

Nutrition: Prunes contain substantial amounts of vitamin A and iron.

Though their laxative properties are well-known, fewer people are aware of the fact that prunes – with only 35 calories per ounce – have only half the calories of most dried fruits, which makes them an excellent choice for anyone watching their weight. Try to avoid those with extra shiny skins; they may well have been treated with potassium sorbate.

How to use: Add prunes to a salad of Chinese leaves, cucumber and tomato. Make a purée of cooked prunes and stir into natural yogurt. Prune juice is delicious, especially with a little lemon or orange juice added. Soak prunes in diluted molasses and serve with yogurt or cream. Stuff lightly-cooked (or well-soaked) prunes for a party.

PRUNE FLAPJACKS

115g/4oz/¹/₂ cup margarine
85g/3oz/¹/₂ cup raw cane sugar
3 tablespoons honey or golden syrup
225g/¹/₂ lb/2 cups rolled oats
pinch of salt
4 large prunes, soaked overnight

Melt the margarine in a saucepan. Stir in the sugar and honey and mix well. Add the oats and salt.

Remove the stones from the prunes and chop the flesh. Add this to the oat mixture, distributing it evenly.

Spoon onto a greased and floured swiss roll tin. Press down gently, making sure it is as even as possible. Bake at 170°C/325°F (Gas Mark 3) for 35-40 minutes, or until cooked.

Cut into bars but leave to cool in the tin briefly. Transfer to a wire rack to get completely cold before storing in an airtight container.

See also Dried fruit compôte.

PULSES
See also **individual varieties**

Pulses is the collective name for the dried seeds of certain pod-bearing plants – usually peas, beans and lentils. Cheap and nourishing, pulses have long been a staple food for millions of people. Broad beans can be traced back to the Bronze Age; chick peas grew in Egypt in the time of the Pharaohs. In Britain, in the Middle Ages, beans were ground to a powder and mixed with wheat, rye or barley to make a kind of bread. For many people they are still a very important food, though in the more affluent West they are vastly underrated. They are not only highly nutritious, very versatile and easy to store; they also cost considerably less than most foods because they are easy to grow. Indeed, it may well be their low price that has resulted in the mistaken belief that they are inferior and dull.

Nutrition: Exact nutritional breakdowns vary from one pulse to another, depending on where it was grown and how old it is. In general though, all pulses are a good source of protein, though only soya beans are a complete protein. Serving pulses with cereals, nuts or dairy products does, however, make up any deficiencies, so the meal as a whole is perfectly balanced. Pulses also contain good amounts of iron and mineral salts, plus the B vitamins riboflavin and niacin. They are low in fat, high in dietary fibre, and on average contain approximately 25 calories per ounce when cooked.

Buying/Storing: Even though pulses will keep indefinitely if stored in a sealed container in a cool place, it is a good idea to buy them from a retailer who has a fast turnover, and aim to use them within a reasonable time. Younger pulses cook in less time, and retain more goodness. Because cooking beans takes a long time, make a habit of preparing more than you need, and keeping the extra to use at a later date. They will last for up to a week in the fridge, several months in the freezer. Soak beans overnight, or bring them to the boil, simmer briefly, and set aside for an hour. All beans should be fast-boiled for 10 minutes first, then simmered until tender, which can take anything from 1 to 3 hours. When cooking beans, do not add salt until the end, as this slows down the cooking process. Gram flours are widely used in India and are usually made from soya or mung beans, or split peas.

How to use: See individual varieties.

PUMPKINS
See also **Pumpkin seeds**

Though much revered in China – where they are called 'Emperor of the Garden' – these large winter squashes with their bright orange flesh actually originated in North America, where they can grow to huge sizes. They grow well in Britain too, but not to such monster sizes; it is surprising to find one that weighs much above 7 kilos (15 lb). They are becoming better known as we make more of a celebration of Halloween, the autumn festival at which hollowed out pumpkin shells are cut into faces and lit from inside with candles. However, in Britain pumpkin is still not very popular as a food.

Nutrition: As members of the same family as marrows, they also have a high water content – about 95%. This means that a pumpkin has only a fifth of the calories of potatoes, yet the firm, sweet orange flesh can be made into a variety of filling dishes. Pumpkins are also a good source of carotene and calcium.

Buying/Storing: Because of their size, they are often sold in ready-cut sections. When buying pumpkin like this, check that it has only recently been cut, and that the flesh looks firm and non-fibrous. Cut pumpkin should be used as soon as possible, though if you do not need it for a day or two you can cook it to a purée, then keep it in the fridge, or even freeze it. When buying whole pumpkins check that the skin is a good colour and has not been damaged. Stored in a cool dry place they should keep for weeks.

How to use: Peel and de-seed pumpkin before cooking. The best known way to eat pumpkin is in the sweet, spicy pie that is traditionally served in America at Thanksgiving. Puréed pumpkin can also be mixed with onion, pepper, nuts and cheese to make a savoury pie. Cream of pumpkin soup can be flavoured as you like (it has a bland taste so needs a pinch of chilli, some herbs or maybe curry powder to liven it up). Slices of pumpkin can be baked or fried and served as a vegetable. Cubed pumpkin can be added to stews, or served in a cheese sauce or tomato sauce.

PECAN PUMPKIN PIE

pastry:
55g/2oz/^{1}/$_4$ cup butter or margarine
45g/1^1/$_2$oz/just under ^{1}/$_4$ cup vegetable suet
200g/7oz/1^3/$_4$ cups wholemeal flour

filling:
340g/^{3}/$_4$ lb pumpkin, cooked and puréed
115g/4oz/2/3rd cup raw cane sugar
2 eggs, beaten or equivalent egg substitute
^{1}/$_2$ teaspoon ground ginger
1 teaspoon ground cinnamon
^{1}/$_4$ teaspoon ground cloves
55g/2oz/^{1}/$_2$ cup pecan nuts, coarsely chopped
55g/2oz/1/3rd cup raw cane sugar

Rub the two fats into the flour to make a breadcrumb-like mixture. Add a few spoonsful of cold water and mix well to make a soft dough. Wrap in a polythene bag and leave in the fridge for 30 minutes.

In a bowl mix together the pumpkin purée, sugar, eggs or egg substitute and spices. Roll out the pastry and use to line a medium flan ring standing on a baking tray. Pour the pumpkin mixture into the flan. Bake in an oven already heated to 220°C/425°F (Gas Mark 7) for 15 minutes. Lower the heat to 180°C/350°F (Gas Mark 4). Sprinkle the flan with the nuts and sugar and cook for 30 minutes more, or until the filling is set. Eat warm or cold.

See also Black bean and pumpkin stew.

######## PUMPKIN SEEDS ########

These flat green seeds are taken from the inside of pumpkin gourds. In America pumpkin crops are grown specially for this purpose – they have even bred a shell-less variety to make it easier to reach the seeds. If you are eating fresh pumpkin, save the seeds, which should be clean and dry, then grill or cook them in a dry pan until they pop. Getting the seeds out is a fiddly job but fun – and they taste wonderful.

Nutrition: Pumpkin seeds are rich in iron and B vitamins, and are composed of about 30% protein.

How to use: Add to salads, granola, and muesli. Sprinkle over savoury or sweet crumbles, or over vegetables. Dry-roast to give them extra flavour.

THREE SEED NIBBLE

140g/5oz/1 cup pumpkin seeds
140g/5oz/1 cup sunflower seeds
soy sauce
140g/5oz/1 cup sesame seeds

Mix together the pumpkin and sunflower seeds, then sprinkle with just enough soy sauce to moisten, making sure it is evenly distributed. Spread the mixture across a heatproof plate or shallow tray and put under a hot grill. Cook for about 5 minutes, stirring frequently, then add the sesame seeds. Continue cooking, still stirring, until the seeds are browned and the sauce had dried to make a coating. (If the pumpkin seeds explode too energetically, lower the heat slightly.)

Leave to cool, then store in an airtight jar. Nice as a nibble, but also convenient as a topping for rice and vegetable dishes, or any kind of stir-fries.

▦▦▦▦▦ QUINCES ▦▦▦▦▦

From a tree that is a member of the rose family, quinces are small hard fruits that have a sweet and delicious taste. Imported quinces are available late winter to early summer, and these can be used in many ways, as they are around the world. Homegrown quinces are available usually in October and November. Closely related are japonicas or Japanese quinces, which are smaller, with hard gritty yellow flesh that is acid. These cannot be eaten raw, but have a good pectin content which makes them ideal for use in jams and jellies.

Buying/Storing: Quinces are ripe when they are yellow. If purchasing them under-ripe store them in a cool airy place, making sure they do not touch each other. You can also ripen them on a sunny window sill.

How to use: Imported quinces can be used to make a sweet paste. Poach them in syrup. Add them to stewed or baked fruit (blanche and freeze a few slices for use in this way when fresh quinces are no longer available). In North Africa they are stuffed with cinnamon-spiced lentils. Brush cut quinces with lemon to stop them discolouring.

JAPONICA JELLY

1 kilo/2 lbs japonicas
juice of 1 lemon
water
raw cane sugar

Wash and halve the japonicas, put them into a saucepan with enough water to cover, and cook gently until they are soft. Check the water every now and again so that they do not dry out, and mash the fruit at the same time.
Transfer the fruit to a jelly bag, suspend over a bowl, and leave to drain overnight. Measure the juice and transfer it to a preserving pan, adding 455g/1 lb/2$^{1}/_{2}$ cups sugar for every 570ml/1 pint/2$^{1}/_{2}$ cups juice. Add the lemon juice. Boil the mixture until it begins to set, use a spoon to skim the top. Pour into clean, warmed jars and cover with waxed paper before sealing.
A lovely tangy jelly for spreading. Also goes well with cheese.

QUINOA

Though most people are unfamiliar with this tiny golden grain, quinoa has been in existence since 3,000 BC. It comes from the South American Andes, one of the highest regions of the world, where it has been and still is a staple for the native populations. Along with potatoes it was the basic food of the ancient Incas. It grows on deep-pink coloured stalks on a plant that can reach 1$^{1}/_{2}$ metres (5 feet) in height. The seeds, which are highly coloured by nature to repel insects, are stripped of an outer coating. When cooked quinoa is light and fluffy, with a slightly nutty taste; its unusual flecked appearance is due to the germ of the seed spiralling out.

Nutrition: It has a higher protein content than most grains, and is a good source of calcium, phosphorus, the B vitamins and vitamin E. It is also easy to digest.

Buying/Storing: Quinoa comes in dried form and therefore will keep for ages if stored in a cool, dry place.

How to use: Use it in any way you would use other grains – it has a subtle flavour that blends well with most ingredients. As well as serving it as a base for stir-fries and curries, try using it in pilaffs, as a stuffing, added to stews and soups. Makes an unusual breakfast porridge. Use cold in salads, try in combinations with other grains, bake as a creamy milk pudding. Ground to a flour it can be used in baking.

STUFFED PEPPERS

1 large red pepper
2 large green peppers
1 large yellow pepper (or use one colour only)
115g/4oz/¹/₄ cup quinoa, cooked
1 tablespoon vegetable oil
2 spring onions (scallions)
1 large stick celery, finely chopped
55g/2oz/¹/₂ cup almonds, chopped
55g/2oz/1/3rd cup raisins
fresh parsley
seasoning to taste
55g/2oz/¹/₂ cup Cheddar cheese, grated

Cut the peppers lengthwise, remove stems and seeds. Blanch them in boiling water for 2-3 minutes, then drain, rinse in cold water, and drain again. Arrange close together in an ovenproof dish.

Heat the oil and sauté the onions for a few minutes, then add the celery and cook for a few minutes more. Stir in the almonds and cook gently until they begin to colour. Add the cooked quinoa.

Remove from the heat and add raisins, a good amount of chopped parsley, and seasoning to the mixture. Use to fill the pepper halves. Sprinkle with cheese. Bake at 180°C/350°F (Gas Mark 4) for 35-40 minutes or until the peppers are cooked.

RADICCHIO

This attractive red, crinkly vegetable is actually a member of the chicory family, and once grew wild in the north of Italy – though imported crops are now most likely to come from Holland. It is the leaves that are eaten, which – with their pleasantly bitter taste – make an excellent salad ingredient. One of the more expensive vegetables.

Nutrition: A good source of vitamin C and other vitamins, radicchio is also thought to have diuretic qualities.

Buying/Storing: Look out for crisp leaves with a good colour and no sign of damage or browning around the edges. Can be kept for 3 or 4 days in the fridge, but the fresher it is the better it will taste.

How to use: Break off the leaves, wash, pat dry, shred and add to other salad ingredients. Apart from the unusual flavour of radicchio, its bright leaves will make a lovely contrast to the usual greens. Can also be lightly cooked and served as a vegetable. For a special meal try stuffing the leaves.

RADICCHIO SALAD WITH BLUE CHEESE DRESSING

1 small head radicchio
1 small endive
2 heads chicory
1 large yellow pepper
black olives

dressing:
285ml/¹/₂ pint/1¹/₂ cups vinaigrette dressing (oil and lemon)
approx. 55g/2oz/¹/₂ cup blue cheese
drop of cream – optional
walnuts or croûtons – optional

Wash and shred the radicchio and endive leaves coarsely. Chop the chicory into rings, the pepper into strips.
Arrange all the ingredients in a salad bowl, sprinkle with olives.
The dressing is easiest to make if you use a blender. Otherwise, mash the cheese so that it is smooth and whisk it into the vinaigrette dressing. Add more cheese if you prefer a stronger flavour (though a dressing should never be so powerful that it kills the taste of the salad ingredients). Add a drop of cream if you prefer a milder taste, or if you want a more liquid dressing.
Spoon a little of the dressing into the centre of the salad to be mixed in at the table. Any extra can be served in a jug. Walnuts or croûtons can be added for texture contrast.

RADISHES

These small red root vegetables have a crunchy texture, and a peppery taste that comes from the mustard oil they contain. They are thought to stimulate the appetite, aid digestion – and in the 17th century they were also recommended for asthma. Radishes are now available all year round.

Varieties: British radishes are gradually being supplemented by more exotic varieties from abroad, each of which has a slightly different appearance, though all have the distinctive peppery taste.

Buying/Storing: They should be firm, smooth, free from cuts or other damage. Buy radishes with their leaves attached if possible, and do not remove these until you are ready to serve them. Store in a cool place and use within 3 to 4 days.

How to use: Radishes are mostly served in salads. Boil older ones and serve them topped with butter or parsley sauce. Radishes are also popular as a garnish.

RADISH 'ROSES'

Clean and pat dry however many radishes you need, choosing those that are well shaped and even-sized. Use a sharp knife to cut a star shape across the top of each one. Drop them into a bowl of iced water and leave for half an hour or until the flesh curls back to make a 'rose'. Use them to add colour and interest to salads or patés, or other savoury dishes.

RAISING AGENTS

These are either methods or ingredients that are used to give both sweet and savoury dishes lighter textures. The most obvious examples of this are whisking egg whites to make a soufflé or mousse (the yolks contain fat and therefore are not included), or beating a batter to make a Yorkshire pudding or pancakes. In fact, the process of combining fat with flour (either rubbing in or blending) helps lighten cakes too, as does sieving the flour before you begin. Flaky pastry gets its lightness from the repeated folding and rolling that traps air between the layers.

Certain cakes, however, need stronger measures if they are to be as light and soft in texture as they should. It is when cooking these that such ingredients as bicarbonate of soda, cream of tartar and baking powder are useful. What they do is expel a gas when heated, and as the gluten in wheat flour is very stretchy it expands, so opening out the texture of the cake.

Bicarbonate of soda can be used on its own. It does, however, have a strong flavour and will colour the flour, so is best used in such recipes as gingerbread when such effects are covered by the spiciness of the cake. When bicarbonate of soda is used with cream of tartar, however, the effect is much the same yet there is no residue taste and the colour is not affected. Baking powder is a commercially-prepared combination of the two, with something like rice flour added to absorb moisture and therefore prevent the powder going lumpy. There is a standard strength so that, once you know how much you need to get a desired effect, you can be sure of success time and again.

Though baking powder is a processed product that offers no nutrients, it is rarely used in large amounts. As its effects cannot be obtained in any other way, it seems illogical to stop its use completely unless, of course, you are one of those rare people who finds it affects them adversely.

See Fruit and nut bran muffins, Lemon honey squares, Pineapple fritters, Buttermilk muffins, Apple oatmeal biscuits.

RAISINS

These are very popular and widely-used. Large and sweet, chewy in texture, they are made from various varieties of grapes, the best coming from muscat grapes. Raisins are produced for export in the eastern Mediterranean, Australia, South Africa and the USA.

Nutrition: They are a good source of calcium, phosphorus, potassium, and some contain vitamin B6 and iron.

Buying/Storing: Buy from a shop that has a fast turnover, and use reasonably quickly although raisins will keep well enough if stored in a dry place. Try to avoid those that have been coated in oil to make them shine (or remember to wash them before using).

How to use: Raisins are one of the most versatile of dried fruits, and can be added to many dishes as well as eaten raw. Try them in curry sauces, as part of a stuffing mixture for vegetables such as peppers or aubergine, and they go well with cheeses. Also nice with root vegetables as they both sweeten and moisten. A few spoonsful of raisins soaked in fruit juice, with wheatgerm and yogurt added, make a quick and nutritious breakfast.

BROWN RICE PUDDING

225g/¹/₂ lb/1 cup brown rice, preferably short grain
570ml/1 pint/2¹/₂ cups milk
55g/2oz/1/3rd cup raw cane sugar
15g/¹/₂oz/1 good tablespoon butter or margarine
¹/₂ teaspoon ground cardamom
¹/₂ teaspoon ground nutmeg
¹/₂ teaspoon ground cinnamon
55g/2oz/1/3rd cup raisins

Cook the rice in a covered pan of boiling water for 10 minutes. Drain well. Heat the milk gently, add the rice, reduce heat and cover. Cook for a further 20 minutes. Transfer the rice and any remaining liquid to a lightly-greased ovenproof dish. Stir in the sugar, fat, spices and raisins. Bake uncovered at 180°C/350°F (Gas Mark 4) for about 15 minutes by which time most of the milk should have been absorbed, and a skin should be forming on top. Serve hot.

See also Buttermilk muffins, Red and white slaw.

RAPESEED
See **Oils**

RASPBERRIES
See **Berries**

REDCURRANTS
See **Currants**

RENNET
See **Cheese**

RHUBARB

Rhubarb has been grown in Britain for centuries, but for a long time people were nervous of eating it and it was valued for the appearance of its large leaves and the herbal qualities of its roots rather than as a fruit. Queen Victoria, however, liked it so much that two varieties developed during her reign were named in honour of the fact – one after her, the other after her consort, Prince Albert. Even today, though, it is not much used around the world, and is one of our least popular fruits.

Buying/Storing: The early forced rhubarb has the most delicate flavour. Maincrop rhubarb needs more cooking – and usually more sweetening too. Stems should be bought or picked when firm and easy to snap. Fresh looking leaves are a good sign too (though discard these – they contain oxalic acid and are poisonous). Rhubarb can be kept in the bottom of the fridge for a few days. This is one of the few fruits that freezes well, so an alternative idea is to cook and freeze it for later use.

How to use: Rhubarb is not usually eaten raw. Cook chopped rhubarb until soft but still holding its shape. You will need a good amount of sugar or honey – sweeten according to your taste. Use the fruit in a crumble or pie. Can also be used to make an unusual marmalade, for chutneys and jams and – of course – rhubarb wine.

RHUBARB ORANGE CRUMBLE

1 kilo/2 lb rhubarb
juice of 1 orange
grated peel of 1/2 an orange
approx. 115g/4oz/2/3rd cup raw cane sugar
115g/4oz wholemeal oat crunch biscuits
85g/3oz/3/4 cup wholemeal flour
85g/3oz/1/3rd cup margarine or butter
85g/3oz/1/2 cup raw cane sugar
1/2 teaspoon ground ginger

Wash the rhubarb, cut into chunks, place in an ovenproof dish. Pour on the orange juice, sprinkle with peel and sugar.
Use a rolling pin to crush the oat crunch biscuits. Mix the crumbs with the flour and

use your fingertips to rub in the fat. Add sugar and ginger. Sprinkle the crumble
mixture over the rhubarb, pressing it down lightly.
Bake at 180°C/350°F (Gas Mark 4) for 30-40 minutes, or until golden crisp on top.
Serve hot. Good with cream, yogurt, concentrated soya milk, or try it with tahini
custard.

RICE

Probably one of the most widely used of all the grains, rice has been a staple
in Asia, China, Africa, South America, Spain and Italy, for thousands of
years. It is now, however, America that is the largest exporter. This small
pale grain grows especially well in a hot wet climate, even on swamp land.
The seeds of the harvested grass are dried, the outer husk (which is
inedible) and bran removed, then – for white rice – the second husk is
removed. This second process means that many of the nutrients are also
removed and the grain that is left consists mostly of starch, which is why
unpolished (sometimes called brown) rice is nutritionally preferable.

Varieties: Choose from many different long and short grain rices. Long
grain tends to be served with savoury dishes, short grain (having a softer,
stickier texture) being reserved for sweet dishes. Look out also for the rare
and expensive wild rice which is often sold blended with long grain white
rice, and has a much stronger taste than most. Rice flour can be purchased
in many shops now, as can rice flakes and rice bran.

Nutrition: Compared with other grains, rice is very low in fibre, brown
rice containing about 1.5%, white rice about 0.5%. Rice flakes contain
fewer nutrients than the whole grain, but are quicker to use. Rice flour is
rich in B vitamins. Wild rice has been eaten by native Americans for
centuries, and was especially nutritious – it is now being grown commercially with the aid of chemicals, which may make it cheaper and more
widely available, but decreases its food value too.

How to use: Serve the whole grain as a base for Indian and Chinese food,
use it to make risottos, pilaffs and rice loaves. Stuff balls of rice with cubes
of cheese and fry them. Use rice to make sweet puddings. Substitute a little
rice flour for wheat when making biscuits – the result will be a crunchier
texture. Rice flakes can be added to soups and stews to thicken them.

CHEESE RICE BALLS

170g/6oz/³/₄ cup brown rice, cooked until soft
seasoning to taste
2 eggs, lightly beaten
115g/4oz/¹/₂ cup mozzarella cheese, cubed
fine wholemeal breadcrumbs
oil for frying

Make sure the rice is well drained. Season and add the eggs, mixing well. Put a tablespoon of the rice into the palm of your hand, top it with a cube of cheese, and mould the rice around to form a ball with the cheese in the centre. Roll carefully in the breadcrumbs, then deep-fry in hot oil, turning frequently, until the outsides are crisp and brown, by which time the cheese inside should be creamy. Drain and serve while hot.

Note: Rice balls can be made in much the same way without the cheese. Instead, add finely chopped raw or cooked vegetables to the rice, maybe with some chopped nuts or seeds. Flavour with soy sauce or tahini.

See also Almond biscuits, Apricot rice, Wild rice and macadamia stuffing, Hoppin' John, Coconut vegetable rice, Minestrone alla Milanese, Butter shortbread, Brown rice pudding.

ROOT VEGETABLES
See also **individual varieties**

A number of the vegetables described elsewhere are root vegetables, but there are some that are traditionally linked together as winter roots, and are used in combination in stews, hotpots and soups. These include carrots, parsnips, swedes and turnips. A more recent addition to this list is salsify, which looks like a small parsnip and is also called 'oyster plant', because of its unusual taste. All these vegetables, except for carrots, are best and cheapest during the winter.

Nutrition: All root vegetables offer some vitamins, but this will vary with each variety. Carrots are rich in vitamin A. They are also all especially good sources of dietary fibre.

Buying/Storing: Choose firm, undamaged vegetables, and look out for worm holes. The colour should be good. Root vegetables will keep for some time if stored in a cool, dry, well-ventilated place.

How to use: See individual varieties. Or use together in vegetable stews.

ROSEMARY

A bushy garden shrub with spiky leaves which can grow up to 2 metres (6 feet) tall. Although it can be found all over Britain, most of the rosemary on sale is imported. Very fragrant, with a fresh bitter-sweet taste. Rosemary is also used as a powerful medicine that acts on the heart and blood vessels.

How to use: Use fresh or dried leaves, crumbled or finely chopped. Add them to vegetable casseroles and soups – especially good with peas and potatoes. Try rosemary with pastry, dumplings, scones and biscuits for a change. It is traditionally used with rich meat dishes. Instead of adding the leaves loose, you can tie them in a muslin bag and remove them before serving the dish – the flavour will be more subtle and you will not have the sharp bitty texture to contend with. Rosemary is also used in bouquet garni, but when mixing it with other herbs yourself take care that it doesn't overpower them.

BRAN AND ROSEMARY BISCUITS

170g/6oz/1¹/₂ cups wholemeal flour
170g/2oz/¹/₂ cup bran
115g/4oz/1 cup margarine or butter
cold water to mix
1-2 tablespoons dried rosemary, crushed
55g/2oz/1/3rd cup sunflower seeds

Sift together the flour and bran, then use fingertips to rub in the fat to make a crumb-like mixture. Stir in just enough cold water to bind to a dough, knead briefly, then wrap in polythene and set aside in a cool place for 30 minutes. Adjust the liquid if the dough seems too dry and knead to distribute the rosemary and coarsely chopped seeds. Roll out on a floured board and cut into circles.

Arrange on a lightly-greased baking sheet and bake at 180°C/350°F (Gas Mark 4) for 20 minutes, or until crisp and golden. Let the biscuits get completely cold before putting them into an airtight container. Serve them lightly buttered with soup, or topped with nut butter, paté or cottage cheese as a snack.

See also Aduki and leek roll.

ROSEWATER
See **Essences, natural**

RUNNER BEANS
See **Beans, fresh**

RYE

Rye will grow even under the most difficult conditions, and so was grown widely throughout much of Europe. As well as providing a basic food, rye may well have been responsible in the Middle Ages for what were at that time thought to be a series of plagues. This is because rye is subject to attack by a fungus called ergot, which can affect the central nervous system and produce hallucinations and trances. It is now less widely grown than it was, and is only popular in Germany, Scandinavia and Russia, although it is used in the USA to make rye whisky.

Varieties: Whole or kibbled rye are available, though it is easiest to use rye flakes. Even easier is rye flour. Make sure the rye you buy is the whole grain.

How to use: Cook the chewy grains like rice and use as a base for vegetables or bean dishes (you can speed up the cooking process by cracking the grains first with a rolling pin). Or serve cold cooked rye in a salad. Rye can be combined with other grains including barley and wheat berries. Pumpernickel and other black breads are made with rye flour, sometimes combined with other flours such as barley – because rye flour is low in gluten it makes a heavy bread. To use it in other baked foods look out for 'light' rye flour which has had more bran removed. Rye flakes are excellent in soups and vegetable hotpots.

FINNISH FLATBREAD

225g/¹/₂ lb/³/₄ cup rye flour
good pinch of salt
2 teaspoons baking powder
30g/1oz/2 tablespoons raw cane sugar
200ml/1/3rd pint/³/₄ cup milk
30g/1oz/2¹/₂ tablespoons melted butter

Sift together the flour, salt and baking powder. Add the sugar. Stir in the milk and knead briefly to make a smooth dough. Grease a large baking sheet. Use floured hands to shape the dough into a large circle about 12mm (¹/₂ inch) thick, and lay it on a baking sheet. Prick with a fork. Bake at 220°C/425°F (Gas Mark 7) for 10 minutes or until lightly browned. This very heavy traditional type of bread is best eaten whilst fresh. Cut into wedges to serve.

To make a lighter version, replace some of the rye flour with wholemeal.

See also Mixed grain granola.

SAFFLOWER
See **Oils**

SAFFRON

The dried orange stigmas of the crocus flower. As it takes literally thousands of stigmas to make an ounce of saffron, it is not surprising that it is the most expensive spice in the world. Fortunately only a small amount needs to be used to add a delicate flavour, plus of course, that distinctive golden colour. The English town of Saffron Walden took its name from the flower.

Varieties: Saffron can be bought as filaments, or ready ground into powder.

How to use: It is popular in Spanish dishes, also in Indian. Mainly used to add colour to a dish, particularly rice.

SHRIKHAND (SAFFRON YOGURT)

570ml/1 pint/2¹/₂ cups natural yogurt
8 filaments saffron
1 tablespoon rosewater
115g/4oz/1/3rd cup raw cane sugar, powdered in a grinder
good pinch ground nutmeg, preferably fresh
a few chopped pistachio nuts – optional

Put a square of muslin over a sieve, suspend this over a bowl, and pour in the yogurt. Leave for at least an hour, preferably overnight, to allow the whey to drain off.

Soak the saffron strands in the rosewater. Mix the drained yogurt with the sugar, then stir in the saffron flavoured rosewater, stirring continually so that the flavours are well mixed. Chill lightly before serving in individual dishes topped with nutmeg. Chopped pistachio nuts sprinkled on top are delicious.

Goes especially well after a curry meal.

SAGE

A hardy evergreen with broad, flat leaves. When dried these take on an unusual greeny-grey colour. Sage has been grown and used throughout Europe since Roman times, and is valued as an aid to digestion as well as for a flavour that is warm, strong, and a little like eucalyptus.

How to use: Traditionally sage was used with meat dishes, particularly the fatty ones, and as a stuffing for poultry. It can, however, be used with many other ingredients, though do use it sparingly as its powerful flavour can swamp more delicate ones. Try sage with cheese dishes, also with pulses. Mix with cream cheese or cottage cheese and add lemon juice to make a spread. Sage and onion stuffing is delicious with vegetables. If you can get the fresh leaves, chop them and sprinkle over a tomato salad or make herb butter.

PITA PIZZAS

1 tablespoon vegetable oil
1 green pepper, sliced
170g/6oz/3 cups mushrooms
4 wholemeal pita breads
200ml/1/3rd pint/³/₄ cup tomato sauce
approx. ¹/₂ teaspoon dried sage
4 tablespoons cooked sweetcorn
30g/1oz/¹/₄ cup sunflower seeds
a few black olives, chopped
seasoning to taste

Heat the oil and fry the sliced pepper for just a few minutes to soften. Add the mushrooms and cook for a few minutes more.

Spread a spoonful or two of the tomato sauce over each of the pita breads, sprinkle with sage. Divide the pepper and mushroom between the breads, then sprinkle with sweetcorn, sunflower seeds, olives and seasoning.

Bake in the oven at 180°C/350°F (Gas Mark 4) for 10 minutes, or until heated through. Serve at once.

You can, of course, use other vegetables as a topping for these quick and easy 'pizzas'. Add some mashed tofu to the tomato sauce if you like. Or sprinkle grated cheese on top.

SAGO

The sago palm grows in the Philippines and Thailand, and sago flour and pearls are made from its ground bark. These products are especially useful for those wishing to avoid gluten, though as sago flour does not perform in baking in the same way as wheat flour, it may be necessary to experiment.

SALSIFY
See also **Scorzonera**

A little-known winter vegetable that is grown in small quantities in Britain, though most of the salsify you find in the shops will be imported. Look out for long white roots, often tied in bunches. It has a taste reminiscent of oysters which explains why it is also sometimes called 'the vegetable oyster'.

Buying/Storing: The roots should be white, firm, and well shaped. Do not buy any that have been damaged or bruised (and take care when handling them as they are more fragile than they look). Can be kept in a fridge for a few days but best eaten as soon as possible.

How to use: Grate young raw salsify and add to salads (with a squeeze of lemon juice to prevent the white flesh from discolouring). To cook, carefully scrape the skin and then drop the whole root into water immediately –

again adding a drop of lemon juice – then cook until just tender. Good as a vegetable accompaniment, also with mild-flavoured sauces. Try in stir-fries.

ALMOND VEGETABLE CRUMBLE

225g/8oz salsify, scrubbed, peeled and chopped
lemon juice
2 carrots, peeled and chopped
2 leeks, cleaned and chopped
approx. 200ml/1/3rd pint/³/₄ cup vegetable stock
115g/4oz/¹/₂ cup ground almonds

Topping:
115g/4oz/1 cup rolled oats
55g/2oz/¹/₄ cup margarine
seasoning to taste
55g/2oz/¹/₂ cup almonds, coarsely chopped

Drop the salsify into a bowl of cold water to which you have added lemon juice. This stops it discolouring.
Then steam the salsify, carrots and leeks until just tender. Drain well. Mix together the stock and ground almonds to make a thick sauce, and stir in the vegetables. Put this mixture into an ovenproof dish, smooth the top.
Use your fingertips to combine the oats and margarine. Season generously. Stir in the chopped nuts. Sprinkle the crumble over the vegetables and press down lightly.
Bake at 190°C/375°F (Gas Mark 5) for 20-30 minutes, or until crisp.

Note: For a thicker sauce add a tablespoon of flour or arrowroot.

▌▌▌▌▌▌▌▌▌▌▌▌▌ SALT ▌▌▌▌▌▌▌▌▌▌▌▌▌

Salt has been used by man for thousands of years, and for many of them has been considered an item of great value. The word 'salary' is taken from salt money paid to Romans 2,000 years ago. Not only did it add flavour but it was also used to preserve vegetables, fish and meat at a time before there were so many other methods – not to mention fridges.

Varieties: Nowadays you can choose from a selection of different salts. Refined salt is best avoided as it has few nutrients and too many chemicals. Instead look for natural sea salt or rock salts (available ready ground, or in crystal form to be used with a grinder at table). There are also low-sodium salts which, though they may have been processed with chemicals, are useful for those who need to reduce the salt in their diets. Look out too for ready-flavoured salts such as onion and celery.

Nutrients: Natural salt, either sea salt or rock salt, contains a wide variety of trace elements essential to good health (including sodium chloride – common salt – and iodine), though in varying amounts. For everyone, salt intake is best kept to a minimum, and we do get a reasonable amount from many other foods. However, there will be times when you want to add salt – to bring out the flavour of certain foods, and in hot weather especially – and as natural salts have a stronger taste than the refined variety, they are ideal.

How to use: Do not make a habit of cooking with salt. Instead, leave it on the table in a salt mill so that it can be added by each person as and when it is needed. Add a few grains of rice to keep it dry.

See Gomasio.

SATSUMAS
See **Citrus fruit, soft**

SAVORY

A popular herb that grows reasonably well in Britain and has a mild yet spicy flavour. There are two kinds of savory in general use. Summer savory is considered to have more medicinal qualities, and is often added to cough mixtures. Winter savory, which is the stronger of the two, is used as an aid to digestion. It is said that, if savory is planted between rows of bean crops, the smell will keep away blackfly.

How to use: Nice in bean, pea and lentil dishes. Add savory to salads, egg dishes, vegetables and tomato sauces. Use in herb butters. Good when added to rice and used as a stuffing.

STUFFED EGGS

6 hardboiled eggs
85g/3oz vegetarian paté
1 tablespoon margarine or butter – optional
seasoning to taste
¹/₂-1 teaspoon dried savory
cucumber and tomatoes to serve

Carefully cut the eggs in half lengthwise, remove the yolks and put these into a bowl. Mash the yolks and mix with the paté, blending thoroughly. If the mixture seems a little dry (this will depend on the paté you use), add some margarine or butter. Season to taste and add savory.

Pile or pipe the filling back into the egg whites. Put three onto a plate, decorate with cucumber and tomato slices, use the rest of the ingredients in the same way. Serve as a starter. Also, of course, ideal party food.

You can mix the egg yolks with a variety of other ingredients to ring the changes. Try finely chopped spring onions. Peppers, celery, sunflower seeds or chopped nuts can also be used. Mayonnaise or sour cream are good binding ingredients.

SCORZONERA
See also **Salsify**

These are from the same family as salsify, but are black skinned. Originally used as a medicine rather than a vegetable, it is still not widely known, though is worth trying if you can find it.

Buying/Storing: These tapering roots are fragile and should be handled with care. Buy only those that are fresh-looking, avoiding any that look shrivelled or damaged. Store in a fridge and eat as soon as possible.

How to use: Cut off the tops and tails, scrape the skin, cut into small chunks and put at once into boiling water, adding lemon juice to stop the white flesh discolouring. Cooked scorzonera can be served with a knob of butter or in a sauce. Raw young roots are good in salad and are especially good with mayonnaise or sour cream dressings.

SCORZONERA SALAD

4 scorzonera roots, scrubbed, peeled and shredded
lemon juice
small piece of white cabbage, shredded
2 carrots, shredded
55g/2oz/¹/₂ cup salted peanuts
vinaigrette dressing or mayonnaise
2 tomatoes, quartered
dark-green lettuce leaves
watercress

Put the shredded scorzonera into a bowl, add the lemon juice and stir well. Add the cabbage, carrots, nuts, and enough salad dressing to moisten. Stir in the tomatoes. Use the lettuce to line a salad bowl. Pile the scorzonera mixture into the centre. Garnish with watercress.
Good as a side salad with a hot savoury dish.

SEAKALE BEET
See **Swiss chard**

SEAWEEDS

These are edible plants and algae that grow in the sea, usually on the seashore between high and low water marks. Seaweed must be one of the oldest crops eaten by human beings. It was used by ancient peoples, including the Chinese, the Greeks and the Romans, not just as a food, but also as a medicine and as a fertiliser. Nowadays there are over a hundred different kinds being used for culinary purposes. A few of these can be found on British shores, but most of those on sale are imported.

Varieties: Seaweed is usually sold in dried form and packed in cellophane packets which include complete instructions on how to rehydrate and use them. The selection available will vary from shop to shop, but probably the best known are kelp, nori, arame, wakame, kombu and hiziki, all of which have slightly different textures and tastes. Laver is found on the beaches of Scotland and Wales. As they are dried they will keep indefinitely in a cool, dry spot.

Nutrition: Nutrients vary according to the species, where it was harvested, and at what time of year, but all seaweeds are an excellent source of essential minerals and trace elements. The most important of these is iodine, a mineral necessary for the proper functioning of the metabolism, and since iodine is found in very few foods, it may be a nutrient many people are short of. Seaweed also contains the essential twenty amino acids, and is an excellent source of vitamin B12 – the one vitamin that vegetarians and vegans are in danger of missing out on as it is present in very few non-animal foods.

How to use: First rehydrate your seaweed. Then add to sautéed vegetables and serve with noodles. Or fry and use as a crisp garnish. Arame is good added to soups. Wakame goes well with beans, also with miso soup. Laver can be used much like spinach, though it is probably best known as the main ingredient of laver bread.

STIR-FRIED VEGETABLES WITH SEAWEED

55g/2oz wakame seaweed
1/2 small white cabbage
2 onions
1 red pepper
2 tablespoons vegetable oil
1/2 clove garlic, crushed
1 teaspoon mustard seed
pinch ground ginger
115g/4oz/2 cups mushrooms, sliced
soy sauce

Soak the seaweed in hot water for 20-30 minutes. Drain well, cool, then chop into pieces.
Finely slice the cabbage, onions and pepper.
Heat the oil and add the garlic, mustard seed and ginger. Cook gently for a few minutes, then add the prepared vegetables and sauté for 10 minutes, stirring occasionally. Add the wakame, raise the heat, and cook for a minute or two. Lower the heat again, add a spoonful or two of cold water, and cook for 5 minutes. Stir in the mushrooms, sprinkle with soy sauce, and cook just long enough to heat through.
Serve with rice.
Other seaweeds can be cooked in much the same way.

SEEDS
See also **individual varieties**

Seeds are the mature fertilised ovules of certain flowering plants which are suitable for eating, either to give flavour, or for their nutritional value – or both. They have been used as a food for many centuries all over the world. Though not as popular as nuts in Britain, they are becoming better known, especially as an ingredient in biscuits, cakes, and the mueslis and granolas that are now appearing on more and more breakfast tables.

Nutrition: The nutrients vary considerably from one seed to another, but all seeds are good sources of protein, calcium, minerals, some vitamins, and unsaturated fats.

Buying/Storing: Seeds are best purchased in small quantities from a shop that has a fast turnover. Though it is hard to tell by looking at them, they *can* become stale and will then lose much of their goodness and taste. Store them in a screw-top jar in a cool place. Do not chop or crush them until just before using them.

How to use: See individual varieties.

SESAME SEEDS
See also **Tahini**

The tiny seed of an easy-to-grow annual plant that is widespread throughout the Far East, Turkey and the Middle East. In Hindu mythology the god Yama blessed the sesame seed, and it is regarded by Hindus not only as an excellent food, but also as a symbol of immortality.

Nutrition: They are a particularly good source of calcium (containing 10 times as much as milk), and should be eaten regularly, especially by people who do not eat dairy foods.

How to use: Add to any baked goods, including bread and biscuits. Sprinkle a spoonful to add interest to vegetables such as Brussels sprouts – better still, lightly roast them first. Use to coat croquettes or tofu dominoes before frying. Much used in sweets such as sesame crunch bars, halva and Indian sweets.

SESAME CRACKERS

4 tablespoons vegetable oil
200ml/1/3rd pint/³/₄ cup water
225g/¹/₂ lb/2 cups wholemeal flour
115g/4oz/1 cup rolled oats
good pinch of salt
55g/2oz/1/3rd cup sesame seeds
extra vegetable oil

Use a whisk or a blender to combine the oil and water until white. Sift together the flour, rolled oats and salt. Add the seeds.

Mix together the liquid and dry ingredients to make a stiff dough (adjust the consistency if necessary). Turn it onto a lightly-floured board and knead for at least a few minutes before rolling out. Cut into circles or squares and brush lightly with extra oil.

Lightly grease a baking sheet and arrange the crackers on it. Bake at 180°C/350°F (Gas Mark 4) for about 15 minutes. When brown and crisp leave the crackers to cool briefly, then transfer them to a wire rack to get cold. Store in an airtight container.

Ring the changes by replacing half the sesame seeds with poppy seeds.

See also Almond biscuits, Tofu balls, Three seed nibble, Oatcakes with thyme.

SHALLOTS
See **Onions**

SHARON FRUIT
See **Persimmon**

SHOYU
See **Soy sauce**

SORBETS
See **Ice cream**

SORGHUM
See also **Grains**

This large, hard grain is actually a variety of millet. It survives with only the minimum of water, so is widely used in hot, dry countries. In many parts of Africa it is still an important staple, the white grain being eaten as meal, a bitter red grain being used to make beer, and sweet sorghum supplying syrup when the stems are crushed. Although it is the third most important cereal in the world (after wheat and rice), it is little known in Britain, though more shops are now stocking it.

How to use: Sorghum can be cooked like rice, or can be added to stews, soups and casseroles. It can also be ground to make flour which will produce a heavy bread, or can be used in both sweet and savoury porridge-type dishes. Sorghum contains no gluten, so is suitable for a gluten-free diet.

SORGHUM AND GREEN BEAN STEW

225g/¹/₂ lb sorghum
approx. 425ml/³/₄ pint/2 cups water
225g/¹/₂ lb green beans, trimmed and sliced
2 tablespoons vegetable oil
1 red pepper, sliced
1 onion, sliced
approx. 425ml/³/₄ pint/2 cups vegetable stock
2 tablespoons peanut butter, or to taste
1 tablespoon miso
seasoning to taste
chopped chives to garnish

Cook the sorghum in the water, keeping the pan covered and checking every now and again that it does not boil dry. It will take about an hour, by which time the grains should be tender but still chewy. Drain if necessary.

Steam the beans and drain.

Heat the oil and cook the pepper and onion to soften. Add the stock, sorghum and green beans and bring to a boil. Lower the heat, stir in the peanut butter and miso. Season generously. Cook for literally 5 minutes so that all the ingredients are piping hot.

Spoon into soup bowls and garnish with chopped chives.

SORREL

There are two kinds in use, one more popular on the Continent and called French sorrel, the other more widely available in Britain and called garden sorrel. They are very similar, though the former is considered to have a more lemony flavour. If collecting wild sorrel, be sure to pick only young fresh leaves, and to avoid any growing near roads or fields where crops may have been sprayed with chemicals. Though spring sorrel is a useful vegetable, its flavour is less pronounced than it is in summer.

How to use: Sorrel's sharp and lemon-like flavour goes especially well with eggs. Try adding it too to flans, stews, sauces. When using milk always scorch the milk first or the sorrel will make it curdle. Also avoid using aluminium pans when cooking sorrel.

SORREL SOUFFLÉ

55g/2oz/¹/₄ cup margarine
115g/4oz sorrel, washed and trimmed
115g/4oz/2 cups mushrooms, sliced
1 small onion, sliced
1 clove garlic, crushed
2 good tablespoons wholemeal flour
200ml/1/3rd pint/³/₄ cup milk
seasoning to taste

3 eggs, separated
55g/2oz/¹/₂ cup Parmesan cheese, grated

Melt the margarine. Chop the sorrel leaves and add to the fat with the mushrooms, onion and garlic. Cook for a few minutes to soften. Remove from the heat, add the flour, milk and seasoning, then return to the cooker and bring to a boil, stirring continuously. Cook for a minute more.
Off the heat stir in most of the cheese and the egg yolks.
In a separate bowl whisk the egg whites until stiff but not too dry. (This is easiest if they are cold, you use a cold bowl and add a pinch of salt.) Use a metal spoon to fold the egg whites gently into the first mixture. Then spoon into a lightly-greased medium-sized soufflé dish. Sprinkle with the remaining cheese.
Bake at 190°C/375°F (Gas Mark 5) for about 40 minutes, or until well risen and golden brown. Serve at once.

SOYA BEANS

See also **Tofu, Tempeh, Soya milk, Soya cheese, Soy sauce, TVP, Yogurt**

There are two kinds of soya beans grown at present, one used to make oil and flour, the other grown for eating. Although they first appeared in Chinese records over 4,500 years ago, and are still widely grown in China (where they are called 'the meat of the earth') many other countries now have soya crops. It is the USA, however, who lead world cultivation, much of their produce going to feed cattle.

Varieties: The large, round, yellow soya bean is the one found in most shops, though some also offer the smaller darker bean. These are all very slow cooking, so look out too for soya grits and soya flakes which have been broken down to speed up the process. Soya flour is not only nutritious when added to baked goods, but has a binding quality that makes it a good substitute for eggs. It is available in full fat, medium and fat free.

Nutrition: The soya has the highest protein content of all the pulses, this (unlike that of other pulses) being made up of all 8 essential amino acids. It also contains iron in an easily assimilated form, trace elements, vitamins, and lecithin and linoleic acid which helps reduce cholesterol in the blood.

How to use: The beans should be soaked overnight, then allow 1¹/₂-3 hours for them to cook. Add cooked beans to stews, curries and casseroles. Mash them and use as a base for a paté or savoury spread. If you use soya flakes and cook them well, they will break down and are therefore useful for thickening a sauce or soup. Add soya flour to sauces and soups to add protein. In bread, use 30g/1oz soya flour to 225g/¹/₂ lb wheat flour.

SESAME SOYA FUDGE

115g/4oz/³/₄ cup sesame seeds
55g/2oz/¹/₂ cup soya flour
honey to mix
1 tablespoon finely chopped orange peel
30g/1oz/¹/₄ cup sunflower seeds

Put the sesame seeds into a bowl, stir in the flour, then add enough honey to make a firm mixture. Add the orange peel and sunflower seeds, and knead briefly so that all the ingredients are well blended.

Lightly grease a shallow tin, spoon in the sesame soya mixture, and press down, smoothing the top. Leave it in a cool place until it beings to firm up. Cut into squares and eat within a few days.

This basic recipe can be adapted in numerous ways. Maple syrup gives a completely different flavour, or try tahini with chopped raisins or dates to sweeten the fudge. Lemon peel can replace the orange. You can omit the sunflower seeds and add vanilla essence for extra flavour, or a spoonful of ground almonds and some almond essence. A pinch of ground cardamom gives an exotic taste.

SOYA CHEESE

There are now a number of these 'cheeses' on the market, all of them based on soya but with additions that endeavour to capture the taste and texture of the real thing. Some of them even come in flavours such as Cheddar. Though they can be grated, sliced and cooked like cheese they wouldn't convince a mouse! However, they are interesting foods full of nourishment, and do expand the choice for vegans or anyone wanting to avoid dairy produce.

SOYA MILK

Soya milk is relatively new in Britain, and is made from soya beans with oil and sometimes raw sugar added. It offers a welcome alternative for the growing number of people who have doubts about the way in which cow's milk is produced (for both ethical and health reasons); also for those who are allergic to cow's milk. Though it can be used in much the same way, it is better to think of it as something completely different. Anyone expecting soya milk to taste like cow's milk may well be disappointed.

Varieties: As the interest in soya milk grows, so does the range of alternatives. Usually packed in long-life packs soya milk can be sweetened or unsweetened, can be made with mass-produced or organically-grown beans, can be light or creamy. Soya milk is also available in extra creamy form which can be diluted with water to normal consistency, or used in concentrated form as a substitute for thin cream. Look out too for powdered soya milk – excellent for camping or keeping in the cupboard for emergencies.

Nutrition: Like the soya bean from which it is made, this milk contains protein, including all the essential amino acids. It has been known to affect thyroid function, so should be given sparingly to young children.

How to use: Use in exactly the same way as milk. Try it in drinks such as milkshakes, sweet rice puddings and other 'milk'-based dishes. Pour onto muesli or other breakfast dishes, use it in tea or coffee. Makes an excellent white sauce (add herbs, mushrooms, etc.) In fact, you can replace dairy milk in almost all recipes with soya milk. Also makes reasonable yogurt.

WHITE SAUCE AND VARIATIONS (DAIRY-FREE)

2 tablespoons vegetable oil
30g/1oz/¹/₄ cup wholemeal flour
approx. 285ml¹/₂ pint/1 1/3rd cups soya milk
seasoning to taste

Heat the oil in a saucepan and sprinkle in the flour. Cook briefly then stir in the milk and continue cooking gently until the sauce thickens. Add seasoning to taste. Adjust the consistency of the sauce, if necessary, by adding a drop more milk.

Alternatively a white sauce can be made by combining all ingredients in a saucepan and bringing gently to a boil, whisking all the time as you do so. This one-step sauce is quicker, but by cooking the flour in the fat first you do get a slightly richer flavour.

Mushroom sauce Cook 2 medium mushrooms, chopped fine, in the oil before adding the milk.

Onion sauce Cook 1 onion, coarsely chopped, in boiling water for 10 minutes, then drain and add to the cooked sauce.

Parsley sauce Add 2 teaspoons chopped parsley and a squeeze of lemon juice to the cooked sauce.

Creamy tomato sauce Gently heat a few tablespoons of tomato purée or thick sauce, then stir into the hot white sauce. Do not boil.

Herb sauce Use 1 or 2 tablespoons fresh herbs, chopped coarsely. Add them at the same time as the milk so that they are lightly cooked.

Béchamel sauce Lightly cook some chopped carrot, onion and celery in the milk, then strain and use the milk as described above.

Mustard sauce Stir in a teaspoon of made-up mustard, or to taste.

Curry sauce Stir in a teaspoon of curry paste, or to taste, and some chopped peanuts.

See also Banana milkshake, Creamy potato soup with pistachios.

▌▌▌▌▌▌ SOY SAUCE ▌▌▌▌▌▌

Like miso, soy sauce is made by fermenting soya beans. Wheat and salt are added, and the process is a lengthy one – both tamari and shoyu sauces, which are the best, take at least 18 months to ferment. Commercial soy sauces are also available widely nowadays, and though they do add flavour they may well contain chemical residues. A few of them also contain monosodium glutomate to which some people are allergic. (It is said you can tell a genuine soy sauce by shaking the bottle – the bubbles should remain!) Use soy sauce with a variety of savoury dishes to give a savoury, salty flavour.

Nutrition: The sauce is rich in protein and other nutrients. In the Orient, where soya sauce is still used widely, it is believed to help digestion, to improve circulation and strengthen the contractions of the heart.

How to use: Add to such dishes as casseroles, soups, stews and stir-fried vegetables whilst cooking. A bottle of soy sauce on the table can replace salt. Try sprinkling it over egg rolls or tempura fried vegetables. Use it as a marinade for tofu slices.

TAMARI HONEY SALAD DRESSING

200ml/1/3rd pint/³/₄ cup vegetable oil, preferably safflower
3 tablespoons lemon juice
4 tablespoons tamari soy sauce, or to taste
2 tablespoons honey, or to taste
1 spring onion, finely chopped
good pinch cayenne pepper
1 tablespoon caraway seeds – optional

Put all the ingredients into a screw-top jar and shake well. They can also be put into a bowl and whisked. Store in the fridge until needed. Shake or whisk again before serving.

A particularly good salad dressing to use with white cabbage salads.

See also Cashew nut butter, Stir-fried vegetables with seaweed, Tofu balls, Three seed nibble.

SPICES
See also **individual varieties**

Spices are the fruit, berries or bark of plants grown in the tropics. They have been used to enliven dull foods, cover the taste of less-than-perfect food, and to aid digestion, for many thousands of years. Nowadays they are used principally as a way to add variety, to enrich and enhance the flavour of ingredients that may be all too familiar. In addition, of course, spices add authenticity to the many exotic recipes that form part of the cuisine of countries around the world, but which are now so popular also in Britain.

Buying/Storing: If you are buying ready-ground spice, buy only a small quantity and store it in an opaque airtight jar, preferably in a cupboard. (Or, if you want to have some handy in a spice rack, decant it from a bigger jar that is kept in the dark.) Smell the spices every now and again; if the aroma is fading throw them out. It is better to buy your spices whole if possible and grind or grate them as needed. Though they are not widely available they *can* be found, and an increase in demand will persuade shopkeepers to stock them more often.

How to use: See individual varieties.

SPINACH

Popeye's favourite food, of course. Its reputation as a health food may have done it more harm than good. Yet spinach is a popular food in Mediterranean countries where it is the main ingredient in many traditional dishes. Spinach does also grow well in Britain, either naturally or forced. It is available much of the year, but at its best in summer.

Varieties: There are numerous varieties ranging from the soft, delicately flavoured summer spinach to the coarser winter spinach (the stalks can be very tough and are best removed before cooking). Perpetual spinach and Swiss chard are actually members of the beetroot family; they should, however, be treated and cooked in the same way as spinach.

Nutrition: Even though its iron content may have been somewhat over-rated, it is still a good source of this mineral. It also contains vitamins A and C, potassium and calcium.

Buying/Storing: Look out for fresh, crisp leaves – if any are wilted or torn, or if any of the shoots are flowering, do not buy it. Spinach will keep for a short time in the fridge (preferably wrapped in polythene), but it is best eaten as soon as possible after buying or picking. Always handle it with care – spinach is delicate and is easily damaged.

How to use: Do not wash until just before using it. Spinach contains a lot of water and should therefore be cooked in the absolute minimum – just shake the wet leaves, drop into a pan, replace the lid and cook gently for a short time, checking that it isn't burning. Mix with onions, flavour with nutmeg, use to fill pancakes and top with cheese sauce. Combined with ricotta cheese and egg spinach makes a delicious stuffing for pasta rolls. Try spinach in a curry. Add to soups and soufflés. Do remember that spinach shrinks considerably when cooked, and allow extra to account for this. Young leaves can be washed, dried, shredded and eaten raw, maybe with a sprinkling of almonds.

SPINACH LASAGNE

170g/6oz lasagne, preferably wholemeal
approx. 2 tablespoons vegetable oil
1 onion, sliced
1 red pepper, sliced
680g/1¹/₂ lbs fresh spinach, washed and shredded

2 tablespoons margarine
2 tablespoons wholemeal flour
285ml/¹/₂ pint/1 1/3rd cups milk
seasoning to taste
good pinch of nutmeg
55g/2oz/¹/₂ cup walnuts, coarsely chopped
55g/2oz/¹/₂ cup Cheddar cheese, grated
wholemeal breadcrumbs

Add a drop of oil to a large pan of boiling salted water, then drop in the sheets of lasagne one at a time. The oil will help stop them sticking together. Cook them until tender – how long this takes will depend on whether they are home or commercially made. Rinse each sheet in cold water, pat dry, and spread them on clean tea towels, not touching, until needed.

Heat the oil and gently sauté the onion and pepper until soft. Meanwhile, cook the spinach in the minimum of water until it too is tender. Combine the pepper and onion mixture with the spinach, add seasoning.

In another pan melt the margarine, stir in the flour, then gradually add the milk, stirring continually. As it comes to the boil the sauce will thicken. Season and add nutmeg, plus most of the walnuts.

Layer a third of the lasagne across the base of a small well-greased ovenproof dish or tin. Top with half the spinach mixture and some of the white sauce. Repeat this. Add the final sheets of pasta and the rest of the sauce, making sure the top is well covered. If necessary, make up some more sauce, or thin down the sauce you have left. Sprinkle with the remaining nuts, cheese and breadcrumbs.

Bake at 190°C/375°F (Gas Mark 5) for about 30 minutes, or until the top is golden. To make this suitable for vegans simply use soya instead of dairy milk, and replace the cheese with crumbled tofu.

Note: Some lasagnes are now available pre-cooked, which means you can skip the first step and simply layer the dry sheets with the other ingredients. When using these be especially careful to cover them completely with vegetables and sauce.

See also Scrambled tofu florentines.

SPROUTED SEEDS, GRAINS AND BEANS

Though not widely used in the western world until recently, sprouted seeds, grains and beans have been used in the East for at least 5,000 years and are an important part of their national cuisine. When treated with moisture and warmth, seeds become activated and manufacture the vitamins and elements needed to produce a new plant. In this highly active state the amount of such nutrients is dramatically increased within just a few days.

Varieties: In theory any seed, grain or bean can be sprouted. Some, however, are far easier to sprout than others, and these are the ones you are most likely to find in your local wholefood or healthfood shop (or, nowadays, supermarket or greengrocers). Mung beans are probably the best known, though look out too for alfalfa (which looks like green shredded wheat!), and the increasingly popular bean mixes. As they are not difficult to make, you can save money and have an instant supply always on hand if you grow your own.

Nutrition: Sprouts are low in calories, high in protein, vitamin A, some of the B complex vitamins and in particular vitamin C. A few sprouts also contain the important vitamin B12 which is rarely found in non-meat sources, and so are invaluable for vegetarians and vegans.

Buying/Storing: They are usually pre-packed in polythene bags. Look carefully to make sure none of the sprouts are brown or rotting, also that bad handling hasn't damaged them. A few shops sell them loose to be weighed up as you need them. Though this makes it easier to see the state of the sprouts, and you can buy exactly the quantity you need, such sprouts – unless fresh that morning – will have begun to dry out and grow stale, so be extra careful. Store your sprouts in a jar or airtight bag in the fridge for a few days (even under these conditions the vitamin C content can go on increasing).

How to use: Sprouts can be lightly steamed or sautéed just like fresh vegetables. They are tasty raw in salads and sandwiches. Sprinkle them into soups, stews, add them to sauces at the last moment (never over-cook sprouts or they will disintegrate). Include sprouts in nut roasts, rissoles, veggie burgers. They make an unusual filling for omelettes.

GROWING YOUR OWN SPROUTS
You will need:
- 1-2 tablespoons of the ingredient of your choice:
Pulses – aduki beans, whole lentils, chick peas, mung beans, soya beans, whole peas, etc.
Grains – wheat berries, barley, buckwheat, corn, oats, rice, triticale, rye, etc.
Seeds – alfalfa, fenugreek, sunflower, sesame, etc.
- a fine-meshed sieve
- a small dish
- a large jam or kilner jar
- muslin, cheesecloth or nylon net
- an elastic band

Put the beans, grains or seeds into the sieve and wash under running water to remove all dust. Check for small stones, wild seeds or foreign objects! Then put your chosen ingredient into a small dish, cover with tepid water, and leave overnight, preferably in a warm dark place.

Pour off the water, then put them into the jar. Use the elastic band to secure the muslin across the top. Pour fresh water into the jar through the muslin, then gently tip so that the water drains away. You can either return the jar to the warm dark place or leave it out in the light. Sprouts grown in the light have more vitamin C and chlorophyl but less vitamin B. Growing them in the dark might take a little longer.

The sprouts will need to be rinsed 2-3 times a day so that they are always just damp. In summer, or if the jar is in a warm spot, take care they do not dry out.

The shoots will begin to appear in a day or two and will be ready to eat in anything from 3-5 days. You eat the whole thing, though alfalfa should be put into cold water to release the small, hard husks which will float to the top and can then be scooped up.

All sprouts not intended for immediate use should be rinsed again, drained (all the while handling them with care as they are fragile little things), then stored in the fridge in a polythene bag or container with a screw-top. They will keep for a few days.

Tips: Buy only fresh untreated seeds from a wholefood or healthfood shop. Seeds intended for pets or for agricultural use may well have been treated with chemicals. Choose the right size jar – sprouts can increase in volume up to eight times! Heavily chlorinated water should be boiled and then left to cool before you use it to rinse your sprouts.

A specially-made sprouter makes the rinsing a lot easier.

Some seeds are a lot harder to sprout than others. Virtually foolproof are alfalfa, whole lentils and mung beans.

See Chinese fried vegetables with eggs, Meal-in-a-salad, Bean sprout omelette, Chinese spring rolls.

SQUASHES
See also **Pumpkins**

These small marrow-type vegetables are very popular in the USA, but are only just becoming available in Britain. They come in a wide variety of colours, shapes and sizes, some at their best in summer, others (which have harder skins) considered to be winter vegetables.

Varieties: There are too many to name. However, two of the most popular (and easy to recognise!) are the pear-shaped butternut squash, and the unusual daisy-shaped custard squash. Look out too for spaghetti marrow which looks more like a yellow elongated pumpkin. When cooked the inner flesh is removed with a fork at which point it separates into long spaghetti-like strands – delicious with a knob of butter and lots of black pepper.

Buying/Storing: Buy only if firm, glossy and undamaged. Summer squashes should have a skin that yields slightly. They will keep fairly well in a cool dry spot.

How to use: Summer squashes can be eaten with or without their skin; when preparing winter squashes, always remove the skin first. Then slice and boil, steam or fry. Add chunks of squash to soups and casseroles. Cut in half or into thick rounds and stuff with a favourite mixture. Serve as a vegetable by baking and then puréeing, adding butter and herbs to taste.

BUTTERNUT AU GRATIN

2 medium-sized butternut squashes
30g/1oz/2¹/₂ tablespoons margarine or butter
seasoning to taste
good pinch of nutmeg
85g/3oz/³/₄ cup Cheddar cheese, grated
30g/1oz/¹/₂ cup wholemeal breadcrumbs

Cut the squashes in half lengthways. Lay them cut side down on a lightly-greased baking tray and bake at 180°C/350°F (Gas Mark 4) for about 30-40 minutes, or until just tender.

Carefully scoop out the flesh and mash it to a purée with the fat, the seasoning and nutmeg.

Refill the skins. Sprinkle the top of each one with some cheese and breadcrumbs. Put under a hot grill for a few minutes, then serve at once.

STAR FRUIT

One of the prettiest fruits of all, this one grows in much of Southeast Asia, Israel, Brazil and also America. It is a pale yellow-green and has five ribs so that when it is cut crossways, you get star-shaped slices that are crisp and lemony. The seeds in the middle should be removed before eating, and it is a good idea to also trim the very edge of the ribs as these can be hard and also may be brown. Also called carambola.

Nutrition: Good source of vitamin C.

How to use: Best in fruit salads. Make an interesting addition to a green salad – add a creamy dressing.

See Tropical fruit salad.

STEAMERS
See **Utensils, cooking**

STOCK, VEGETABLE

A good stock has always been the basis of many if not most recipes. This used to be the liquid left over after cooking vegetables, and which was full of the goodness leeched out of them by the water and heat. Nowadays it is more likely to be from a stock cube (the vegetable water having been thrown down the sink!). For healthy eating, try to make a point of preserving the water whenever you cook vegetables.

Vegetable stock also makes a delicious drink, either just as it is or with herbs or soy sauce added. There is, in fact, now a company making a vegetable stock that comes in a tagged bag like tea, all ready to make an instant additive-free and nutritious drink.

Buying/Storing: When buying stock cubes look out for those that are additive-free. The better the quality (in other words, the higher the price) the more likely they will have been made from good quality vegetables. As these are dried, they will keep indefinitely and it is always useful to have a few in your store cupboard. If you usually make your own stock – or, even easier, make it a habit to save the water in which vegetables were cooked – you can keep any unused liquid in the fridge for a day or two, or pour it into ice trays and freeze until needed.

How to use: Stocks can be used with soups, stews, sauces. They are useful for moistening ingredients when making bean burgers or nut loaves. Add a drop when sautéeing vegetables. Soak TVP in vegetable stock to give it extra flavour. Have a cup of stock as a healthy alternative to that mid-morning coffee.

STRAWBERRIES
See **Berries**

STRING BEANS
See **Beans, fresh**

SUET, VEGETABLE

This is made from vegetable oils rather than animal fats and is therefore very useful for vegetarians. It is also good for anyone who is trying to reduce their intake of saturated fats, although palm nut oil – which is usually a key ingredient – doesn't have an especially high polyunsaturates content. Still, though, vegetarian suet is certainly a healthier option than the more traditional kind.

Buying/Storing: Buy from a shop with a good turnover and read the pack to make sure it really is vegetarian. Store in the fridge.

How to use: Can be used in all those dishes where suet really does result in a different texture. Steamed puddings, Christmas pudding, certain pastries, stuffing mixes.

MINCEMEAT

455g/1 lb/3 cups mixed dried fruit
1 large cooking apple
115g/4oz/2/3rd cup raw cane sugar

grated peel of 1 orange
grated peel of 1 lemon
2 teaspoons mixed spice
115g/4oz/³/₄ cup brazil nuts
115g/4oz/¹/₂ cup vegetable suet
2-4 tablespoons brandy

Mince the dried fruit, grate the apple, and combine with the peel, spice and sugar. Coarsely chop or grate the nuts, grate the fat, and stir into the other ingredients together with the brandy. Spoon into clean, dry jars and seal well. Keep in a cool place (preferably a fridge) until needed.

See also Pecan pumpkin pie.

SUGAR

Sugar is the sweetener extracted from sugar cane, a perennial plant that grows naturally in the West Indies and around the Indian Ocean. The use of sugar cane dates back to around 300 BC, and for many years it was valued not so much as a sweetener but as a food. Workers in the field would chew on the cane for nourishment and energy. When the sugar refining process was developed white sugar became a 'status' food that only the affluent ate, but it soon came down in price. Everyone wanted it and everyone could afford it. What made matters worse was the fact that it was now possible to consume large amounts of concentrated sucrose. Sugar's reputation as a 'naughty but nice' food had begun.

Although brown sugar and white sugar are made from cane, white has been refined to such an extent that it is almost pure chemical, with no nutritional value whatsoever. Raw brown sugar, on the other hand, still contains some of the goodness of natural molasses and nutrients, and is free of added chemicals. It is only in recent years that raw brown sugar has been rediscovered as an alternative to white sugar.

Nutrition: All sugars, including the more 'natural' honey and maple syrup, dull the appetite and the taste buds when consumed in excess, and all are harmful to teeth, so therefore should be consumed sparingly. However, raw brown sugar does contain some nutrients such as calcium, phosphorus, magnesium, sodium, potassium and iron. It also has a better taste and can therefore be used in smaller amounts. In general, the darker the sugar the more nutrients it will contain, and the stronger will be its flavour.

Buying/Storing: Many people confuse brown sugars. There are some on the market which are no more than dyed white sugar, and have no nutritional benefits at all. Look for the word 'raw' on the pack, which should also give the country of origin. The sugar itself will tend to be sticky in texture as it has not been washed after crystallisation. Choose from four varieties: demerara, light muscovado, muscovado and molasses. Sugar is best transferred to an airtight container. When the lighter texture of caster sugar is required, powder raw cane sugar in a grinder.

How to use: Use wherever a recipe calls for white sugar – in drinks, dessert dishes, jams and marmalades. Add to baked dishes. Make healthier sweets. Use just a pinch to flavour savoury dishes such as relishes, sauces, red cabbage and apple casserole. Ideal when making cakes and biscuits. Good in ice cream. Always question whether it is necessary to add sugar to a recipe, and add as little as you need to – remember that we are nearly all hooked on sugar, so adding sugar 'to taste' will almost always be more than is necessary either for flavour or for health.

LEMON PANCAKES (EGG-LESS)

115g/4oz/1 cup wholemeal flour
55g/2oz/¹/₂ cup soya flour
1 teaspoon baking powder
285ml¹/₂ pint/1 1/3rd cups water
vegetable oil to cook
2 lemons
raw cane sugar

To make the batter, sieve together the flours and baking powder, then gradually stir in the water. Beat for a few minutes before leaving in the fridge for at least 30 minutes. Whisk the batter again before using. It should be the consistency of single cream, so add a drop more water if it is too thick.

Heat a spoonful of oil in a small heavy-based pan. When a faint haze rises, pour in a paper thin covering of batter, tilting the pan to spread it. Cook for a minute or two, shaking the pan occasionally to prevent sticking. Flip, or use a spatula to turn the pancake, and cook the other side. Keep it warm whilst using the rest of the batter in the same way. This is best done by placing cooked pancakes on a covered plate over a pan of hot water.

Sprinkle each pancake lightly with sugar, roll up, and serve at once accompanied by wedges of lemon, and the sugar bowl for those who might want more.

Note: This basic pancake recipe can be used by vegans (or anyone wanting to avoid eggs) to make a variety of sweet pancakes. It is also ideal with savoury fillings such as ratatouille, tofu and beansprouts, whatever you fancy.

See also Almond biscuits, Butterscotch cream, Molasses toffee apples, Gooseberry brulée, Buttermilk muffins, Cardamom and rosewater icing, Caramellised satsumas, Mulled wine, Key lime pie, Tropical cream dessert, Tempeh in sweet and sour sauce.

SULTANAS

See also **Dried fruit**

Made from white seedless grapes, sultanas are soft and sweet. They are widely grown in the eastern Mediterranean, Australia and South Africa, though the best come from Turkey.

Nutrition: Sultanas contain calcium and vitamin B6.

How to use: Add to apple strudel, or use with cashews in a muffin batter. Sultanas are good in tomato chutney and nice in curry sauces, especially when served with eggs. Eaten in small quantities they make a healthy treat for children to nibble – maybe combine them with nuts and flaked coconut.

DRIED FRUIT COMPÔTE

85g/3oz/¹/₂ cup prunes, soaked overnight
85g/3oz/¹/₂ cup apricots, soaked overnight
85g/3oz/¹/₂ cup dried apple rings, soaked overnight
85g/3oz/¹/₂ cup sultanas
55g/2oz/1/3rd cup raw cane sugar, or to taste
2 teaspoons rosewater
1 tablespoon of finely chopped preserved ginger
55g/2oz/¹/₂ cup flaked almonds

Put the prunes and apricots into a saucepan. Add the sugar and just enough water to cover the fruit.
Bring to the boil, stir to dissolve the sugar, then lower the heat and cover the pan.
Simmer, stirring now and again, for 10 minutes. Add the apple rings and sultanas and cook 10 minutes more, or until all the fruit is just tender. You may need to add a drop more water during the cooking process, but keep it to a minimum.
Stir in the rosewater and ginger. Allow to cool and then chill the compôte in the fridge. Serve sprinkled with flaked almonds.

See also Green tomato chutney, Lemon honey squares, Fruit and nut bran muffins.

SUNFLOWER SEEDS

North American native peoples once cultivated sunflowers, feeding the leaves to animals, using the petals as dye, and obtaining oil and food from the seeds. Although still widely grown in North America, sunflower seeds mean especially big business in Russia. In fact, you can take the seeds from the sunflowers in your own back garden, but removing them from the husk is a fiddly job.

Nutrition: They contain a rich concentration of nutrients including B complex vitamins, many minerals, protein, and vitamin D.

Buying/Storing: Buy from a wholesaler who has a fast turnover, and only take home a small quantity at a time. They are best purchased raw. Store them in an airtight container and they will keep fresh for some time, though don't leave them until they begin to look or smell stale.

How to use: Sunflower seeds have a sweet taste which goes well with many dishes. Sprinkle them over crumbles and soups, mix them into pastry and baked goods, add them to muesli. Unusual but tasty added to a tomato sauce and served with spaghetti. Ground sunflower seeds can be used to bake very nutritious biscuits. Try dry-roasting them to get a fuller flavour. Mix them with other seeds to make a nibble to serve with drinks or take when you're out rambling.

SUNFLOWER MAPLE BISCUITS

225g/^{1}/$_2$ lb/1^3/$_4$ cups sunflower seeds
170g/6oz/1^1/$_2$ cups wholemeal flour
1 egg
2 tablespoons maple syrup
2 tablespoons vegetable oil
cold water to mix

Use a grinder to powder the seeds. Mix this with the flour.
Whisk together the egg, syrup and oil. Combine the two mixtures adding enough water to bind them to make a firm dough.
With floured hands break it into 3 pieces, shape into rolls about 50mm (2 inches) wide, wrap them in polythene bags and chill for an hour at least.
Use a sharp knife to cut them into thin rounds. Arrange these on a lightly-greased baking sheet. Bake at 180°C/350°F (Gas Mark 4) for about 20 minutes or until just browned. Transfer the biscuits to a wire rack to cool completely.

See also Filo parcels, Millet and sunflower croquettes, Sunflower and celery paté, Sesame soya fudge, Pita pizzas, Three seed nibble.

SWEDES

Also called 'yellow turnips', swedes probably arrived in Britain in the late 18th century when they were used for cattle fodder. They are still not very popular as a vegetable, though they are the traditional accompaniment to the Scottish haggis which is eaten on Burns night. They are known in Scotland as 'neeps'.

Nutrition: As with all root vegetables they are a good source of dietary fibre, but they also contain a fair amount of vitamins B and C, plus some iron.

How to use: Swedes have a distinctive sweet taste that is also fairly strong. They can be steamed, puréed and used as a sauce, either alone or combined with other root vegetables. Add a couple of spoonfuls to a casserole or soup. Try them too sliced and lightly fried, roasted, or grated raw and used in a salad.

SWEDISH SHEPHERD'S PIE

85g/3oz/good 1/3rd cup brown lentils, soaked overnight
85g/3oz/good 1/3rd cup green split peas, soaked overnight
1 tablespoon vegetable oil
¹/₂ clove garlic, crushed – optional
1 small onion, sliced
1 carrot, sliced
1 small leek, sliced
seasoning to taste
¹/₂ teaspoon mixed herbs
1 teaspoon fresh parsley
455g/1 lb swedes, peeled and diced
approx. 30g/1oz/2¹/₂ tablespoons margarine or butter
tablespoon cream or concentrated soya milk

Cook the lentils and split peas in fresh water, simmering them gently for about 45 minutes, or until soft. Meanwhile, heat the oil and fry the garlic, onion, carrot and leek until cooked. Drain the lentils and combine the two mixtures. Season them well, add herbs and parsley. Transfer to an ovenproof dish.

Steam the swedes for about 15 minutes, then mash well together with the fat, cream or milk and some seasoning. Spread this mixture over the top of the lentils and smooth the top. Dot with a little extra fat – this helps the top to brown.

Bake at 190°C/375°F (Gas Mark 5) for about 20 minutes.

SWEET CICELY

A fern-like herb that grows mainly in the north of England and Scotland – it is easy to grow even in damp, shady spots – and has clusters of pretty white flowers. It is also popular in France. The taste it adds is sweet and rather like aniseed.

How to use: Sweet cicely can at least partly replace other sweeteners in many dishes. Use with sharp fruits such as gooseberries, greengages and plums. Also good in fruit juices. Cicely can be used with savoury dishes like bakes, salads and vegetable casseroles – it marries especially well with parsnips.

SWEETCORN, FRESH
See also **Maize**

Sweetcorn originated in America over 5,000 years ago and it is still eaten there on a huge scale. Although it is known in Europe, Britain is the principal consumer of corn-on-the-cob on this side of the Atlantic. Locally-grown crops usually appear only for a short season in late summer, though corns are sometimes imported, so extending the season.

Varieties: Apart from fresh sweetcorn, look out too for the baby sweetcorn that is harvested when very young, and that features frequently in Oriental cookery. These should be eaten whole and have an especially sweet taste. They need the minimum cooking. Sweetcorn kernels are also removed from the cob and then sold either in tins or frozen.

Buying/Storing: Buy plump, well shaped cobs with kernels that are a golden yellow. These are best eaten on the day of purchase as the natural sugars soon turn to starch once the vegetable is picked, and the taste will fade. Do not remove the husks until just before cooking.

How to use: There is nothing to beat lightly-cooked corn-on-the-cob. Just remove the husks and cook in a pan of boiling water for 15-30 minutes, or until just tender. (Do not add salt as this will make the kernels tough.) Top with a little butter, margarine or tahini and eat at once – taking care not to burn your fingers. Alternatively, the kernels can be sliced off with a sharp knife to be used in soups, stews, vegetable casseroles and flans, or to be added to egg dishes or stuffings to add colour. Also good added to fritters. Or mix with broad beans and a dressing to make succotash. Nice in salads, especially combined with bean sprouts, tomatoes and roasted sunflower seeds. Baby sweetcorns can be eaten raw in salads, or added to stir-fries, or curries (Thai curry sauces are especially suitable).

CHINESE SPRING ROLLS

4 small pancakes, cooked on one side only (see page 219)
2 tablespoons bean sprouts
2 tablespoons cooked sweetcorn
1/2 red pepper, finely chopped
2 spring onions, finely chopped
1 small stick celery, finely chopped
1 teaspoon fresh ginger, freshly grated
seasoning to taste
85g/3oz/just under 1/2 cup tofu, drained and mashed
oil for frying
soy sauce to serve

Mix together the bean sprouts, sweetcorn, red pepper, onions, celery, ginger, seasoning and tofu.
Spread some of the mixture on the cooked side of the pancake, then roll it up half way, tuck in the sides and continue rolling to make a small neat package. Brush the edges with either water or egg white, and press them to secure. Use the rest of the ingredients in the same way.
Deep-fry in hot oil for a few minutes only until golden and cooked. You can also shallow-fry them if you prefer, turning them over after a few minutes. Drain them well. If eating them as a snack, dip them into soy sauce. Can also be served as part of a meal with rice, stir-fried vegetables, and a scattering of cashew nuts.

Note: Chinese spring rolls can also be made using puff pastry – these are then baked in the oven, rather than fried. You can also buy specially made pastry wrappers in some speciality shops.

See also Red and white slaw, Corn and peanut gumbo, Pita pizzas, Mexican flan.

SWEET PEPPERS

Also called capsicums, these colourful bell-shaped vegetables are native to South America and the West Indies. They first became known on a wide scale in Britain in the 1950s and are now grown here commercially – although some say the sweetest ones are those that are imported.

Varieties: Most varieties start out green and then turn yellow or red, the taste being sweeter as they ripen. It is now possible to buy peppers in other and more unusual colours including white, orange and deep purple. They also vary considerably in shape, some long and thin, others round and fat.

Nutrition: A good source of vitamins B1 and B2, C and D.

Buying/Storing: Buy peppers that are firm and smooth. If they are wrinkled or soft they are past their best. Once cut peppers should be put into a plastic bag and kept in the fridge, but only for a day or so.

How to use: Peppers can be cut into strips and served in salad. Fried peppers make a good topping for pizza, or can be served as a vegetable. Use in quiches, flans and soups. Cook with onions and walnuts and use to stuff crêpes. Make a Mediterranean-style ragoût and sprinkle with seeds. You can also stuff whole peppers and bake them.

MEDITERRANEAN PEPPERS

2 red peppers
2 yellow peppers
1 clove garlic, chopped fine
approx. 20 black olives
parsley
olive oil
lemon juice
seasoning to taste
225g/¹/₂ lb/1 cup smoked tofu, drained well

Grill or roast the peppers whole, turning as necessary, until their skins are black and blistered. Wrap them in a cloth and leave for 30 minutes or so to cool down. Their skins will come off easily.

Cut the flesh into strips and arrange them in a serving dish. Sprinkle with the garlic, olives, a generous amount of parsley. Mix the oil, lemon juice and seasoning and poor a little over the salad (any extra can be put on the table so people can help themselves).

Cut the tofu into thin strips and grill until crisp, then arrange decoratively over the peppers. Serve.

Note: Smoked tofu makes an unusual and delicious addition to this salad. In Mediterranean countries, however, it is more likely to be replaced by hardboiled eggs which is an idea you might also like to try.

See also Autumn salad, Butter bean pie, Artichoke salad, Mexican flan, Vegetable stew for couscous.

SWEET POTATOES

Often confused with yams, these potatoes have a smoother reddish-brown skin, they taper at one end, and have a much sweeter taste. Originally grown in South America, they are now more popular with the North Americans who not only use them in many of their favourite dishes, but also export them regularly.

Nutrition: They have more vitamin C, dietary fibre and carotene than ordinary potatoes.

Buying/Storing: The tubers should be firm and undamaged. They will keep for a week or two if stored in a cool dry spot.

How to use: Wash carefully – their skin is delicate. Then boil, steam, or fry them. Like ordinary potatoes they can also be roasted in their skins. As they are so sweet try them in dessert dishes, jams and preserves.

SWEET POTATO DESSERT

4 medium-sized sweet potatoes
30g/1oz/2¹/₂ tablespoons butter
2 tablespoons raw cane sugar
¹/₂ teaspoon ground cinnamon
¹/₂ teaspoon ground ginger
30g/1oz/1/3rd cup hazelnuts, roasted and coarsely chopped
natural yogurt to serve – optional

Cook the potatoes (in their skins) in a saucepan of boiling water for 30 minutes. Drain them, peel, and mash the flesh. In a bowl combine the sweet potato purée with butter, sugar and spices.
Divide the mixture between 4 bowls or glasses. Garnish with the hazelnuts.
Put yogurt on the table so that those who want it can help themselves.

SWISS CHARD

One of the spinach or leaf beets, which are members of the beetroot family. Swiss chard is rather like spinach, though it has fleshier stalks that are paler in colour and are mild in flavour. It is sometimes also called seakale beet. Closely related is a red chard which has similar leaves but centre stalks that are more the colour of rhubarb, and perpetual spinach.

Nutrition: If it is fresh, lots of vitamin C.

Buying/Storing: Like spinach the leaves should be a good colour, un-damaged and not too limp. Keep it in the fridge for a day or so if you must, but try to eat it as soon as you can.

How to use: The stalks, which are crisper, can be added to salad or used with dips. The leaves should be very lightly cooked in the minimum of water and then served as a vegetable – add a knob of butter and pinch of nutmeg.

TAHINI

Tahini is a pale creamy paste made from crushed sesame seeds, sometimes with a little sesame oil added. If made from roasted seeds, the colour is darker and the flavour stronger. It has been an important food for centuries in such countries as Turkey, Greece and Cyprus, and is also a popular ingredient in Arab cookery.

Nutrition: Tahini contains all the goodness of sesame seeds in a concen-trated form, including vitamins, minerals, calcium, protein and iron. It is easy to digest, and considered by some to be soothing for the stomach. As it is very high in fat, however, it should be used sparingly.

Buying/Storing: Buy it in screw-top jars from healthfood, wholefood and some speciality shops. Make sure it is always covered, keep in a cool spot, and it will keep well for some time.

How to use: Tahini is a very versatile food with a distinctive and delicate flavour. Try it with spicy falafels, or make into a sauce for vegetables and rice. Make a dip by adding oil, lemon juice, and garlic or herbs. Mix with water and lemon to use instead of milk in tea or coffee (it will give your drink a nutty taste). It also goes well with sweet recipes. Make a spread by mixing it with honey or maple syrup; add water and you have a cream to pour over fruit salads or fruit crumbles. Mix with cake crumbs, orange peel and spices, and roll into balls for a quick nutritious treat.

SAVOURY WALNUT BALLS

140g/5oz/1 cup walnuts, ground
55g/2oz/1 cup wholemeal breadcrumbs
1/2 teaspoon ground cumin
1/2 teaspoon cayenne pepper
seasoning to taste
approx. 2-3 tablespoons light tahini
sesame seeds
paprika

In a bowl mix together the nuts, crumbs, spices and seasoning. Add just enough tahini to make a firm but pliable dough. Continue kneading briefly for a minute or two, then divide the dough into small even-sized pieces and roll these into balls. Mix together some sesame seeds and paprika, and use this mixture to coat the balls. Chill them briefly before serving. Good at parties – spear each one with a cocktail stick.

See also Kasha and cabbage, Cauliflower paté, Hummus, Endive and butter bean soup, Tahini custard.

TAMARI
See **Soy sauce**

TANGELO
See **Ugli**

TANGERINES
See **Citrus fruit, soft**

TAPIOCA
See **Cassava**

▌▌▌▌▌▌▌▌▌▌ TARRAGON ▌▌▌▌▌▌▌▌▌▌

Tarragon is a small bushy herb with long, slender, pointed leaves which – when added to food – give a fresh and very distinctive flavour. It is native to parts of Russia. The variety called French tarragon is best for cooking.
How to use: The most popular use is in tarragon vinegar which can also be used to add interest to such sauces as hollandaise and bernaise. Tarragon goes well with mayonnaise too. Try tarragon butter with young asparagus or broccoli to enjoy these vegetables at their best. Chopped leaves can be added to egg dishes and salads.

TARRAGON VINEGAR

570ml/1 pint/2¹/₂ cups white wine vinegar
approx. 55g/2oz fresh tarragon sprigs

Put the wine vinegar into a small screw-top jar or bottle.
Wash, dry and slightly crush the tarragon leaves. Drop them into the wine vinegar,
screw on the top. Leave in a cool spot for at least a few weeks, preferably longer, for
the wine vinegar to absorb the tarragon flavour.
This classic herbed wine vinegar is good in salad dressings, of course, but can also
be used in sauces. Try adding it in small amounts to soups and stews.

See also Asparagus with hollandaise sauce.

TARTAR, CREAM OF
See **Raising agents**

TEAS
See also **Cash crops**

Tea is the most popular drink in the world. In Britain alone we drink 107
million cups per day. Yet most teas – like coffee – do us little good, and some
do us positive harm.

There are two main kinds of commercial tea. Green tea, especially
popular in China, is produced without fermentation and contains few if
any chemicals. In fact, it is both refreshing and good for the digestion. It is
the black tea that we import in such vast quantities that is more likely to
have been sprayed and treated in other dubious ways.

Quite apart from the way in which it has been processed, though, black
tea contains tannic acid, up to twice the caffeine found in coffee, plus
another substance called theophylline that is even more of a stimulant.
These have much the same effects on the body as coffee: an excited nervous
system, palpitations, the over-secretion of gastric juices. Like coffee, black
tea can also become an addiction that is hard to break.

If you feel you would like to try alternative drinks, consider first some of
the green teas that are now available in wholefood and healthfood shops.
Three year tea (also called twig tea) in particular is full of flavour, and it also
has a soothing effect on the nerves. Yogi tea is an excellent alternative, even
when made with black tea (this is diluted, and the spices help counteract
any harmful effects). And as herb teas become increasingly popular the
range grows, not just of single herbs but combinations that can be sweet,
flowery, spicy, sharp, most of them available in tea bags for convenience.
Try a selection – there is sure to be at least one that suits you.

TEAS, HERB

Herb teas, unlike ordinary tea, do not contain tannin or caffeine, and are not dyed. Like the herbs from which they are made, they have many very effective medicinal qualities and therefore not only provide a refreshing drink but can also be used to sooth, calm, stimulate, help digestion, etc.
Varieties: Herb teas are best made from fresh leaves; they need only be washed lightly, torn and then left to steep for a few minutes in boiling water. Alternatively, dried herbs can be used either singly or in combinations of your choice. You can also now choose from a wide range of herbal tea bags which are on sale not only in wholefood and healthfood stores, but also in chemists and supermarkets. Though some contain just one herb, most are in imaginative and delicious combinations, often with spices added. Do not forget that herbs are powerful – it is best not to drink the same kind all the time, but to vary them.

Some favourites to try are:

Chamomile   Antiseptic, soothing; a good nightcap
Dandelion   Make it from fresh young leaves
Elderflower   Good for colds; tastes a little like lemonade
Fennel   Especially good after a meal, or for stomach cramps
Hibiscus   A delicious fruity taste
Lemon balm   A fresh summery taste; helps balance the nervous system
Lemon verbena   An excellent relaxant that is also a mild digestive
Mallow   A diuretic and helps with internal inflammation
Mu tea   A classic mixture containing ginseng and other exotic Oriental herbs
Nettle   Not as strange as it sounds; a good source of iron and vitamin C
Orange blossom   Soporific qualities, so good at night
Peppermint   One of the best known herb teas; a good tonic
Raspberry leaves   Considered to be strengthening; especially good before and just after childbirth
Rosehip   Another favourite, sweeter than most
Sage   Excellent for nervous exhaustion
Spearmint   Helps the digestion
Banchu   A twig tea but can also be found in leaf form; good for digestion
Valerian   The most effective herbal sedative

TEMPEH

A fermented soya bean product that is especially popular in Indonesia where it is served in a wide variety of different recipes. Though similar in some ways to the better known tofu, it has a thicker texture and a stronger, sweeter flavour.

Varieties: It is sold in blocks that can usually be purchased fresh, refrigerated or frozen.

Nutrition: Tempeh is high in protein, vitamins and minerals and is gluten-free. As the culture has already started to break down the proteins and fats, it is especially easy to digest. It is also an excellent source of vitamin B12.

How to use: Tempeh can be marinated in soy sauce, flavoured with herbs and garlic, and then deep- or shallow-fried. If cut into very thin strips and fried until golden it goes crisp and has a salty taste rather like that of bacon. It can also be combined with vegetables and an egg or egg substitute to make burgers or a savoury loaf. Mix it with cooked grains and use as a stuffing. Serve in a variety of sauces.

TEMPEH IN SWEET AND SOUR SAUCE

vegetable oil for frying
225g/¹/₂ lb/1 cup tempeh
2 tablespoons vegetable oil
1 small onion, finely chopped
3 tablespoons cider vinegar
1 tablespoon raw cane sugar
parsley to garnish

Heat the oil. Cut the tempeh into dominoes and deep-fry until golden.
Meanwhile, in another pan heat 2 tablespoons of oil and fry the onion to soften. Stir in the cider vinegar and sugar and cook for about 10 minutes. Add the tempeh, stir, and cook gently for 10 minutes more.
Serve with a grain dish and green side salad.

See also Chicory salad with tempeh.

THYME

A small garden bush with tiny grey leaves that is grown widely in Britain as well as in most Mediterranean countries and America. Its pungent fragrance, with its warm and sweet undertones, is attractive to bees, hence the wide variety of thyme honeys that are available. Because of its powerful antibiotic and antiseptic properties, thyme oils feature frequently in commercially-made germicides. Most bouquet garnis contain thyme.

How to use: Cream sauces are particularly good with thyme added. It also goes well with soups such as borscht, stuffings, nut roasts and salads. Aubergine, peppers and courgettes is a vegetable combination that tastes delicious with a little thyme added – try it in ratatouille. As it has a strong flavour, use it sparingly.

OATCAKES WITH THYME

225g/¹/₂ lb/2 cups rolled oats (fine)
3 tablespoons vegetable oil
pinch of salt
¹/₂-1 teaspoon dried thyme, crushed
1 tablespoon sesame seeds
water to mix

Put the oats into a bowl and use your fingertips to rub in the oil so that it is well distributed. Stir in the salt, the thyme and sesame seeds.
Add water and knead briefly. The dough should be soft but able to hold its shape.
Roll out on a lightly-floured board. How thick or thin you roll it is up to you. (Thinner oatcakes will hold together less well, and will be crisper.) Cut into small circles and place on a lightly-greased baking tray.
Bake at 150°C/300°F (Gas Mark 2) for 20-30 minutes, or until firm and lightly coloured. Cool, and store in an airtight container.

▌▌▌▌▌▌▌▌▌▌▌ TIGER NUTS ▌▌▌▌▌▌▌▌▌▌▌

Once very popular in Britain, the tiger nut has somehow gone out of fashion. It is still imported from Spain where it is grown on a small scale (though adverse weather conditions over recent years have badly affected the crops, and tiger nuts are in even shorter supply than usual).

These small wrinkled brown nuts are extremely hard and have a white sweet flesh that is reminiscent of coconut. To make them easier to eat (and yet somehow crisper) soak them in water for 24 hours.

How to use: Though best eaten as a snack, tiger nuts can be ground up and used in savoury dishes.

TIGER NUT LOAF

1 medium onion, peeled and chopped
2 cloves garlic, crushed
2 sticks celery, finely chopped
115g/4oz/1 cup tiger nuts, coarsely ground
55g/2oz/1 cup wholemeal breadcrumbs
200ml/1/3rd pint/³/₄ cup cottage cheese or yogurt
1-2 tablespoons soy sauce
1 tablespoon chopped parsley
seasoning to taste

In a bowl mix together the onion, garlic, celery, ground nuts, breadcrumbs, cottage cheese, soy sauce, parsley and seasoning. The mixture should be thick and moist.
Pour into a greased loaf tin and bake at 180°C/350°F (Gas Mark 4) for 40 minutes.
Cut into wedges to serve. Add a white, cheese or tomato sauce if liked.

TOFU

Tofu is a bean curd made by grinding soya beans into an emulsion, then using salt or a mild acid to curdle it. The result is a firm white curd, usually sold in pre-packed slabs. It has a mild flavour, so it can be used in both sweet and savoury dishes. Tofu is thought to have originated in China more than 2,000 years ago, and is still used in both China and Japan as a staple, being one of the first solid foods given to babies. It is only in recent years that it has become known in the West, though as interest in natural healthy foods grows, so does its popularity.

Varieties: There are two main kinds of tofu on sale in Britain. One is a firmer version which is more suitable for savoury dishes. The other, called silken tofu, is a blend of soya curds and whey, and is softer and therefore ideal for when a creamier texture is required. The better stocked stores may also offer organic tofu (made from organically-grown beans), and possibly smoked tofu which has a definite taste and a firmer than usual texture. A new variety is dried tofu, ideal for camping or your store cupboard as it is light and compact, will keep for ages, and yet needs to be soaked in warm water for just 10 minutes before being used. If you can get it, do also try braised tofu which is delicious and comes tinned and ready to eat.

Nutrition: Like the soya bean from which it is made, tofu is an excellent protein food, yet is low in calories. It contains the 8 essential amino acids found in soya beans, and is easy to digest. As many manufacturers use calcium sulphate to start the coagulation, tofu also contains a small but useful amount of calcium.

Buying/Storing: Check that the tofu you buy is fresh. If there is no sell-by date on the pack, ask. Once the pack is opened, keep tofu in cold water in the fridge, changing the water daily. It should keep for up to a week in this way.

How to use: The firm variety is best shallow- or deep-fried, added to flans and quiches, or eaten raw with soy sauce. Use the softer tofu to make sweet cheesecakes or whips, or as a substitute for cottage cheese. Make your own tofu mayonnaise. Perfect in spring rolls or with other Chinese or Japanese dishes, of course. Smoked tofu with rice makes an excellent vegetarian version of kedgeree.

FRIED TOFU CUTLETS

455g/1 lb/2 cups tofu
wholemeal flour
seasoning to taste
1-2 eggs
approx. 55g/2oz/1 cup breadcrumbs

vegetable oil for frying
tomato sauce to serve

The tofu must be well drained. A good way to do this is to wrap it in a clean tea towel, put a weight on top, and leave it for an hour. Cut into 4 same-sized pieces and dust with flour, seasoning this first. Whisk the eggs and dip the tofu into them, then drop into the breadcrumbs and turn so the tofu is thickly and evenly coated. Set aside briefly.

Heat vegetable oil and shallow-fry the tofu, turning it once. When crisp and golden, drain well on paper towels. Serve with hot tomato sauce.

See also Scrambled tofu florentines, Mushroom and tofu tacos, Mediterranean peppers, Autumn salad, Kasha and cabbage, Aubergine fritters, Tofu balls, Kohlrabi bake, Tomato and tofu soup.

TOMATOES

Once used only as a decorative plant, tomatoes were considered dangerous to eat, and are still shunned by macrobiotics. Though most of us use them as a vegetable, they are in fact a fruit. Now grown in a wide variety of shapes and flavours, tomatoes are a popular ingredient in many parts of the world, particularly in Mediterranean countries.

Varieties: Besides the usual selection there are 3 special varieties that are sometimes available, and are worth trying if you come across them. Beefsteak are very large tomatoes, often imported from America. Cherry tomatoes – as their name implies – are small, very sweet, and mostly used whole. Plum tomatoes have an elongated shape and are the ones we are most used to buying in tins. They are widely used in Italian cookery and though fresh tomatoes are obviously more nutritious, there are occasions when it is worth using the tinned variety – just to get that subtle but unique taste.

Nutrition: They are an excellent source of vitamins A and C, and when eaten raw also offer some vitamin E.

Buying/Storing: When buying any kind of tomatoes, check that they are firm and undamaged. Under-ripe tomatoes can be left in the fridge if you want to slow down their ripening process, but soft fruit should be kept at room temperature and used as soon as possible. A glut of soft tomatoes can be made into a sauce and frozen.

How to use: Use the tastiest ones raw in salads. Over-ripe tomatoes can be cooked to make a sauce to serve with pasta, or to spread over pizzas before adding the topping. (To peel tomatoes, soak them briefly in boiling water – the skins will split and be easy to remove.) Tomatoes go well with aubergines, as in Middle Eastern dishes – add spices and serve with yogurt. Use them in stews, flans and quiches. Make cream of tomato soup, or gazpacho, which is a chilled soup. An unusual starter is a savoury tomato sorbet. Large tomatoes can be stuffed and served raw or cooked. Green tomatoes make tasty chutney.

TOMATO SAUCE

2 tablespoons vegetable oil
680g/1¹/₂ lbs tomatoes, peeled and chopped
1 onion, sliced
1 clove garlic, crushed
1 tablespoon fresh basil or 1 teaspoon dried basil
1 bay leaf
seasoning to taste
140ml/¹/₄ pint/2/3rd cup vegetable stock or water
1 tablespoon tomato purée
30g/1oz/¹/₄ cup wholemeal flour
water

Heat the oil and add the tomatoes, onion and garlic. Stir well and cook gently for 5 minutes. Add herbs, seasoning, vegetable stock and purée. Cook for 15 minutes more. Remove the bay leaf. Pour into a blender and blend to make a smooth sauce. Return it to a clean saucepan. Stir the flour into a few spoonfuls of water and add to the sauce. Bring to the boil, then simmer until thick and creamy, adjusting the consistency and seasoning as necessary.

This is a basic tomato sauce, and can be served in many ways, including over spaghetti or rice, or as part of a stuffing mix. You can adapt it by using yogurt, tahini or blended tofu instead of flour as a thickener. Other ingredients can also be cooked with the tomatoes – peppers, carrots or mushrooms for example. An apple gives an unusual sweetness. Try different herbs. Make up large amounts of tomato sauce and freeze the extra until needed.

TORTILLA CHIPS
See **Maize**

TRITICALE

This is a grain first produced in the 1930s, when wheat and rye, two crops that grow well together, were crossbred. It is now being grown in North America and Russia, and on a small scale in Britain.

Varieties: Comes as a whole grain, flakes, and flour.

Nutrition: Triticale is a grain that contains 2% more protein than either wheat or rye, and has an improved amino acid balance.

How to use: It has a lighter, softer gluten than wheat so recipes need to be adjusted accordingly. When baking bread try using half and half with wheat flour. It is a very good sprouting grain, and gives a delicious harvest that can be added to salads, vegetables and soups.

CHINESE FRIED VEGETABLES WITH EGGS

30g/1oz/2¹/₂ tablespoons margarine
4 eggs, lightly beaten
seasoning to taste
2 tablespoons vegetable oil
¹/₂ clove garlic, crushed
1 yellow pepper, sliced
1 onion, sliced
¹/₂ small head broccoli, broken into florets
3 tablespoons peas, cooked and drained
55g/2oz/1 cup triticale sprouts
soy sauce
good pinch raw cane sugar

Melt the margarine in an omelette pan, tilting it so that the base is evenly covered.
Pour in the seasoned eggs and cook gently until just set. Transfer the omelette to a
plate, roll up, and use a sharp knife to cut into thin strips. Keep them warm.
At the same time, heat the oil in another pan and cook the garlic, pepper and onion
for 5 minutes. Add the broccoli, cover the pan and continue cooking for 5 more
minutes, or until all the vegetables are just beginning to soften (they should still be
crisp). Stir in the peas, sprouts, soy sauce, sugar, and season to taste. Cook gently
for just long enough to heat through.
Serve with a grain dish such as rice or bulgur. Top with the vegetables and a
scattering of omelette strips.

▌▌▌▌▌▌▌▌▌▌▌▌▌▌ TURMERIC ▌▌▌▌▌▌▌▌▌▌▌▌▌▌

The ground root of a plant native to India that is a member of the ginger
family. Though the resulting powder has a subtle and aromatic taste,
turmeric is principally used for the distinctive bright yellow colour it gives
to food, curries in particular. In fact, in the Far East turmeric is used to dye
fabrics besides also being valued for its medicinal properties.
How to use: One of the main ingredients in commercial curry powder.
Use when pickling or making relishes. Adds interest to a white sauce. Good
with rice and vegetable dishes, unusual in salad dressings. It can be used
instead of saffron for colouring dishes.

SCRAMBLED TOFU FLORENTINES

455g/1 lb/2 cups tofu, drained and crushed
2 tablespoons vegetable oil
soy sauce
good pinch of turmeric
seasoning to taste
garlic salt
455g/1 lb spinach, washed and shredded

Put the tofu into a small saucepan with the oil and cook briefly, stirring continually.

Add the soy sauce, turmeric, seasoning and garlic salt. Continue cooking for 5 minutes.

Meanwhile, cook the spinach in a covered saucepan using just a spoonful of water. It should be soft in 5 minutes or so.

Divide the drained spinach between 4 small plates, topping each one with some of the scrambled tofu. Serve with fresh wholemeal baps or toast as a light snack.

See also Apricot rice, Spicy cauliflower.

TURNIPS

Before potatoes arrived, turnips were what the poor of Europe lived on. This may be why they are not very popular these days, though they can be used in a variety of ways, and as they are still one of the cheapest vegetables around, they offer very good value for money. Early summer roots are green and white, and are tender; maincrop turnips may be more of a violet colour and have a thicker skin and coarser flesh.

Buying/Storing: Look for firm roots that are free from bruises, holes or spongy patches. The smaller ones will have the best flavour and be less inclined to stringiness. Can be kept in a cool dry place for a reasonable time.

How to use: Young turnips can be cooked whole and then served as a vegetable with a knob of butter. Or try them raw, sliced thin or grated and added to other ingredients. Older turnips can be cooked and then puréed with butter and yogurt. Add them to winter stews and casseroles, make them into a creamy soup. Turnips are surprisingly good in stir-fries. In combinations, take care the strong flavour of maincrop turnips doesn't swamp that of other ingredients.

TURNIP AND CHEESE CROQUETTES

680g/1¹/₂ lbs turnips
55g/2oz/¹/₂ cup Cheddar cheese, grated
seasoning to taste
1-2 teaspoons fresh chives, chopped
1 egg yolk
1 egg, beaten
approx. 85g/3oz/1 cup fine wholemeal breadcrumbs

Peel and slice the turnips. Either steam or boil them for about 15-20 minutes, or until soft. Drain well and then mash the flesh and transfer it to a bowl.

Stir in the cheese, seasoning, herbs and egg yolk. Use floured hands to divide the mixture into equal-sized portions, and roll them carefully into croquettes. If you have time, leave them in the fridge briefly – this will help firm them up.

Drop each croquette into the egg and then the breadcrumbs, making sure it is well and evenly coated.

Grill them, turning them often so that the whole croquette is cooked and golden. If you prefer you can bake them in the oven, or even fry them.

▓▓▓▓▓▓▓ TVP (TEXTURED ▓▓▓▓▓▓▓ VEGETABLE PROTEIN)

TVP is made from soya or field beans which are processed (either by extrusion or spinning) in such a way as to give the texture of meat. Sometimes artificial meat flavouring is also added. TVP can be used in a variety of ways, is quick to prepare, and compares well with meat for its high protein content, whilst being much lower in price. It can be used to replace some or all of the meat in various dishes, and is understandably popular with the catering trade, particularly as an extender.

Varieties: At one point TVP was available in a range of flavours but nowadays it is rare to find it in any other than beef, which is the one manufacturers find sells best. You can flavour plain TVP yourself very successfully by soaking it in vegetable stock or water with miso or soy sauce added, then cooking with onions, garlic, herbs, or whatever you fancy. Choose also from chunks and finely minced TVP.

Nutrition: This depends on the beans used to make the TVP, and will vary from one product to another. In general, though, TVP is low in calories (being low in fats) whilst providing a fair amount of protein, minerals and vitamins. The most nutritious is TVP made from soya beans.

Buying/Storing: TVP is dehydrated – soak it in water or vegetable stock when you want to use it. This means it will keep indefinitely if put in a cool dry place, preferably in a closed container. Hydrated TVP will keep for a few days in the fridge.

How to use: Use minced TVP as you would use minced meat – in shepherd's pie, a bolognese sauce for spaghetti, to make burgers. Chunks can be used in stews, pies, and curries. Be imaginative with the sauces you serve with TVP and you will find it tasty and quick to prepare – a useful 'convenience food'!

MOUSSAKA

225g/¹/₂ lb/2 cups minced soya TVP
3-4 tablespoons vegetable oil
1 leek
2 teaspoons dried mixed herbs
seasoning to taste
cold water
2 aubergines
115g/4oz/1 cup grated Cheddar cheese
285g/¹/₂ pint/1 1/3rd cups thick white sauce
tomatoes to garnish
parsley to garnish

Hydrate the minced TVP according to the instructions on the packet. Heat half the oil and sauté the very finely chopped leek until it begins to soften. Add the drained TVP and cook for a few minutes more. Stir in the herbs, seasoning, and a few spoonsful of water to moisten. Cover and cook for 20 minutes.

Meanwhile peel the aubergines, cut into thin slices, and fry on both sides in the remaining oil, using more if necessary. Drain well. Layer a third of the aubergines in an ovenproof dish, top with half of the TVP mixture and some of the cheese. Repeat, and then finish with aubergine. Pour on the white sauce, making sure it is well-distributed. Top with a final sprinkling of cheese. Bake at 190°C/375°F (Gas Mark 5) for 30 minutes. Garnish with slices of tomato and parsley.

UGLI

There are a number of hybrids of citrus fruits, this one probably being the best known in Britain. It resulted from crossing a tangerine with a grapefruit. (A tangelo is a similar hybrid, but the tangerine side dominates.) Round and medium-sized, the ugli has a loose fitting knobbly green and orange skin. The pink flesh inside is juicy and sweet (it actually consists of thousands of swollen hairs). There are a few seeds. Ugli fruits are especially popular in Jamaica.

Buying/Storing: Look for fruits that have not been damaged or bruised. They should not feel too soft. Store in a cool place for up to a week.

How to use: Best eaten raw. Can be added to sweet and savoury salads. The peel can be candied.

UMEBOSHI
See **Pickles**

UTENSILS, COOKING
See also **Grinders**

Despite what the advertisers would wish us to believe, it is not necessary to splash out on a vast array of utensils and tools in order to be a good cook.

The food processor that will do everything not only takes considerable time to understand let alone use – it also prevents you enjoying touching, smelling, really getting close to the foods you are cooking. Most professional cooks prefer to do things the old-fashioned way, even if it takes a little longer.

Still, though, you will need a few basics. Always buy the best quality you can afford; if you choose with care such utensils will last you a lifetime.

Whether you cook with gas or electricity you will need saucepans. A set giving you a choice of different sizes is ideal, but just a couple will do to start with. The very best are earthenware or cast iron, both of which conduct the heat superbly. Enamelled iron is also good, though there is a chance that it could contaminate food, especially if coloured (watch out too that it isn't chipped). Other good alternatives are stainless steel and glass. Non-stick coated pans, when heated, may release toxic fumes; to avoid this problem, use only with gentle heat. Aluminium pans are best avoided – the aluminium may leave a poisonous deposit on food, and in any case, such pans are usually too thin to cook evenly. If you already have one and cannot or do not wish to replace it, at least make a point of never leaving cooked food stand in it.

Other important basics for your kitchen are a couple of knives of different sizes, the heavier the better. A solid chopping block. A good quality grater for grating cheese, breadcrumbs, apples for muesli, and so on. Add to these a wooden spoon (for stirring food in your saucepan without scratching it), wooden spatula, a whisk, measuring jug, rolling pin, mixing bowls and casseroles. A mortar and pestle is a nice way of grinding herbs and spices, also nuts if you haven't got a grinder. Your choice of extras depends very much on the kind of food you enjoy.

All vegetables are better steamed than boiled, and the easiest way to do this is to buy one of the many fold-up steamers that can be slipped into saucepans of different sizes, washed out in seconds.

However, for vegetables cooked to perfection, nothing can beat a wok. Again, the better the quality the tastier will be the results. Woks can be used with gas or electricity, many coming with special stands to help them balance on today's modern cooker tops. They originated in China where cooking fuels were in short supply, the wok needing only the minimum heat. To cook stir-fried vegetables you add just a tiny drop of oil, and cook them briefly – the design and material of the wok will do the rest to ensure they are cooked to perfection. Many vegetarians and vegans use them almost exclusively, finding they have no need of other saucepans.

Because the more natural diet also includes slow cooking beans, it might be an idea to invest in a pressure cooker. Look for one made from enamelled or stainless steel. Pressure cookers will cook not just beans but vegetables and grains too, all in the shortest possible time, and will seal in the goodness as they do so.

VANILLA

Originally this was the pod of a tropical climbing orchid native to Central America, though nowadays the vanilla you find in the shops is more likely to be part of a crop grown commercially in another tropical region. The pod is picked before it is ripe and is then cured over a period of time, ending up as a long black bean-like strip. Some people use the whole pod to flavour food, others use an extract – either way vanilla's sweet yet delicate taste is known around much of the world, and is a favourite with manufacturers of ice cream, confectionery and cakes.

Varieties: It is better to use whole vanilla pods than vanilla essence, as the latter may well have additives included – some vanilla flavourings are pure chemical. Although fairly expensive, vanilla pods can be used time and again. If, however, you prefer to use vanilla extract, there are some now coming onto the market that claim to be entirely natural in origin, and though they too are expensive, they are well worth the extra money. Look out too for ground vanilla.

How to use: Add the pods to rice puddings, custards and other sweet dishes, then remove the pods before serving, rinse and pat dry. Store a pod in a jar of sugar so the sugar absorbs some of the flavour. (Vanilla sugar is the finely ground pod mixed with sugar.) When making cakes and biscuits use ground vanilla which gives a stronger, fuller flavour. Vanilla is invaluable when making sweets, ice creams, mousses, and is said to actually bring out the taste of chocolate.

COCONUT CREAM PIE

170g/6oz/1 1/2 cups wholemeal flour
pinch of salt
85g/3oz/1/3rd cup margarine
3-4 tablespoons water

filling:
170g/6oz/1 cup raw cane sugar
4 heaped tablespoons wholemeal flour
710ml/1¹/₄ pints/3 cups milk, warmed
3 egg yolks
2 tablespoons butter
¹/₂-1 tablespoon vanilla essence
85g/3oz/1 cup desiccated coconut

To make the pastry, sift the flour and salt together into a bowl, then use fingertips to rub in the fat to make a mixture like breadcrumbs. Add enough water to make a dough, knead briefly, wrap in a polythene bag and chill for 30 minutes.
Meanwhile, prepare the filling. In a saucepan mix together the sugar, flour and milk and heat gently, stirring continually with a wooden spoon until you have a thick sauce. Remove from the heat and leave to cool slightly.
In a bowl whisk the egg yolks, then add a few spoonsful of the sauce and continue whisking briefly. Pour this back into the saucepan and cook gently for 3 more minutes, stirring continually. Add the butter, vanilla essence, and most of the coconut. Set aside.
On a floured board roll out the prepared pastry and use to line a medium-sized pie dish. Prick the base with a fork, and bake blind at 200°C/400°F (Gas Mark 6) for 15 minutes. Remove from the oven and spoon in the prepared coconut cream. Sprinkle with the remaining coconut. Continue baking at the same temperature for about 20 minutes, or until set. Serve cold.

See also Almond biscuits, Butterscotch cream, Cardamom and rosewater icing, Brown bread ice cream.

VEGANISM
See also **Meat, Fish**

The vegan is someone who lives entirely on the products of plants, avoiding not just the flesh of animals and fish, but also any ingredients that are in any way associated with them. This means vegans do not consume milk, cream, yogurt, cheese, butter, anything containing whey (most commercial margarines do), nor eggs and honey.

Most vegans also consume few processed foods as so many of these contain animal-derived ingredients.

Though a vegan diet may sound difficult to follow, it can in fact be both tasty and varied. The range of vegan foods grows daily, especially items based on soya. More exotic fruits and vegetables are being imported. Recipe ideas from around the world are reaching our shores, plus the spices and other ingredients necessary to put them together.

However, anyone adapting to a vegan diet from eating meat on a regular basis should do so slowly, letting their body get used to this new way of eating. It is also well worth studying at least the basic principles of nutrition. Protein intake in particular must be watched. Though we need considerably less protein than used to be thought, we do need some, and plant foods contain less than flesh foods. Nutrients such as vitamins and minerals are generally plentiful in plant foods, though vitamin B12 is found almost exclusively in animal foods. Some vegan foods – barmeme yeast extract is a particular favourite with vegans – have B12 added, so this need cause no problems. On the plus side, the vegan diet is extremely low in saturated fats, high in natural fibre, and can actually help with many complaints and illnesses.

The main reason upwards of 20,000 people in Britain have chosen to be vegan is their reverence for life, a concern that includes taking individual responsibility not just for the animals, but for the planet itself. Veganism promotes a caring use of the earth's resources in a way that goes beyond words to direct action. Vegans eat to save the planet.

VEGETABLES
See also **individual varieties**

Vegetables are edible plants, and come in many varieties – roots, stems, leaves, pods, seeds or fruits, some needing to be specially cultivated, but many growing wild in the countryside even today. Though sometimes unpopular in the past with the wealthy – who were busy filling themselves with pheasant and boar and had no space left for bulky vegetables – they have long been the mainstay of the poor, who always had a pot of vegetable broth bubbling over the fire. The Romans introduced many new varieties, together with imaginative ways of cooking them, and the British became masters at growing vegetables. By the 16th century, however, interest in vegetables had waned again, and during the reign of Henry VIII they were hardly used at all. They became popular again during the Elizabethan period, and have now become very much a part of the British pattern of eating, though they are still considered little more than a trimming to go with the meat.

Until quite recently many people grew their own vegetables in gardens and on allotments, and considerably more varieties of vegetables were available. Do-it-yourself vegetable growing has declined enormously since the Second World War, though there has been a renewed interest over the past few years, chiefly as a result of the concern many people feel about the over-use of chemicals and pesticides by commercial vegetable growers. In addition, many of the vegetables sold in greengrocer's shops today are restricted to the easiest-to-cultivate and therefore most lucrative varieties, and many of the older – and tastier – favourites are in danger of dying out.

Nutrition: Although most vegetables contain some vitamins and minerals, not all of them are particularly good sources. Green vegetables do usually offer some folic acid, a B vitamin found in almost no other foods. Some contain vitamins A and C, and many are useful for their mineral salt content, especially iron. Dietary fibre is present in vegetables, but in rather small amounts as most are at least 90% water – the best sources are root vegetables. As much of the vitamin content is destroyed by cooking, try to eat some raw vegetables each day in the form of a salad. When you *do* cook do so quickly (steaming is ideal) and make use of the vegetable stock that remains, either as a savoury drink, or by using it as a base for soups, stews or casseroles.

Buying/Storing: Choose only fresh, undamaged vegetables and buy from a greengrocer or supplier you know to have a fast turnover. Whenever possible buy organically-grown vegetables which are usually richer in nutrients and – maybe even more important – have not been adulterated with chemicals. Do not, however, let the absence of organically-grown vegetables in your neighbourhood stop you from eating vegetables – almost any source of vegetable is better than none. Most vegetables will keep for a short time if placed in a cool, well-ventilated spot. Some will keep for a long time, but do not forget that they will rapidly lose their vitamin content. Anything packed in polythene should either be unwrapped, or holes should be made for ventilation.

How to use: See individual varieties.

VEGETABLE STOCK
See **Stock, vegetable**

VEGETARIANISM
See also **Meat, Fish**

The definition of a vegetarian is someone who does not eat the flesh of any creature that once lived, nor products derived from its corpse. Obviously this means vegetarians do not eat meat, fowl, or fish. It also includes such ingredients as lard (made from the fat of animals), gelatin (produced by boiling hooves, tendons and ligaments), cochineal (a food dye made from the bodies of insects), and so on. Unfortunately it is almost impossible to avoid some of these ingredients as – until labelling laws insist that not just ingredients are listed, but their source also – there is often no way of knowing exactly what we are eating.

The reasons people choose to become vegetarians are various. Probably the majority in Britain do so for moral reasons, finding the way in which living creatures are exploited both repulsive and wrong. At the same time there is increasing concern that – with modern farming methods relying so heavily on drugs and chemicals, and with genetic engineering producing animals that are lightyears away from their origins – flesh foods are no longer natural foods, nor healthy. Many feel they may actually pose health risks.

As we as a nation become more aware of Green issues, there is also the question of how much damage the consumption of flesh foods is causing to our planet. Most certainly it is having effects, both direct and indirect. It is also directly responsible for much of the starvation in the Third World, where vegetable protein that could feed the native people is being grown instead to become feed for our factory-farmed animals.

At present there are getting on for 3 million people in Britain who have chosen to eat in a way that involves the minimum exploitation of animals, other people and the planet. Their numbers are increasing daily.

VINEGAR

A rather sharp acidy liquid, obtained by fermentation from a fruit or vegetable source. Both wine and cider ferment naturally to form vinegar, and the preservation of food in vinegar is a technique which has been used for many centuries. Nowadays vinegar is used more often as a seasoning, or as an ingredient in salad dressings.

Varieties: Malt vinegar is a highly-processed variety and best avoided. Wine vinegar is probably the most widely used, especially in Mediterranean countries. It can be either red or white and usually contains a blend of wines. Best of all, however, is cider vinegar which is made from the whole apples and can vary in colour from yellow to dark amber.

Nutrition: Cider vinegar has been used in healing for many years, and is said to have germ-killing and antiseptic qualities as well as helping to lower blood pressure.

Buying/Storing: Read labels and buy only vinegars with the minimum of additives. Store in a sealed bottle in a cool, dark place. Unless you use vast quantities of it, buy only in small amounts at a time.

How to use: Use in salad dressings, add in small amounts to stews, sauces and soups. Perfect for pickling things. Both wine and cider vinegar can be flavoured by the addition of herbs – the chosen herbs should be steeped in the vinegar for 3-4 weeks – or spices, garlic, chilli peppers, whatever you have handy. Use cider vinegar also as a gargle for sore throats, make a hot drink with honey, or inhale the steam.

MUSHROOMS À LA GRÈCQUE

340g/12oz/6 cups firm button mushrooms
¹/₂ teaspoon coriander seeds
2 black peppercorns
¹/₂ clove garlic, crushed
3 tablespoons vegetable oil
2 tablespoons water
2 tablespoons red wine vinegar
2 tablespoons tomato purée
1 tablespoon lemon juice
fresh marjoram and parsley
seasoning to taste

Wipe the mushrooms and set aside. In a mortar crush together the seeds, pepper and garlic with the pestle. Put the oil, water, wine vinegar, tomato purée, lemon juice, herbs and seasoning into a saucepan. Add the seed mixture. Bring to the boil, then cover and simmer for 5 minutes.

Stir the mushrooms into the sauce, cover again, and continue cooking gently for 5 to 10 minutes, or until the mushrooms are cooked but still firm.

With a slotted spoon take out the mushrooms and divide them between 4 saucers or ramekins. Without covering the pan boil the remaining juice to thicken. Spoon this over the mushrooms.

Cover and leave in the fridge, preferably overnight, to marinate. Serve cold – nice with pita bread.

See also Marinated beans, Gado-gado, Pickled onions, Red cabbage with sour cream, Tarragon vinegar, Tempeh in sweet and sour sauce.

WAKAME
See Seaweeds

 # WALNUTS

Walnuts probably originated in ancient Persia, though numerous varieties of walnut tree now grow throughout the northern hemisphere. Fresh (wet)

walnuts are available only for a limited time each year, and are creamy and sweet. The shelled nuts that are so popular at Christmas are much drier. Most walnuts are purchased ready-shelled.

Nutrition: They are the highest of all nuts in polyunsaturated fats.

Buying/Storing: Fresh walnuts should have damp shells, but be careful of mould, and certainly avoid any that have been damaged. They should be kept in a cool spot and eaten within a reasonable time. Shelled dried walnuts, if kept in an airtight container, will keep for ages, though they will undoubtedly not taste as good as when they were just bought.

How to use: Walnuts have a dry, rather savoury taste, and can be used in many ways. Try them in Waldorf salad or add them to vegetable dishes. Mix them with lightly-fried onions and mushrooms to make a pancake filling, add them to cheese sauce. Try them with Middle Eastern dishes instead of the more expensive pine or pistachio nuts. They also make a good alternative to pecan nuts in American recipes. Good with sweet dishes, and very popular in cakes, especially when combined with dates or bananas.

WALNUT CHEESE ROULADE

225g/¹/₂ lb/1 cup curd cheese
115g/4oz/¹/₂ cup mild blue cheese (such as dolcelatte)
1 small red pepper, coarsely chopped
115g/4oz walnuts, coarsely chopped
watercress to garnish

Mash together the curd and blue cheese until well combined. Add the pepper, distributing it evenly. Shape the mixture into a smooth roll and coat with the nuts. Chill in the fridge to firm up. Serve garnished with watercress.
Slice and eat with salad as part of a light lunch. Also delicious after dinner with biscuits and a bowl of fresh fruit.

See also Moulded salad, Fruit and nut bran muffins, Lettuce dolmas, Bazargan, Ricotta cheese and spinach pasties, Spiced mooli, Spinach lasagne, Pea and carrot loaf, Savoury walnut balls.

WATER

In an age when recycling is an increasingly popular concept, it might be thought that the Water Boards are in the forefront of the movement. Our water is treated so that it can be used again and again. The trouble is that, to make it safe to drink, chlorine is added in amounts that can affect the taste, making it anything from unpleasant to downright disgusting. (Some people are actually allergic to it.) Chlorine, of course, kills bacteria, which means it is powerful stuff. So quite apart from the taste, what might it be doing to our insides?

The state of British water has come in for a lot of criticism lately. Apart from the deliberate additives there are those that sneak in on their own. Copper from old pipes, nitrates that have seeped through the soil and joined underground water supplies.

Yet water is essential to life – a person can live for weeks, even months without food, yet for only a few days without water. You need to drink, and yet your tap water contains only a few health-giving minerals and a lot of dubious additives.

Public awareness of the importance of good drinking water is growing, and as it does it can only be hoped that the standard of our tap water will improve. Meanwhile, there are a number of mineral waters on sale to fill the gap. Less expensive, both of time and money, are the many water filters you can now buy. The simplest is a jug over which a charcoal filter is slotted through which the tap water is poured. Others can be fitted to your tap, or beneath the sink. Nitrates, fluorides and other such additives cannot be completely removed that easily, but most filters will at least reduce them until the Water Boards clean up their own act.

WATER CHESTNUTS

You may find fresh water chestnuts – if you are lucky – in Chinese stores. They look like slightly flattened gladioli corms, though in fact they are the roots of a water plant. Remove the brown and peeling scales and you will find the white flesh which has a crunchy texture and a sweet taste. However, most people have only ever tried the tinned variety which has little taste, though it does still add interest to traditional Chinese dishes.
How to use: Slice fresh or tinned water chestnuts and add to stir-fries, sweet and sour dishes. Chop them up and combine with other vegetables and tofu to fill spring rolls.

See Chinese style kale.

WATERCRESS

The Romans believed watercress helped them to make decisions, as well as being a cure for mental illness. Nowadays it is still popular, though for its spicy and rather bitter taste rather than anything else. It is native to Britain and still grows wild in places, though most of the watercress on sale has been specially cultivated.
Nutrition: Though it is famed for its iron content, this is in fact no higher than that of many other green vegetables – parsley has 5 times as much. It also contains vitamins A and C, phosphorus and some calcium.
Buying/Storing: Look for glossy dark-green leaves and long stems. Be-

cause of spraying and poisonous effluents, wild watercress should be avoided unless it is clearly growing in clean water. Watercress should really be eaten while fresh, but can be kept for a day or so in a perforated polythene bag in the fridge.

How to use: Usually added to salads and sandwiches. Try it also in watercress soup; use as a filling for flans or make a watercress quiche. Adds interest to stir-fried vegetables. Chop leaves and stir into mayonnaise or butter. Traditionally used as a garnish for a wide variety of savoury dishes because of its lovely dark-green colour.

WATERCRESS AND POTATO SOUFFLÉS

1 bunch watercress, washed and trimmed
30g/1oz/¹/₄ cup almonds
225g/¹/₂ lb potatoes, cooked
4 tablespoons milk
2 teaspoons parsley, chopped
good pinch nutmeg
4 large eggs, separated

Chop the watercress and almonds. Mash the potatoes; add the watercress, almonds, milk, parsley, nutmeg and seasoning.
Stir in the egg yolks, mixing well.
Put the egg whites into a cold bowl, add a pinch of salt and whisk until stiff enough to hold small peaks. Use a metal spoon to carefully fold the egg whites into the watercress and potato mixture.
Grease 4 individual ramekins and divide the mixture between them. Place on a baking tray and bake at 180°C/350°F (Gas Mark 4) for 20 minutes, or until well risen and crisp on top. Serve at once.

See also Flageolet salad.

WATER ICES
See Ice cream

WHEAT
See also **Bulgur, Bran, Wheatgerm, Couscous**

This is a hardy plant that grows well in most climates – hence its popularity. In fact, half the population in the world relies on wheat as a staple, and it is the most widely-used grain in Britain, supplying about a quarter of our protein intake. Wheat is usually consumed as bread of one kind or another, a food that was first produced around 4,000 BC, when the Egyptians discovered how yeast lightened the end-product. To get the right balance, most of our bread is made with a combination of the soft wheat which grows best in the British climate, plus hard wheat imported from the USA, Canada or Russia.

Varieties: Wholewheat berries (the complete grain) are on sale in most wholefood and healthfood stores, and can be used like rice. Kibbled wheat is the cracked grain which is easier to cook. Ground wheat is called semolina. Wheat flakes are crisp and dry and used in breakfast cereals. Wheat flour comes in many varieties. Refined bleached flour has had the bran and wheatgerm removed, and is an inferior food – avoid it. Stone-ground wholemeal is the best as this has been gently ground between two large flat stones resulting in less damage (and more nutrients). Wholemeal flour is flour that has been refined in the usual way, but then the bran and wheatgerm have been put back. Wholemeal flour is usually available in 100%, which gives heavier results but contains all the original grain, 85% or 81%, which has had some bran removed to give lighter results. Wholemeal flour is also available in a self-raising variety. Unbleached white flour has had the bran and wheatgerm removed but has not been bleached; it makes a softer, moister loaf with a yellow tinge, nice for a change.

Nutrition: Wholewheat berries and wholemeal flour are good sources of iron, thiamin and nicotinic acid, plus protein. Wheat has the highest fibre content of any grain.

How to use: Wholewheat berries are tough and chewy – allow an hour at least for them to cook. They go well with eggs, and vegetables of all kinds, especially peppers. Try draining the cooked grains well and then frying them for an interesting texture. Frumenty is a sweet recipe introduced by the Romans and is made by boiling wheat in milk with cinnamon and honey (or raw sugar). Kibbled wheat is best used in cereals and breads, while wheat flakes – besides being served with milk at breakfast – can make a quick topping to a vegetable crumble. Semolina is used in desserts, and also makes good cheese fritters. Do try making your own bread sometimes too – it's easier than you think, and very therapeutic!

WHEAT BERRY SALAD

225g/¹/₂ lb/1 cup wheat berries
1 tablespoon vegetable oil
2 spring onions, finely chopped
1 stick celery, finely chopped
4 mushrooms, finely chopped
1 courgette, finely chopped
55g/2oz/¹/₂ cup almonds, chopped
French dressing
seasoning to taste

Rinse and drain the wheat berries. Heat the oil in a saucepan, add the wheat berries, stir and cook briefly, then cover with water, bring to the boil, and simmer for about an

hour or until just tender, adding more water if necessary. Drain, rinse in cold water, and drain again.
Put the wheat berries into a bowl. Add the vegetables and nuts, stirring well. Add enough French dressing to moisten, season generously.
Chill briefly before serving.

See also Mixed grain granola, White sauce, Butter shortbread, Homemade pasta, Sesame crackers, Wheatgerm bread, Carob cake.

WHEATGERM

This is the germ of grains of wheat, a tiny embryo weighing only one-fortieth of the whole grain, but containing all the nutrients needed to grow a new plant. It is highly perishable, which is why it is removed from commercially-made white flour; this enables its shelf-life to be extended considerably.

It was only when flour refining began in earnest around 1870 that wheatgerm was 'discovered'. Up until then it had been an integral part of all flours, and though its special nutritional value may not have been appreciated, the bread that was baked from it was far more nutritious. Though nutritionists fought to have it returned to its rightful place, they were scorned for most of the early part of this century, and it is only with the recent interest in wholemeal flour and bread that wheatgerm has again become popular.

Varieties: Best is raw unprocessed wheatgerm, which is usually pre-packed in small cellophane packs. Stabilised wheatgerm has been treated to stop rancidity and has lost some of its nutrients in the process, though it is still a valuable food. Toasted wheatgerm is also now becoming available, sometimes with added sweetening.

Nutrition: Wheatgerm oil is the richest known source of vitamin B6, also of vitamin E. In addition, wheatgerm contains vitamin A, iron, calcium and 12 amino acids.

Buying/Storing: Buy from a retailer you know to have a fast turnover and, once the pack has been opened, transfer the wheatgerm to an airtight container and store in the fridge. Throw it out if it smells at all stale. Toasted wheatgerm has slightly better keeping qualities.

How to use: Add wheatgerm to everything – it has a mild flavour and is easy to digest. Goes well with breakfast cereals, muesli, sauces, stuffings, baked goods, bread, scrambled egg, yogurt, honey, peanut butter. Use instead of flour when rolling out pastry – this will give it a nutty texture. Coat fritters or croquettes with it when frying. Use to thicken soups.

WHEATGERM BREAD

15g/¹/₂ oz/1 tablespoon dried yeast
1 teaspoon honey or raw cane sugar
425ml/³/₄ pint/2 cups warm water
565g/1¹/₄ lbs/5 cups wholemeal flour
115g/4oz/1 cup wheatgerm
pinch of salt

Cream together the yeast, honey or sugar, and a little of the warm water, then set aside in a draught-free spot for 10 minutes, or until frothy. Sift together the flour, wheatgerm and salt. Make a well in the centre and pour in the yeast, plus the rest of the water. Use your hands to mix well. Turn the dough onto a floured board and continue kneading until it is smooth. Leave covered in a warm spot until doubled in size. Knock the dough back, knead again briefly, then flour hands and shape dough into a loaf. Put into a well-oiled tin and leave in a warm place to rise to the top. Bake at 190°C/375°F (Gas Mark 5) for 35-40 minutes, or until the loaf sounds hollow when tapped. Put on a wire rack to cool.

See also Cauliflower paté, Muesli.

WINE

The consumption of wine in Britain has increased dramatically over recent years, and is still doing so. Yet though food manufacturers are required by law to indicate what additives their products contain, those who make wine are subjected to no such restrictions. We tend to assume that the wine-making process is a natural one – after all, all you really need to make wine is some grapes, right? Wrong. True though that once used to be, things have changed.

Many of the commercially-produced wines that are sold in bulk at reasonably low prices are, in fact, highly processed. The grapes from which they are made may well have been treated with chemical fertilisers and pesticides. Once picked and taken to the factory, a whole army of additives might have been used to transform them into wine. (The winemaker can legally 'improve' his wine with 20 permitted additives!) The most commonly used is sulphur dioxide which is a sterilising and preserving agent. If a small amount is helpful, large amounts (which is what many manufacturers use) may not only give the wine an 'off' smell and a nasty aftertaste, but will almost certainly result in hang-over effects such as a headache and stomach upset. Other additives are used to give the wine body, colour, taste. In northern Europe sugar – not allowed as a sweetener – can however be added to the grape must before fermentation to make the wine stronger. Tannin is added to some red wines.

Many of the cheaper wines will have been clarified with the help of such substances as dried blood powder and isinglass (sturgeons' air bladders) making them not only rather unsavoury, but completely unsuitable for vegetarians and vegans. Whether or not these additives are dangerous is hard to say. What we *can* say is that they detract from both the naturalness and the quality of the finished product.

Though certain standards are obviously maintained, it is important that wines should be subjected to the same labelling laws as foods. We have a right to know what we are drinking. We need information to be able to make informed choices.

There are now some excellent organic wines coming onto the market, and though they are more expensive than the real cheapies, many of them still compare well with better quality wines. As yet there is no one body co-ordinating standards for producers of organic wines in different countries. Most countries do, though, have their own. Yet as their products arrive on our shelves it is hard to be sure just what they do and do not contain. Even so, their aims are shared. Vines are grown without the use of pesticides or chemical fertilisers. Chemical additives are kept to a minimum, though a small amount of sulphur dioxide is usually still used. Many of them are vegetarian or vegan.

Identifying these wines at the off-license or supermarket is not always easy. Look out for bottle labels or tags that actually state the wine is organic. Hopefully, in time, there will be a shared and easy-to-spot symbol that will indicate to the buyer that a wine has come up to certain standards.

See Mulled wine, Cucumber and strawberry salad, Grapes in wine, Cheese and horseradish fondue.

WOKS
See **Utensils, cooking**

WORCESTER SAUCE

This is a very salty sauce that is flavoured with anchovies. There is, however, a vegetarian Worcester sauce now available, though not widely stocked. Made from natural ingredients, it is also low in salt and contains no sugar. Look out for it – worth having in the cupboard even if just for those occasions when nothing but the flavour of Worcester sauce will do.
How to use: A vital ingredient for a Bloody Mary; also good in tomato juice even without the vodka. Adds interest to soups, stews, casseroles. Stir it into dips, patés. Add to salad dressings.

YAMS

These are the tubers that grow under certain tropical vines. Though not well known in Britain, more are now being imported from various parts of the world including the West Indies (principally for sale to immigrants used to cooking with yams as an alternative to potatoes, though also to help satisfy the growing interest in exotic ingredients).

Varieties: Rather strange looking, often hairy, with a thick skin that can be fawn, pink, red or brown, and up to 30cm (1 foot) in length, all yams have flesh that is moist and creamy. The taste is also similar – a cross between that of ordinary and sweet potatoes.

Nutrition: Yams are an especially good source of vitamin A.

Buying/Storing: Check that there is no damage, and that the yams are firm. They will keep well in a cool dry place.

How to use: Cook yams much as you would cook potatoes. They can be steamed, boiled, fried. Add vegetables and nuts and make yam fritters. Mash them with sugar and flavour with spice. As the flesh tends to discolour once exposed to the air, a drop of lemon juice added to the cooking water is a good idea.

BAKED YAMS WITH YOGURT SAUCE

2 medium yams, scrubbed and pricked
285ml/¹/₂ pint/1 1/3rd cups natural yogurt
1 tablespoon raw cane sugar
1 good teaspoon ground cinnamon

Cook the yams in a moderate oven – 180°C/350°F (Gas Mark 4) – until just tender. The time this takes will depend on the size of the yam. For more evenly cooked yams, push a skewer through the centre of each (or wrap them in silver foil).
Make up the sauce by mixing the yogurt with the sugar and cinnamon.
Cut the yams into thick slices and serve either topped with a spoonful or two of the yogurt sauce, or with the sauce served separately in a jug.
A perfect accompaniment for such dishes as burgers or courgettes, good with omelettes, great with flans and nut loaves.

▓▓▓▓▓▓▓ YEAST, BAKING ▓▓▓▓▓▓▓

Though heavier breads *can* be made, in Britain we tend to prefer a lighter textured loaf, and for this we need yeast. Yeast is a fungal growth which produces fermentation by the use of enzymes. As liquid and warmth activate it, it gives off carbon dioxide, making the dough rise. Besides being used in baking it is also an important ingredient in brewing and winemaking.

Varieties: Once live yeast was mostly available only as tiny dried granules, but as interest in baking grows more speciality shops now sell fresh cake yeast. This looks like a small piece of putty. Dried yeast is a good alternative, however, and a new easybake dried yeast has recently appeared on the market, a blend that also contains vitamin C to encourage fermentation.

Nutrition: Contains some B vitamins.

Buying/Storing: Fresh yeast should be used fairly shortly after buying, though it will keep for a week or two in the fridge. If it begins to go brown around the edges it can still be used, but trim off the discoloured part first. You can also freeze it. Dried yeast is usually in a tin or individual packets and if stored in a dry spot, will keep for months.

How to use: Use yeast in breads, rolls and pizza bases.

HOT CROSS BUNS

15g/¹/₂oz/1 tablespoon dried yeast or 30g/1oz/2 tablespoons fresh yeast
285ml/¹/₂ pint/1 1/3rd cups lukewarm milk and water
55g/2oz/1/3rd cup raw cane sugar
455g/1 lb/4 cups wholemeal flour
1 teaspoon cinnamon
1 teaspoon mixed spice
115g/4oz/2/3rd cup currants
2 large tablespoons candied peel
1 egg
55g/2oz/¹/₄ cup margarine or butter, melted

Crumble the fresh yeast into a bowl and mix to a paste with a drop of the warm milk and water and a teaspoon of sugar, then add the rest of the liquid and set aside in a warm spot for 5 minutes or until frothy. Dried yeast should be sprinkled onto the liquid with a teaspoon of sugar, stirred until it has dissolved, then set aside in the same way.

Meanwhile, take a large warmed bowl and mix together the flour and spices. Add the rest of the sugar, the currants and peel. Beat the egg and add it to the yeast mixture with the melted fat; add these to the dry ingredients, mix well. Turn the dough out onto a well floured board and knead for a few minutes, then return it to the bowl, cover with a tea towel, and leave in a warm spot for about an hour or until risen. Lightly knead the dough again, divide into 12 even-sized pieces, and shape them into buns. Arrange them on lightly-greased baking sheets, and use a knife to mark each one firmly with a cross. Set them aside again in a warm draught-free place; within about half an hour they will have doubled in size. Meanwhile, heat the oven to 200°C/400°F (Gas Mark 6). Bake the buns for about 15 minutes until golden on top. Though delicious like this (served warm or cold) they can also be glazed with a syrup made of sugar and milk. If not to be eaten that day, you can re-heat them briefly in a hot oven just before you need them.

See also Wholemeal baps, Wheatgerm bread.

YEAST, BREWER'S

Fresh brewer's yeast is used as part of the beer making process (it is this same yeast that is mixed with salt, the soluble residue being evaporated to leave the sticky mass that is known as yeast extract).

Also used as a natural nutritional supplement, brewer's yeast is exceptionally rich in B vitamins. It also contains 16 of the 20 amino acids and 14 essential minerals.

It can be purchased in inexpensive pill form, and many people take it this way. However, it also comes as a powder which is highly concentrated and excellent as an instant pick-you-up. As this has a yeasty flavour not everyone likes, try adding it to fruit or vegetable juices, or stirring into yogurt.

TOMATO ZIPPER (FOR ONE)

200ml/1/3rd pint/³/₄ cup tomato juice
squeeze of lemon juice
soy sauce or Worcester sauce
1 tablespoon powdered brewer's yeast

Flavour the juice generously with lemon and sauce, stir in the brewer's yeast so that it is well mixed. Drink at once.

YEAST EXTRACT

When fresh brewer's yeast is mixed with salt it is broken down by its enzymes. The soluble residue is evaporated under pressure by a process invented in Germany at the turn of the century, but now popular throughout the world. Sold in jars, its salty and rich savoury taste is used to add flavour to food.

Varieties: There are many varieties of yeast extract on sale, most of them with a very high salt content, though some manufacturers are now offering reduced salt products.

Nutrition: Yeast extract is an excellent source of several B vitamins. In addition, some are fortified with vitamin B12 which makes them very useful for vegans who – as this vitamin is found almost exclusively in animal products – may be in danger of a deficiency. To meet recommended requirements of this vitamin they should aim to consume 55g/2oz of fortified yeast extract per week.

How to use: Dissolve in liquid and add to soups, stews and casseroles. Use in patés and nut loaves. Also makes a good drink for cold wintry days. Spread thinly on toast or use to add interest to salad sandwiches. A tiny bit added to nut butter, especially peanut, is delicious. Always go easy with yeast extract – it has a very strong and salty taste.

See Borlotti bean burgers, Split pea spread.

YOGI TEA

Not only does this taste delicious but it has all sorts of healing properties. Indians have been using it for centuries to help cure mild ailments such as coughs and colds, to give energy as well as to relax. It can be made in many different ways but always contains a selection of spices. An especially good tea for anyone with digestive problems might include ginger. Sometimes it contains black tea, other versions are made with just the flavourings. A delicious yogi tea that contains no black tea (and is therefore especially healthy) is now available loose in packets, and also in convenient-to-use tea bags.

BASIC RECIPE

4 mugs cold water
2 cardamoms
2 cloves
small stick cinnamon
2 black peppercorns
small pinch fennel seeds
2 tea bags
milk – optional
raw cane sugar or honey – optional

Simply combine the water and spices in a saucepan, bring to the boil, throw in the tea bags. Lower the heat and simmer the mixture for at least half an hour. Strain off the spices and pour into small cups. Add milk and sweetening if liked, but it can be drunk just as it is.

As this is a slow process, why not make up larger quantities of the tea at one time and store it in the fridge? It will keep well provided you do not add milk.

YOGURT

Yogurt is thought to have been used first by the nomads of eastern Europe at least a thousand years ago. It is still one of the most popular foods there, but is also widely used in many other countries where it goes under a variety of names (for example, tako, laben raid, zabady and kefir) and has numerous different tastes and textures. Made from milk that has been treated with bacterial cultures, it is a thick creamy substance that is versatile, inexpensive, and one of the finest natural foods available.

Varieties: Yogurt can be made from whole, semi-skimmed or skimmed milk. It can then be left plain or flavoured (usually with artificial colourings and flavourings, which are best avoided, though better quality fruit yogurts are worth trying). Greek yogurt is a variety that has been strained and is therefore more concentrated and creamier; it is better for cooking than low fat yogurts as it is less inclined to curdle. As people become more wary of consuming too much cow's milk, manufacturers are now offering yogurt made from the milk of sheep or goats, both of which are produced on a small scale and less likely to be treated with antibiotics and hormones. Many who suffer from digestive or allergy-related problems find these a boon. Yogurt can also be made with soya milk.

Nutrition: Yogurt is high in protein, and low fat varieties are widely available for anyone who is concerned about keeping their fat consumption down. Greek yogurt, however, which has the highest protein content, also has the highest fat content, so think of it as a nutritious lower-calorie alternative to cream and use it sparingly.

Some nutritionists believe that the bacteria and enzymes in yogurt help to maintain a healthy intestinal environment. There is no difference in nutritional terms between yogurts labelled 'live' and those that have been pasteurised, though you may prefer your yogurt to be bacteriologically alive rather than sterile.

Buying/Storing: Yogurt is sold just about everywhere these days, though live unflavoured varieties are usually only available from healthfood and wholefood outlets. Those sold in supermarkets may still be live – it depends whether they have been pasteurised after bacterial action or not. Make sure any yogurt you buy is well within its sell-by date, and store it in the fridge where it should stay perfectly edible for a week or two.

How to use: Most people tend to think of yogurt in connection with sweet dishes, and it does go especially well with fresh fruit. Or flavour natural yogurt with fruit spread, honey or maple syrup (adding a pinch of spice, maybe, or some crystallised ginger). Try yogurt too in savoury sauces, stirred into soups and casseroles, as a topping for vegetables or jacket potatoes. It makes a good contrast with spicy dishes such as curries or chilli, either on its c .vn or with chopped cucumber or tomatoes added. Yogurt salad dressing is delicious, especially with grated root vegetables.

HOMEMADE YOGURT

570ml/1 pint/2¹/₂ cups milk (whole, skimmed, cow's, ewe's, goat's, long-life or soya)
1 tablespoon natural yogurt or packet of yogurt culture
1 tablespoon single cream or skimmed milk powder – optional
flavourings of your choice (i.e. honey, maple syrup, lemon curd, raw cane sugar, jam, fruit purée, etc.)

Easiest to use is an electric yogurt maker which will come either as one flask-like container or several smaller ones. Alternatively you can use a wide-neck vacuum flask or glass jars. Whatever you use should be spotless before you begin.

Take a heavy saucepan (which should also be absolutely clean) and pour in the milk, adding the cream or skimmed milk powder if using it. Slowly bring the milk to the boil, stirring to prevent a skin forming. Either cool the milk slightly, or simmer uncovered for 10 minutes (which will help thicken the yogurt) and then set aside to cool. When the milk reaches just above blood heat (approx. 43°C/110°F) whisk in the yogurt or culture. Pour at once into the vacuum flask or jars (all of which should have been warmed first), seal and put in a warm place. An airing cupboard is ideal – if using jars, you might like to put hot towels around them. If using a yogurt maker, seal it according to instructions.

The yogurt will set in anything from 3 to 8 hours (the average time is about 6 hours) depending on the milk, the starter, and where the container is kept. Though flavouring can, of course, be added when the yogurt is served, you might prefer to give it more time to be absorbed, in which case do it now. Store the yogurt in a fridge where it should thicken a little more. Eat within 4-5 days.

Although a spoonful of yogurt can be used with milk to make more, it is a good idea to use a fresh yogurt culture every now and again. Bulgarian is best.

See also Frozen banana yogurt, Blackcurrant mousse, Yogurt rarebit, Tiger nut loaf, Baked yams with yogurt sauce, Kiwi raita, Shrikhand (saffron yogurt), Flageolet salad.

ZUCCHINI
See **Courgettes**

Also by Janet Hunt

The Diet-free Diet Book

Are you a diet freak? Starve one week, binge the next? Counting calories, fats, proteins, vitamins?

It's all unnecessary. The Diet-free Diet Book helps you make use of all the information contained in The Green Cook's Encyclopedia. It explodes all the myths of dieting, and offers you a realistic alternative. You can learn to be friends with your body, enjoy your food, and banish the scales for ever.

You'll discover why you eat the way you do; how to find your natural weight; how fat feelings can catch you out; and how to cut your partner down to size.

Janet Hunt offers a positive and creative approach to your body and the food you eat, all based on easily available wholefood and vegetarian ingredients. By avoiding the hazards associated with meat, and offering many alternatives to dairy products, she comes up with lots of ideas for tasty, wholesome eating. And the book is rounded off with useful menu planners and a selection of mouth-watering seasonal recipes.

Available from your bookseller.

£5.99   1-85425-042-6

For a complete catalogue of Green Print books, write to Green Print, 10 Malden Road, London NW5 3HR.